D0205669

FUNDAMENTALS OF SPORT MARKETING

Brenda G. Pitts, Ed.D.
University of Louisville

David K. Stotlar, Ed.D.
University of Northern Colorado

Fitness Information Technology, Inc.
P.O. Box 4425, University Avenue
Morgantown, WV 26504-4425

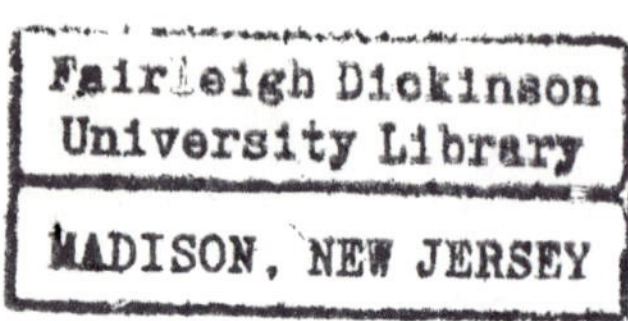

Library of Congress Card Catalog Number: 95-61902

ISBN 1-885693-02-8

Cover Design: James M. Williams/Micheal Smyth
Copyeditor: Sandra R. Woods
Printed by: BookCrafters
Production: Pepper Press

Printed in the United States of America
10 9 8 7 6 5 4 3

Fitness Information Technology, Inc.
P.O. Box 4425, University Avenue
Morgantown, WV 26504 USA
(800) 477-4348
(304) 599-3482 (phone/fax)
E-Mail: FIT@access.mountain.net

Sport Management Library

The Sport Management Library is an integrative textbook series targeted toward undergraduate students. The titles included in the Library are reflective of the content areas prescribed by the NASPE/NASSM curriculum standards for undergraduate sport management programs.

Forthcoming Titles in the Sport Management Library

Case Studies in Sport Marketing
Communication in Sport Organizations
Ethics in Sport Management
Financing Sport **(Now Available)**
Legal Aspects of Sport Entrepreneurship
Management Essentials in Sport Organizations
Sport Facility Planning and Management
Sport Governance in the Global Community
Sport Management Field Experiences **(Now Available)**

ABOUT THE AUTHORS

Dr. Brenda G. Pitts is a graduate of the University of Alabama, and is currently the Chair of the Department of Health Promotion, Physical Education, and Sport Studies at the University of Louisville. She developed the sport management curriculum at the University of Louisville and served as director from 1984 to 1993. Dr. Pitts teaches graduate and undergraduate courses in sport marketing, sport administration, and research in sport administration and has taught Sport Marketing in Hong Kong, Singapore, and Malaysia. Dr. Pitts' research has been published in numerous journals including the *Journal of Sport Management, Sport Marketing Quarterly, Leisure Information Quarterly, Journal of Legal Aspects of Sport, Women in Sport and Physical Activity Journal,* and the *Journal of Applied Research in Coaching and Athletics.* Dr. Pitts co-authored a chapter titled "Strategic Sport Marketing: Case Analysis" and is currently writing and editing a book titled *Case Studies in Sport Marketing.* She has made numerous presentations at national and international conferences.

Dr. Pitts' professional service has included organizing the first research and arts conference held in conjunction with the Gay Games IV in 1994 as well as serving as President of the North American Society for Sport Management, Co-Chairof the NASPE-NASSM Task Force on Sport Management curriculum Standars, and member of the Sport Management Program Review Council. She frequently serves as a management and marketing consultant to Louisville sport organizations.

A former collegiate and professional basketball player, Dr. Pitts is a member of the Huntsville-Madison County Sports Hall of Fame. She continues to pursue her lifelong interest in sports through participation in soccer, golf, boating, softball, camping, and volleyball.

Dr. David K. Stotlar has a Doctor of Education degree from the University of Utah, and serves as the Director of the School of Kinesiology and Physical Education at the University of Northern Colorado. He teaches on the faculty in the areas of sport management and sport law. He has had over forty articles published in professional journals, and he has written several textbooks and book chapters in sport, fitness, and physical education. He has made numerous presentations at international and national professional conferences. On several occasions, he has served as a consultant to fitness and sport professionals; and in the area of sport law, to attorneys and international sport administrators. He was selected by the USOC as a delegate to the International Olympic Academy in Greece and the World University Games Forum in Italy. He has conducted international seminars in sport management for the Hong Kong Olympic Committee, the National Sports Council of Malaysia, Mauritius National Sports Council, the National Sports Council of Zimbabwe, the Singapore Sports Council, the Chinese Taipei University Sports Federation, the Bahrain Sport Institute, the government of Saudi Arabia, the South African National Sports Congress, and the Association of Sport Sciences in South Africa. Dr. Stotlar's contribution to the profession includes having served as the Chair of the Council of Facilities and Equipment of the American Alliance for Health, Physical Education, Recreation and Dance and as a Board Member and later as President of the North American Society for Sport Management.

Table of Contents

FOREWORD

Twenty years ago few institutions of higher education had a course in sport marketing at the graduate level, much less a course for undergraduates. Even then, the concept of sport marketing was limited primarily to selling tickets to athletic events and marketing sporting goods. Marketing by the sporting goods industry was either dependent on a conservative application of standard business concepts or the practice of high risk entrepreneurial strategies. When it came to the methodology of selling events, sport marketing was more art than science. The "*creative hustler*" was the stereotypical success story. There appeared to be little "*method to the madness*" and few trained professionals to guide the development of the sport industry.

Undoubtedly, much of this lack of sophistication reflected the relatively small size and simplicity of the industry--from unimaginative white canvas athletic shoes with rubber soles, to wooden baseball bats, to a world without ESPN. Today's $100 billion dollar sport industry is considerably broader in scope and light years away--from in-line skates, to leather athletic shoes form-fitted with the use of an air pump, to graphite clubs and rackets. This new world of sport business demands highly educated and experienced professionals willing to master its intricacies.

Fundamentals of Sport Marketing is an excellent textbook geared to serve the undergraduate population aspiring to sport management and marketing careers. Brenda Pitts and David Stotlar have put together a gem of a book from several perspectives:

- This is the first text to present a comprehensive picture of the depth and breadth of the sport industry. All of the activities, goods, services, people, places, and ideas related to sport, fitness, recreation, and leisure are included in the scope of this work.
- The approach to all subject matter is solidly grounded in curriculum standards, an absolute "must" for any text that focuses on the fundamentals of sport marketing.
- The authors and editors have embraced diversity and avoided the traditional tendency to marginalize important trends and previously underdeveloped consumer groups, such as women in sport.
- The text integrates many important marketing elements typically overlooked or treated apart from the subject matter to which they refer (i.e., ethics, legal concerns, relevant professional associations and publications and current and future technology issues).

- The grammar, writing style and structure of each chapter make evident the fact that Dr. Pitts and Dr. Stotlar are teachers first and foremost. The book is laced with examples, learning activities, reference lists and suggested readings.

In short, the undergraduate student and teacher will be more than pleased with this book that meets every requirement of a basic text in sport marketing. The outstanding player is the person who understands and masters the fundamentals. Master *Fundamentals of Sport Marketing* and you are on your way to becoming an outstanding sport marketer.

Donna A. Lopiano, Ph.D.
Executive Director
Women's Sports Foundation

Preface

You are surrounded by the sport industry. As a matter of fact, you and the sport industry are so well integrated, you probably don't even notice it! As you read this preface, you are probably wearing sports shoes, a team logo cap, a team logo T-shirt, sports shorts; have just come from or are going to a work-out or a game; or are going to watch or have just watched a sports event on TV.

The sport business industry is tremendously vast and diverse. In 1988 it was estimated to be a $62 billion dollar industry and ranked 22nd among the top 50 industries in the United States--larger than the automobile industry! How can this be? At the time the industry was growing at the average rate of 6.8% per year. If it keeps growing at that rate, it will be a $136-billion dollar industry by the year 2000! The reason is that the sport industry is everywhere. There are millions of people who participate in hundreds of sports. There are hundreds of professional sports. There are people, organizations, and companies involved in producing, organizing, facilitating, and promoting everything that makes up the industry.

Think, for example, about what you would do on vacation were it not for sports and recreation activities like surfing, snow skiing, hiking, camping, boating, cruising, white water rafting, horseback riding, rock climbing, volleyball, sailing, in-line skating, aerobics, and basketball.

What would you do if there were no recreational leagues or weekend tournaments or competitions for softball, basketball, volleyball, tennis, golf, bowling, track and field, aerobics, swimming, biking, sailing, and boating?

What would you do if there were no sports equipment to use or sports facilities at which to participate? What would you wear for participation if there were no uniforms, sports apparel, or sports shoes?

What would you do if there were no sports to watch on TV or in person? What would you do if you did not have auto racing, basketball, golf, tennis, sailing, or fishing events to attend at your annual company outing? What would you do if you could not read about sports events or sport business news in the newspapers, magazines, or books?

This is the sport industry today. All products, people, and businesses that organize, facilitate, produce, or promote sports, fitness, recreation, or leisure activities or enterprises make up today's sport industry.

As we prepared *Fundamentals of Sport Marketing*, we kept the year 2000 in mind. Undergraduate sport management students who are reading this text will be completing their degrees and starting careers in the sport industry just as the year 2000 is upon us. They will be the executives who take over the industry at the beginning of a new century. They will be facing many years of potentially rewarding careers and personal lives. Just how rewarding that time will be depends on two factors--the sport management and sport marketing foundation of knowledge gained from the research of sport management and sport marketing scholars of today and the ability to adapt and embrace the changes and challenges of the world and the sport industry in a new century. We want those students to carry into the new century the knowledge and skills needed to succeed. Therefore, this book has been written with particular emphasis on the changing social, political, economical, and legal environments that will challenge the sport marketing management graduates.

In this book you will find the face of the sport industry presented through a multicultural approach. You will also find the depth and breadth of the industry through our presentation and utilization of a vast array of examples across a multitude of settings. For example, you will not find a chapter on women in sport. Women have been in sport throughout history. Therefore, women are interwoven throughout the text just as they are throughout the industry. To set women apart in one chapter would give the perception that they are not just as much a part of the industry as males, but rather, a group of people to be studied separately. We have presented many other populations in the same way throughout the text.

This book represents an original and creative work including sport marketing concepts and theories from many years of experience in the industry, in research, in teaching, in working with students, and in working closely with practitioners who spend every day working in the sport industry.

Fundamentals of Sport Marketing is part of a very important textbook project, the Sport Management Library (SML), based on the Sport Management Program Curriculum Standards of the National Association for Sport and Physical Education-North American Society for Sport Management (NASPE-NASSM). The SML will include 10 books written by some of the top scholars in sport management. It is being published by Fitness Information Technology. When these books are published, sport management faculty will have specialized topic textbooks for their classes.

Overview

Chapter 1 is an introduction to the sport industry. The terms *sport*, *industry*, *sport industry*, and *sport management* are defined as concept terms according to how they are used in the field of sport management. We believe if the student does not have a true perspective of the sport industry, the student's success can be jeopardized. Many factors that have been a positive influence on the growth and development of the sport industry and those that will affect the future growth and development are presented.

The sport management and sport marketing students of today will be challenged in their careers with the internationalization--or globalization--of the sport industry. Although the largest portion of the sport industry in the United States comprises leisure and participant sports and sporting goods, the student in a career in the sport industry will encounter sports activities and products of many cultures and countries introduced into the United States or will encounter U.S. sport businesses or organizations taking their product to other countries. Chapter 2, "The Global Market for the Sport Industry," offers an overview of the global marketplace for the sport marketer, what the sport management or sport marketing person needs to know to enter the global market, and what is in store for the sport industry as it moves into the global market.

To ignore history would leave the student with a gaping hole in understanding sport marketing as it is today. Chapter 3, "Historical Eras in Sport Marketing," fills the gap. Written by guest authors Dr. Lawrence W. Fielding and Dr. Lori K. Miller, the beginnings of sport marketing come alive and offer the reader the answer to the question "How did sport marketing get here?" The authors use a real company, the Hillerich & Bradsby Company, to present an historical picture of sport marketing in the United States. Further, the authors concentrate on two areas within the industry they found to have had the greatest impact on sport marketing in the sport industry--spectator sports events and sporting goods. A result of their research is the development of a model that illustrates what they identify as three distinctive eras in the historical development of sport marketing.

Chapter 4, "Sport Marketing Theory," marks the first discussion of a "theory" of sport marketing. In this discussion, the student learns that academicians have not yet agreed on what sport marketing is. Some have a narrow perspective and some a broad perspective. This, of course, influences the perspective that a student will learn. We have taken the broad perspective, believing that sport management graduates who take a career in the sport industry will potentially be much more successful if they have a more comprehensive perspective. Finally, a unique and original model of sport marketing management is presented. This model illustrates every aspect of sport marketing and serves as the working principle from which the functions of each aspect are detailed throughout the rest of the book.

The contents of Chapter 5, "Sport Marketing Research and Segmentation," are presented in two parts. The basis of every decision for the sport marketer must come from solid and current information. This information is gathered through research. Therefore, research is the foundation of sport marketing. The sport marketer uses this research to make decisions on segmentation--consumer segmentation and competitor segmentation--and for most areas within the sport enterprise.

Chapter 6, "Marketing Information Systems," describes marketing information systems and where and how to store and retrieve the data generated by the research.

Chapter 7 briefly describes the marketing mix elements and their functions within an organization and the marketing plan. Chapters 8, 9, 10, and 11 then detail each of the elements of the marketing mix.

Chapters 12, 13, 14, and 15 present details about promotional methods that have become practically synonymous with sports and the sport industry. Because these promotional methods are so prevalent, it is important that the student be exposed to such detailed information.

Structure of the Chapters For Learning -Each chapter takes the student through a logical outline of material specific to each chapter. Questions for study are at the end of each chapter. Students can used these questions as a study guide. There is also a set of learning activities. Students should use these activities to apply many of the concepts presented in the chapter.

ACKNOWLEDGMENTS

There are many people who made a variety of contributions to the writing and development of our book. We want to express our gratitude to them. First, we want to recognize the leadership of Janet B. Parks (Bowling Green State University). As the Editor-in-Chief of the SML project, Dr. Parks worked very hard to put it on track. Thanks to her guidance and determination (and occasional browbeating), the books in the SML will make a significant contribution to the sport management literature.

We want to thank the major reviewers, Wayne Blann (Ithaca College) and Richard Irwin (Memphis State University), for their work and insight. The final manuscript is much improved due to their suggestions and comments.

We want to thank Drs. Lawrence Fielding and Lori Miller for their contribution to this text--chapter 3. We believe this marks the first time a sport marketing textbook has offered a chapter on the history of sport marketing.

We want to thank the students in our sport marketing classes. We tested the book by using the material as it developed over the years. The students pointed out errors and questioned the concepts and models. Therefore, changes over the years resulted in very strong material.

In addition, we want to thank our colleagues who have reviewed and used our material over the years and made suggestions for improvement. We know you have been waiting for the finished book, and we are happy to finally get it to you. We know it is still not quite perfect, and we know you will let us know. You are the ultimate judge. As you use the book for your classes, let us hear from you. We will continue to improve the material.

Finally, we want to thank the efforts of people who did technical work on the material. Thank you, Michel Ball, at the University of Louisville, for your diligent work on the figures and tables. And thank you Fitness Information Technology, Inc. and Andy Ostrow for the original idea for this project and for seeing it through into print.

Brenda G. Pitts
David K. Stotlar

CHAPTER 1

THE SPORT BUSINESS INDUSTRY

THIS is a book about the fundamentals of sport marketing. Before you attempt to apply the fundamentals of sport marketing to a sport business, you must understand the sport business industry. What is it? What exists in the industry? What is the size of the industry? How has it developed? How does it compare to other industries? What does it offer the consumer? The answers to these questions are an important first step in sport marketing.

To develop an understanding of the term *sport industry*, we will first define the terms *sport* and *industry* and derive our definition of the sport industry. Second, we will discuss why the sport industry is so large and diverse by looking at the factors that influence the growth and development of the industry. You will learn that the growth of the sport industry has been phenomenal and that it continues to grow. As it grows, competition for the consumer dollar grows fierce. There is no other time than now that is more important for sport companies to become adept at sport marketing. The companies that survive will be those managed and directed by individuals with a sport management education in general and a sport marketing education in particular (Pitts & Fielding, 1991).

WHAT IS AN INDUSTRY?

An "industry," as defined by Porter (1985), is "a market in which similar or closely related products are sold to buyers" (p. 233). Some industries contain only one product. It is more typical that an industry comprises a variety of product items sold to many existing or potential consumers who vary demographically, psychographically, and who may change in need, want, desire, or demand (Porter, 1985).

Housing sales are part of the real estate industry. Other products that are included in the real estate industry are vacant land sales, ownership of rental property, and leasing business office space or warehouse space.

Another industry is the travel industry. Within this industry are travel agencies, airline companies, airplane manufacturers, hotel owners and managers, rental car agencies, limousine services, restaurants, luggage manufacturers and retailers, exhibition hall or conference facility operators, and businesses, such as amusement parks and souvenir merchandise manufacturers.

As you can see in the two examples, an industry comprises a few products or many products. Those products can be very closely related and similar or very loosely related and not so similar. Either way, the products are usually related in some way as defined by those involved in the industry. Later in this chapter, you will learn about the products that constitute the sport industry.

What Are Sport and Sport Management?

It is important that the sport management and sport marketing person understand the concept of sport as it is used in the field of sport management. Otherwise, the sport management or sport marketing professional does not have a true perspective of the industry, which can hurt the success of the sport management or sport marketer's work.

Notice that the title of this book is *Fundamentals of Sport Marketing* and not *Fundamentals of Sports Marketing*. Also note the use of the term *sport management* instead of *sports management*. The term *sport* has a very different meaning than *sports*.

According to Parks and Zanger (1990), the term *sports* "implies a collection of separate activities such as golf, soccer, hockey, volleyball, softball, and gymnastics—items in a series that can be counted" (p. 6). This is the way most people define sports—as sports activities. This typical definition reflects primarily two things: first, exposure to sports in our schools and colleges and second, exposure to sports every day through the media. That is, what the average person sees and hears through television coverage of sports events, the sports section in the newspaper, and the sports report on TV news broadcasts is sports activities as they take place or a report of the outcome. Therefore, *sports* management implies only managing *sports* activities.

Sport, however, is a collective noun and a more all-encompassing concept. Therefore, the North American Society for Sport Management (NASSM), the association composed of university academicians and scholars, chose the word *sport* as a term that more correctly identifies and defines the sport management field of study (Parks & Zanger, 1990).

The term *sport management* therefore implies a much broader concept. It is all people, activities, businesses, and organizations involved in producing, facilitating, promoting, or organizing sports, fitness, and recreation products. This includes, for example, the company that manufactures sports equipment, clothing or shoes; a person or company that offers promotional services for a sports organization; an organization charged with governing a sport; a person who represents a professional athlete as an agent; people who own and manage a sports facility;

people who design and construct those sports facilities; a person who teaches golf; a company that manages the promotional merchandise and licenses for a sports event; and television companies that are involved in broadcasting sports events.

WHAT IS THE SPORT INDUSTRY?

We may now define the term sport industry. The research of Pitts, Fielding, and Miller (1994) and a study by *The Sporting News* and Wharton Econometric Forecasting Association Group (Comte & Stogel, 1990) provide thorough descriptions of the products and buyers that constitute the sport industry. Their research shows that the sport industry includes a wide variety of sport-oriented products and buyers. The product offerings include sports, fitness, recreation, or leisure activities and their related goods and services. The buyers include businesses and consumers from all populations (see chapter 5).

Based on this research and the definitions of sport and industry presented earlier, the definition of sport industry follows.

> The SPORT INDUSTRY is the market in which the products offered to its buyers are sport, fitness, recreation, or leisure-related and may be activities, goods, services, people, places, or ideas.

Here are some examples of the types of products offered in the sport industry:

- sports offered as a participation product, such as participation in a women's recreational basketball league
- sports offered as a spectatorial product (entertainment), such as a baseball game, the American Gladiators, or wrestling
- equipment and apparel needed or desired to participate in sports and fitness activities, such as softball uniforms, ice hockey pads and other equipment, women's body building apparel, roller blade skates, and bicycle helmets
- promotional merchandise used to promote sports, sport events, or fitness activity, such as team logo caps and shirts, fitness club shirts or towels, stadium cushions, and blankets with logo
- facilities needed or desired for producing sport, such as a new sport stadium, or remodeled racquetball courts to accommodate wallyball
- services, such as tennis racket stringing, laundry, or golf club cleaning
- recreational activities, such as mountain bicycling, hiking, camping, horseback riding, boating, cross country skiing, sailing, and mountain climbing
- complete management and marketing for a large marathon offered by a private company that specializes in the management and

marketing of marathons and other running events

- an individual offering to handle the financial, legal, contractual, and promotional affairs of a professional athlete
- magazines about specific sports and other activities offered by publishing companies.

The Size of the Sport Industry

In 1990, a report of a study of the sport industry revealed that the Gross National Sports Product (the sum of output and services generated by the sports industry) totaled $63.1 billion in 1988 (Comte & Stogel, 1990). A summary of the study over a 3-year period from 1986 to 1988 is presented in Table 1.1. This summary shows that from 1986 to 1988 the sport industry grew an average of 6.8% yearly. This is an important figure to note when comparing the sport industry to other industries that usually average a yearly growth of 1 to 3%. If the sport industry were to continue an average yearly growth of 6.8%, by the year 2000 the sport industry will be a $139-billion dollar industry. In other words, it could be over twice the size it was in 1988.

In the 1987 study, the sport industry ranked 23rd among the top 50 U.S.

TABLE 1.1 - The Sport Industry Today

According to the GNSP (Gross National Sports Product): the sum of output and services generated by the sports industry.

1st Study	1986 data	$47.3 billion		
2nd Study	1987 data	$50.2 billion	+6.1%	23rd largest industry in U.S.A.
3rd Study	1988 data	$63.1 billion	+7.5%	22nd largest industry in U.S.A.

Increase yearly of +6.8%

Source: Sports, Inc. & Sporting News with WEFA (Wharton Econometric Forecasting Association)

industries by gross national product (Sandomir, 1988). In 1988, the sport industry improved by one to the 22nd position among the top 50. Table 1.2 illustrates the 1987 position and the industries that were larger and smaller than the sport industry. Table 1.3 illustrates the broad categories of products identified in the study.

Another way to help us determine the size and especially the depth and breadth of the sport industry is to look at the factors that have affected growth and development of the industry and at the situation that exists in the industry.

TABLE 1.2 - The Top 50 Industries in 1987

		(In billions)
1.	Real estate	$519.3
2.	Manufacturing (durable goods)	479.9
3.	Retail trade	427.4
4.	Regulated industry	408.2
5.	Manufacturing (non-durable goods)	373.6
6.	Wholesale trade	313.0
7.	Health services	223.7
8.	Business services	179.3
9.	Communications	120.9
10.	Radio and television	108.3
11.	Insurance	101.3
12.	Miscellaneous professional organizations	86.4
13.	Electrical machinery	85.0
14.	Banking	84.8
15.	Chemicals and allied products	77.1
16.	Food and kindred products	74.0
17.	Insurance carriers	72.7
18.	Trucking and warehousing	64.2
19.	Legal services	62.3
20.	Fabricated metals	60.3
21.	Printing and publishing	58.2
22.	Non-auto transportation equipment	56.0
23.	**SPORTS**	**50.2**
24.	Motor vehicles and parts	49.9
25.	Social and membership organizations	45.3
26.	Paper and allied products	39.5
27.	Auto repair garages	38.9
28.	Security/commodity brokers	36.7
29.	Primary metals	36.4
30.	Lodging	35.7
31.	Personal services	34.4
32.	Air transportation	34.2
33.	Petroleum and related products	33.6
34.	Rubber and plastics	29.9
35.	Educational services	29.6
36.	Insurance agents and brokers	28.6
37.	Lumber	27.7
38.	Stone, clay and glass	27.5
39.	Instrument manufacturing	26.9
40.	Amusement and recreation services	24.0
41.	Apparel	22.5
42.	Textile mills	19.9
43.	Credit agencies	17.0
44.	Holdings and other investment firms	16.2
45.	Tobacco	15.5
46.	Furniture and fixtures	14.9
47.	Miscellaneous repairs	13.9
47.	Miscellaneous manufacturing	13.9
49.	Telephone and telegraph	12.7
50.	Transportation services	12.0

Source: Comte, E. & Stogel, C. (1990, January 1). Sports: A $63.1 billion industry. *The Sporting News,* 208(28), p. 60-61.

TABLE 1.3 - Categories of the Sport Industry 1987-1988

Category	1987	1988 (in millions)	Percent change
Leisure & participant sports	$21,599.5	$22,789.3	+ 5.5
Sporting goods	18,069.3	19,012.8	+ 5.2
Advertising	4,058.6	4,388.5	+ 8.1
Net take from legal gambling	3,504.8	3,618.3	+ 3.2
Spectator sports receipts	3,050.0	3,240.0	+ 6.2
Concessions, souvenirs, novelties	2,100.0	2,348.1	+11.8
TV and radio rights fees	1,209.2	1,415.8	+17.1
Corporate sponsorships	1,012.0	1,140.0	+12.6
Golf course, ski area construction	542.3	946.9	+74.6
Sports insurance	722.0	830.0	+15.0
Magazine circulation revenues	658.6	773.0	+17.4
Royalties from licensed properties	584.0	735.0	+25.9
Athlete endorsements	520.0	585.8	+12.7
Trading cards and accessories	350.0	408.3	+16.7
Sports book purchases	241.0	330.7	+37.2
Stadium and arena construction	250.0	319.3	+27.7
U.S. Olympic Committee, NGB budgets	98.2	114.2	+16.3
Youth team fees	95.3	97.0	+ 1.8
Halls of fame	5.4	6.0	+11.1
Total	**$58,670.2**	**$63,099.0**	**+ 7.5**

Source: (Comte & Stogel, 1990). Note: Several categories have been statistically adjusted with updated 1987 figures, which may vary from previous publications; sports insurance premiums include professional and amateur teams, and individual players, but not multi-purpose facilities.

Factors In The Growth And Development Of The Sport Industry

The sport industry is very large and very diverse. To understand this it is important to look at some of the past, present, and future factors influencing the growth and development of the industry (see Figure 1.4) (Pitts, 1993). The sport marketer must constantly analyze what is affecting the industry because that influence could be something that may impact a product or a business that could lead to success or disaster. If the sport marketer studies and understands how the factors affect the product or business, decisions and strategies can be developed that will lead to success.

1.

Increase in the number of new and different sport, fitness, and recreation activities.

Since the middle 1970s the United States has experienced a consistent and fast growth in the number and type of sport-, fitness-, or recreation-related activity offered to the buyer. Consider the following examples. In the late 1970s, a presumably new way to get fit was offered. This was called aerobics—exercising to music. Today, there must be hundreds of different kinds of aerobics offered for

1. Increase in the number of new and different sport, fitness, & recreation activities.
2. Increase in number of same sports offered.
3. Increase in number and type of sport magazines & trade magazines.
4. Increase in leisure time.
5. Increase in mass media exposure.
6. The fitness boom of the 1970s.
7. Increase in number and type of facilities, events, and participation.
8. Increase in and expansion of sport related goods and services for the variety of market segments.
9. Increase in the number and type of profession level sport, fitness, and recreational activity.
10. The movement from single-purpose to multi-purpose facilities.
11. Increase in sport for the diversity of the populations.
12. Increase in sponsorship & funding of sport from the general business community.
13. Increase in endorsement.
14. Increase in sport education.
15. Increase in profits.
16. Increase in technology in sport related goods, services & training.
17. Enhancement of sport as a consumer product.
18. Increase in marketing and marketing orientation in the sport industry.
19. Increase in competency of management of sport.
20. The globalization of sport and the global market for sport.

FIGURE 1.4 - Factors Influencing the Growth of the Sport Industry - Past, Present, and Future
Source: Pitts, 1993

consumption to a wide variety of consumers; for example, there are soft aerobics, hard aerobics, jazzerobics, elderobics, and baby-robics. Recently, in-line skating made its way across the continent. Boogie-boarding was invented. Consider these new sports offered: snow kayaking, hang gliding, parasailing, windsurfing, ice surfing, knee boarding, 2-person and 3-person beach volleyball, indoor soccer, and even something called bungee-jumping.

With this type of fast and diverse growth in inventions in sport and fitness activities comes increased participation from many populations of consumers. Whereas the traditional sport of outdoor 11-on-11 soccer played for two 45-minute halves might not interest someone, that person might be interested in trying a modified game of soccer indoor, 5-on-5, for four 12-minute quarters.

These new inventions have increased the number and type of sport activity products offered to the consumer and have reached an increased number and type of consumer market segments. This kind of new product development is one key to success in competitive strategy.

2.

Increase in number of same sports.

There has been an expansion in the offerings of existing sports and other activities. In other words, if someone wanted to play volleyball a few decades ago, the few options available were to join a YWCA, YMCA, or a local city parks and recreation league. Today, volleyball is offered by multisport centers, clubs, independent organizations, through individual tournaments, and even by local pubs or bars.

Soccer was a sport almost unknown in the United States just a few decades ago. Today, soccer may be found at many parks and recreation facilities, privately owned facilities, state facilities, and on the campuses of schools and colleges. It is offered to consumers of all ages. There are leagues for children who are 4 years old as well as the fast-growing leagues for the 30-something, 40-something, and 50-something player.

3.

Increase in number and type of sport magazines and trade magazines.

Walk into any local book store and go to the magazine section. How many magazines can you count that are sport-, fitness-, health-, leisure-, or recreation-oriented? If the sport exists, there is or soon will be a magazine for it. The variety includes boating, sailing, in-line skating, hunting, fishing, flying, running, walking, adventure travel, camping, hiking, mountain biking, four-wheeling, canoeing, water sports, snow sports, and a multitude of others.

What are the purposes of the magazines? What purposes do they serve for the consumer? They expose the consumer to a sport. They educate, encourage, and support participating in the sport or becoming a spectator of the sport. They serve as a source of information and as a resource for networking. They serve as a catalogue of sport equipment and apparel and therefore offer to the manufacturers a source of advertising directly to a target market. Of course, there is a profit to be made for the publishers.

This proliferation of information has influenced the popularity of and the growth of participation in sport-, fitness-, and recreation-oriented activity. It also has an effect on sporting goods and services sales.

4.

Increase in leisure time.

Although this factor fluctuates almost constantly and certainly on an individual basis, there is a constant: When leisure time increases, involvement in sports increases. Leisure time is the amount of time a person is not at organized work, their job. Typically, a person is on the job an average of 40 hours per week.

The other hours of the week are used for many activities, including sports and other recreational pursuits.

When a person is working only a part-time job, that person has more leisure time. When a person has lost a job, leisure time increases dramatically.

5.

Increase in mass media exposure.

The advent of television and certainly the broadcasting of sports on television have had a tremendous impact on the growth of the sport industry. Through television, people are exposed to a variety of sports and sport events. The demand for sport on television gave way to advertising dollars for the networks and for the sport enterprise as well. The exposure has influenced the awareness of sport, the popularity of sport, and the participation in sport.

Sport businesses use television as a promotional tool. Sport as an activity and sporting goods and services use television. At the same time television uses sport to attract viewers.

How many industries enjoy this fact: Almost all newspapers around the world include a separate section covering sports. Reading about sports and recreation increases the awareness of sport and the desire to participate in sports and recreation.

6.

The fitness boom of the 1970s.

The United States experienced a fitness boom in the 1970s. As the Baby Boomers began to mature and became aware of their lagging overall fitness and health levels, they became involved in fitness- and health-related activities. In reaction to this increased interest, a number of fitness and health-care products hit the market. There was an increase in the number of sports centers, fitness centers, and health clubs, as well as a proliferation of related products.

The fitness boom has had a lasting effect. It increased the general population's awareness of fitness, wellness, and overall health. Concern over getting into shape resulted in a large number of people taking up a variety of fitness- and sport-related activities.

7.

Increase in number and type of facilities, events, and participation.

The increased interest in sport, fitness, and recreation activity over the last few decades has influenced the number and type of facilities, events and overall participation in sport-, fitness- and recreation-related activity. More sport and fitness facilities have been built. They are much more accessible to the consumer and are accessible in a variety of ways. For example, the number of golf courses built increased during the late 1980s and early 1990s. The largest percentage of these are public courses. Therefore, golf is more affordable and accessible to more consumer segments.

Another factor influencing this growth in building sport facilities and offering events is money. Call any city visitors and convention office, and they can tell you how many conventions were held in the city during the prior year. They can also give you an estimate on the economic impact of each of those conventions. Economic impact includes the money brought into the city because of the convention—money spent by the convention attendees on lodging, food, and transportation. In the last decade, many cities studied the economic impact of sport events and determined there was great potential for positive economic impact similar to that of conventions.

Realizing the money involved, many cities built sports facilities and created committees whose primary responsibility is to attract sporting events. The sporting events might include small events such as a 10K run, a car race, a 3-on-3 basketball tournament, a beach volleyball tournament, or a rodeo. These efforts can also include trying to attract events as large as the Olympics.

8.

Increase in and expansion of sport-related goods and services for the variety of market segments.

It was not so long ago that most sporting goods and sports equipment were designed and made only for the white male participant. Today, sporting goods manufacturers are designing goods and equipment for a variety of consumers. Further, the number of companies, retail or manufacturer, owned and managed by people who are not white males is increasing. These companies are set up to design sports equipment specifically for other populations. A woman, for example, may look for running shoes made for a woman's foot instead of having to purchase a shoe made for a male and modifying it to fit her feet. A child who wants to play soccer can buy soccer shoes made specifically for children.

At the same time, technology and design have influenced sports equipment and apparel. Tennis rackets are available in a variety of sizes: The grip is offered in several sizes, shapes, and materials; the racket head is offered in several sizes and materials; several types of string are offered; and, the weight of the racket varies. Uniforms come in a variety of styles, sizes, and materials. Most sports have clothing or equipment custom designed for enhancing performance. Consider the one-piece vinyl-looking suits used by those in the sport of luge. The style and material are aerodynamically designed for speed.

Sporting goods, as well as the sport activity, are much more available, more affordable, and more accessible to more consumer segments. Historically, tennis was enjoyed exclusively by the wealthy. Today, tennis is affordable to and enjoyed by people of many income levels.

Services surrounding sport and fitness activities have expanded. Services offered in some fitness clubs include laundry service, racket stringing, golf club cleaning, child care, concessions, restaurants, lounges, suntanning beds, valet parking, and massage.

The variety of goods and services are expanding to accommodate the many populations in today's world. The demographics and psychographics of the people in the United States change almost constantly. At one time a marketer could safely assume that the greatest majority of people living in the United States were Caucasian, Christian, and heterosexual, and that a household consisted of a traditional marriage and family of a woman, man, and a few children. In today's world, opposite-sex married couples with and without children comprise only about 55% of U.S. households in 1990 (Ball, 1989). The other 45% include those who are living alone (24%), female-headed households (12%), male-headed households (3%), opposite sex living together (3%), and same sex living together (2%) (Ball, 1989). Knowledge of and sensitivity to current household structures are important in decisions concerning all marketing strategies.

Sports equipment designed for people with disabilities is being developed more frequently today. There are softballs that emit a beeping sound for individuals with impaired vision. There are wheelchairs designed for speed. Materials are very lightweight, and the chair is aerodynamically designed and constructed. The wheelchair is used in activities such as basketball, running, and tennis participation.

9.

Increase in the number and type of professional-level sport, fitness, and recreational activity.

Refer back to Factors 1 and 2. When a new sport activity is invented, sometimes that sport becomes a professional sport activity. A professional sport is one in which the participant is paid to perform or in which the participant is making a career of the activity. Consider the number and range of sport and fitness activity that are professional today: racing cars, trucks, boats, horses, and dogs; Frisbee throwing; water sports, such as water skiing, knee boarding, trick skiing, jet skiing, surfing, boogie boarding, wind surfing, sailing, yachting, and fishing; snow sports, such as downhill and cross-country racing, trick skiing, ice sailing, dog-sledding, and ice fishing; bowling; billiards; hang gliding; aerobics competition; and body building. While the number of professional activities has increased the number of professional sports participants, it has also increased the number of opportunities available for the sport management and sport marketing professional in producing, facilitating, promoting, or organizing the events. In addition, it increases the need for sports equipment and apparel designed for the professional sport and participant.

10.

The movement from single-purpose to multipurpose facilities.

Early sport, fitness, and recreation facilities were typically single sport or single purpose. Today, sport facilities are built with the capability to serve many purposes and to accommodate many sports events as well as nonsports events. Consider today's fitness centers. Most will have the usual weight-lifting room, sauna, and suntanning beds. Further inspection will reveal large multipurpose rooms for aerobics and other activities, an indoor and outdoor pool, steam rooms, whirlpool spas, plush locker rooms and full-service dressing rooms, child-care services, restaurants, lounges, volleyball courts, racquetball courts, basketball courts, tennis courts, massage services, a pro shop, and many auxiliary services, such as racket stringing, laundry services, hair dryers, shampoo, and even toothbrushes and toothpaste.

The multipurpose multisport facility serves today's fitness- and health-minded consumer as a home away from home. These facilities are more accessible, more convenient and, more efficient, and they can accommodate the consumer's changing desires for something different when the consumer gets bored with one sport.

There are still some single-sport facilities built today, the primary purpose of which is to accommodate one sport. As examples, look at the Toronto Sky Dome, the Joe Robbie Stadium in Miami, and the Super Dome in New Orleans. Even though they were built primarily to service one or two sports, however, other events are staged in the facility.

11.

Increase in sport for the diversity of the populations.

As sports are taken up by the variety of populations that exist in the United States and around the world, the increase was and is affected primarily by two factors. One factor is that populations want organizations and services of their own and are organizing sports and managing sport businesses specifically for the people of the population. Another factor is that as populations gain equal rights, legislation has forced increased opportunity in sport, fitness, or recreational activity.

For some populations, sports opportunities increased almost parallel to their fight for their civil rights in this country. The African American population's involvement in sport, fitness, and recreation activity increased as their struggle for civil and equal rights made progress.

Women and girls gained more involvement in organized high school and collegiate athletics because of legislation aimed at stopping discrimination based on gender in educational institutions. The number of women and girls participating in sports and athletics has increased significantly since the early 1970s.

The number of sport businesses, organizations, and events primarily targeting the lesbian and gay population has grown at a very fast rate (Pitts, 1989; 1994). The event that represents and reflects the growth of sport in the lesbian and gay population is their Olympic sporting event, the Gay Games. The Games are held every 4 years, and the number of events, participants, sponsors, and attendance has grown at a phenomenal rate. The Gay Games have been held four times since 1982, and the numbers have increased almost 400% (see Table 1.5). As a matter of record, there were over 11,000 participants in Gay Games IV in 1994, which makes it the largest sporting event, as of 1994, of the 1990s decade.

The passage of legislation such as Public Law 94-142 and other similar legislation aimed at stopping discrimination against people with disabilities has resulted in increased opportunities in sports and fitness activity for these individuals. The passage of the Americans with Disabilities Act of 1990 will perhaps have a significant impact on enhancing the accessibility of sports facilities (Miller, Fielding, & Pitts, 1993).

TABLE 1.5 - Facts of the Gay Games

Date/Site	Participants	Countries	Events	Attendance	Workers
Gay Games I San Francisco 1982	1,300	12	14	50,000	600
Gay Games II San Francisco 1986	3,482	22	17	75,000	1,200
Gay Games III Vancouver 1990	7,300	28	31	200,000	3,000
Gay Games IV New York City 1994	11,000	40	31	700,000	7,000
Gay Games V Amsterdam 1998	?	?	31	?	?

Sources: Coe, R. 1986; Marks, J. 1986; Pitts, B.G. 1989; Pitts, B.G. 1994, June; Schaap, D., 1987.

12.

Increase in sponsorship and funding of sports from the general business community.

Companies are heavily involved in sponsorship today. Watch any race car driver step out of her or his car. Look at the uniform, and what do you see? The uniform is covered with patches of the many companies that provided money to the racing team organization. Look at the car. It is almost impossible to see the car because it is covered with sponsors' logos.

The provision of money usually comes with the agreement that the name or logo of the company will be displayed. Conditions of the contract will include many specifications concerning where and when the logo will be displayed, its size, and how often it will be displayed.

Why do companies get involved in sponsorship? The most common reasons are that the company wants the public to think of it as a caring company; that it wants the public to see and to remember its name; and, in many cases, that sponsorship is less expensive than other forms of advertising.

13.

Increase in endorsement.

Over the last few decades, the use of individuals or companies in sport to endorse a product has increased. The product may or may not be a sport product. The agreement may involve a fee or goods and/or services traded for the individual's or company's time. Use of the endorser brings attention to the product by capitalizing on the popularity of the endorser. There are different categories of endorsement, some of which are:

- individual endorsement: use of an athlete, coach, owner, or other individual person
- team endorsement: use of a full team
- full organization: use of an entire organization, such as the use of the NCAA (National Collegiate Athletic Association), the NFL (National Football Association), the IOC (International Olympic Committee), or USOC (United States Olympic Committee) to endorse a product.

14.

Increase in sport education.

People want to learn how to play sports, games, and other activities. Some want to learn how to officiate, coach, and train athletes. Some want to learn how to organize and manage sporting enterprises. Others want to learn how to produce or promote sports events. These are some examples of what some people want to learn related to sport. When people desire something, it is usually eventually offered for sale. Education in sport also is used as a means of promoting and encouraging participation in sport and of promoting other sport products. The consumer is offered tennis lessons, golf lessons, summer camps for children for almost every sport, and fitness weeks for the adults. Other examples include education for coaches, such as coaching clinics, seminars, conferences, and workshops. There are meetings and clinics to educate officials. There is a vast array of books, videocassettes, and magazines that offer lessons, suggestions, and tips for improving performance. Recently, there has been an increase in the popularity of sport management degree programs for undergraduate and graduate students who want a career in sport management in the sport industry. All of these products have positively affected the sport industry.

Parallel to this, of course, is an increase in related sport products. For example, there are all kinds of equipment offered as teaching apparatus to improve performance. In addition, someone has to produce official's uniforms, caps, whistles, flags, socks, shoes, jackets, and even bags.

15.

Increase in profits.

As sport has become commercialized, the cost of producing sport has increased, and hence, the price of sport and sport-related products has increased. Executives in the sport industry have begun to apply more and better sport business and sport marketing skills, and therefore, profits have increased. The increase in sales of everything related to sport has created increased overall profits in the sport industry. In some cases, the profits have been used to increase services and goods, or as a cost savings to the consumer.

16.

Increase in technology in sport-related goods, services, and training.

The sport industry has benefited from advances in technology. Technology has influenced sports equipment, facilities, clothing, and shoes, and has affected performance through sophisticated training programs. Some specific examples include computer-assisted programs in nutrition, training, skill analysis, and equipment design and materials used in equipment, uniforms, shoes, and other gear.

17.

Enhancement of sport as a consumer product.

Companies with sports for sale have done a much better job of packaging sports to attract a wide variety of consumers. Fitness centers and sports clubs have enhanced their offerings to attract and keep consumers. As you learned earlier, fitness centers have become almost a "home-away-from-home." Every convenience and service are offered to get and to keep the consumer's attention.

Sports for sale as a spectatorial, or entertainment, product are being packaged to attract many more consumers and a greater variety of consumers. For example, consider a minor league men's professional baseball game. The consumer is lured to the park with accommodations for tailgating (partying in the parking lot before and after a game), a chance to be one of the first 2,000 people through the gate to receive a huggie (a plastic can cooler), and the possibility of winning a brand-new truck during the 7th-inning stretch (based on ticket-stub number drawing). Moreover, for one hour after the game, a local country music band will play their hearts out while the consumers two-step on the infield. What a bargain!

In another example, the Kentucky Derby offers over 70 events leading up to and surrounding the Kentucky Derby horse race. The actual race lasts only about 2 minutes, but the events surrounding the race now last about 4 weeks. The primary reason for offering the consumer more than just the sports event is to make the sports event the centerpiece of a larger event. Of course, another reason is money. Many people and businesses profit from the Kentucky Derby. Therefore, everyone cooperates in order to bring in more consumers.

18.

Increase in marketing and marketing orientation in the sport industry.

As sport managers learn and then apply the fundamentals of sport marketing to the sport industry, the sport industry is treated more as a business, and sport products are designed with the consumer needs in mind. Maybe you have heard the expression "Give the consumers what they want!" This applies evermore to the sport industry. Take, for example, basketball rules changes specifically for entertainment value: The dunk was legalized because the fans loved it; there are TV timeouts because television's advertisers need the time for their commercials. Why isn't soccer televised in the United States on a regular basis? Because there are no timeouts in order to assure advertiser's commercials. Television officials are pressuring soccer officials to change the rules in order to make it "TV friendly." In other words, rules in sports are changed to make the sport more marketable.

19.

Increase in competency of management in sport.

Although sport management is still a new field of study when compared to most other disciplines, it will have an influence on the sport industry. The number of undergraduate, master's, and doctoral programs of study in sport management continues to grow at a fast rate. In 1993, curriculum standards were approved by the members of the North American Society for Sport Management, and in 1994 an accrediting process began (NASPE-NASSM Joint Task Force on Sport Management Curriculum and Accreditation, 1993). Students who earn degrees in sport management will fill the jobs in the sport industry. Eventually, there will be more employees and executives in the sport industry with a sport management degree than with other degrees. As appropriately educated sport administrators begin to manage in the sport industry, they will have a positive effect on the industry.

20.

The globalization of sport and the sport industry.

The globalization of sport and the sport industry is here. Consider the attempts of American football executives to expand with teams in Europe and Asia. Who would have ever thought that the 1994 mens World Cup in soccer would be played out in the United States? Consider the sheer size of the modern Olympics: There were just over 10,000 athletes from 172 countries competing in 257 events at the Olympic Games in Barcelona in 1992. Consider sport products like shoes, clothing, and equipment. Around the world, you will find people who know the goods and equipment of Nike, Adidas, Puma, and other companies that have put their products in the hands of people everywhere. (You will learn more about the globalization of the sport industry in chapter 2.)

What Exists in the Sport Industry?

You should have a good start on understanding the depth and breadth of the sport industry. As you discovered in the preceding sections, the industry is quite large and varied. It is so large and diverse that it is necessary to organize what exists in the industry to make it easier to study and easier to understand everything that might be included in the industry.

Consider an experiment in determining exactly everything—sport activity, sport business, and all related products—that is included in this super-large industry. Do this by developing a list. You could get organized by creating categories. The categories could contain products in the industry that have commonalities, such as categories of sporting goods and equipment, clothing, shoes, sport activities, sport marketing companies, and fitness centers. Of course, trying to list everything in the United States would be practically impossible. You would end up with an enormous list! So let's start with your home town. Consider some resources that will help you, such as the yellow pages and copies of your local newspaper. List all the YMCAs and YWCAs and what is offered in each one. Write down every activity, service, good, league, tournament, and other product offered at the Ys. Now list city recreation offices and everything offered. List the fitness centers and health clubs and everything offered. Develop a list of youth sport organizations and everything offered. Add to your list sporting goods outlets (hunting, fishing, general), golf courses and driving ranges, sports clubs, recreation centers, company recreation and fitness centers, sports magazines, newspapers, books, videocassettes, television shows, local college athletics departments, professional sports teams, church-affiliated sports or fitness centers, water sport outlets and marinas, sailing clubs, snow ski outlets and clubs, bowling centers, tennis centers, running clubs and events, and everything else related to sport.

How many pages do you have so far? You should have several even if you live in a very small town. You may not have realized just how much you are surrounded by sport and sport-related products.

Now multiply the number of items on your list by the number of towns and cities in your state. Remember, the lists will increase as population and city size increases. Now you have an idea of the size of the sport industry in your town and in your state.

As you can see, finding a way to categorize your lists is a more effective way to study what exists in the sport industry. As one method, definitions can be used. However, as pointed out earlier in the chapter, sport is defined in many different ways, and most of the definitions include only sports activities. What about everything else in the industry? In other methods there are a few studies that have tried to identify and categorize everything that comprises the industry. Comte and Stogel (1990) categorized the industry according to the amount of money involved. Parks and Zanger (1990) categorized the industry according to career

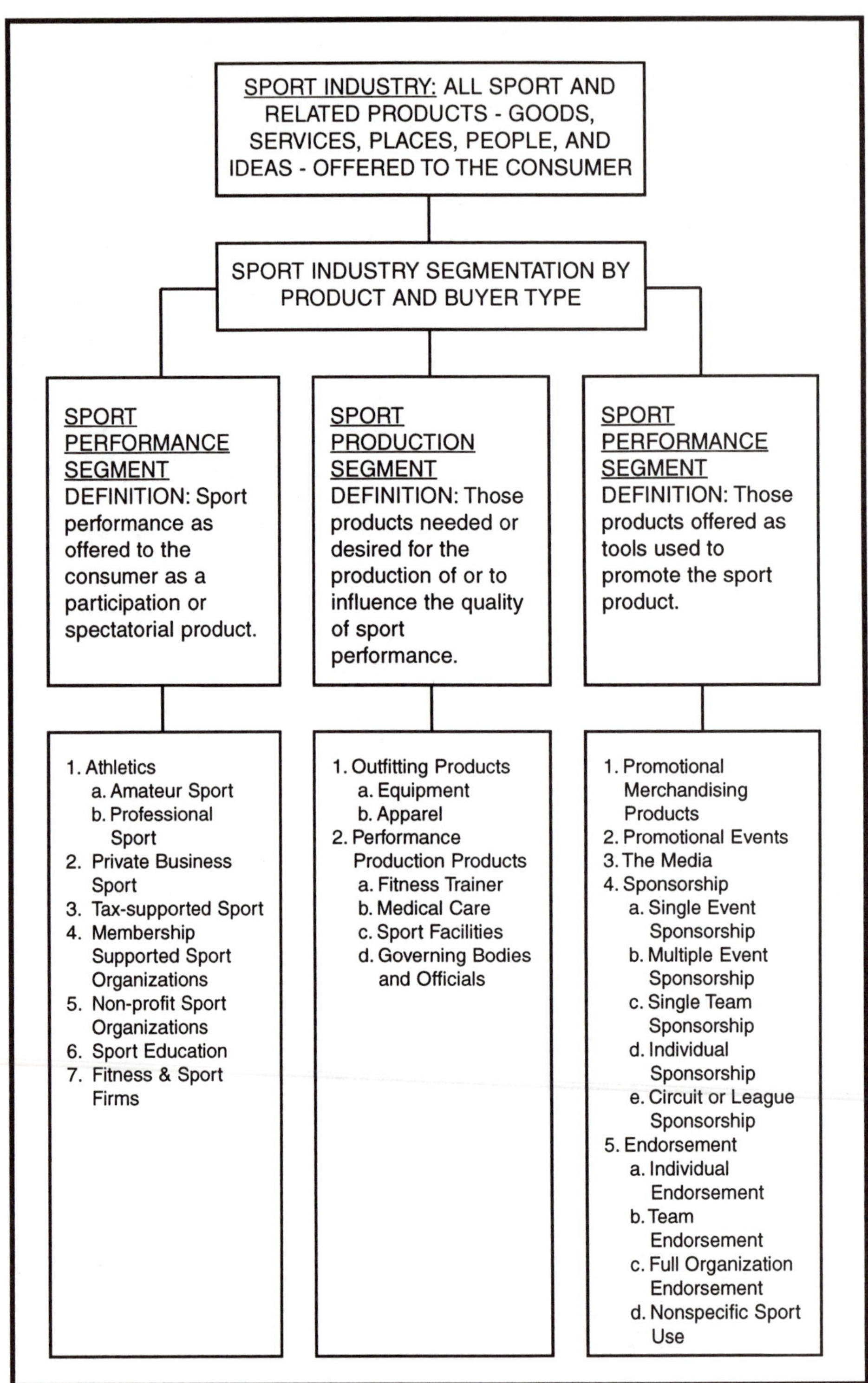

FIGURE 1.6 - The Sport Industry Segment Model

Source: Pitts, Fielding, & Miller, 1994

segments. Pitts et al. (1994) categorized it according to products and buyers.

As shown in Table 1.3 earlier in this chapter, Comte and Stogel (1990) ranked categories in the sport industry according to the largest and smallest amounts of money involved. You can see that they included a variety of categories ranging from gambling to advertising to broadcasting rights fees.

Parks and Zanger (1990) identified 14 career segments in the sport industry according to common skills and knowledge needed specific to an area. The career areas are intercollegiate athletics, professional sport, facility management, campus recreation programs, community-based sport, sports information, sport marketing, sports journalism, sports club management, the physical fitness industry, athletic training and sports medicine, aquatics management, consulting, and entrepreneurship. This type of categorization can be very helpful for a student in sport management in determining which area of the sport industry the student might like to enter in search of a career.

The sport industry was divided into segments based on products and buyers in a study by Pitts et al. (1994). In their study, every product was considered according to its function or benefit to a consumer. Three categories, or industry segments, were identified: the sport performance industry segment, the sport production industry segment, and the sport promotion industry segment (see Figure 1.6). This type of categorization, called industry segmentation, is helpful to the sport marketing professional in planning marketing strategies. An understanding of product function is key to a marketer.

Chapter Summary

Students in sport management and in sport marketing must develop an understanding of the sport industry, sport management, and sport marketing. An industry is a market containing similar products. Some industries contain only one product. The sport industry contains several. The sport industry is the market in which the products offered to its buyers are sport-, fitness-, recreation- or leisure-related and may be activities, goods, services, people, places, or ideas. The sport industry is a very large, very broad, and very diverse industry. Its products serve a large and diverse consumer. There are studies that created categories or industry segments as a way of organizing the sport industry in order to better define and understand it.

There are many factors that have affected and will affect the sport industry. Some had an impact in the past in the growth and development of the industry. Some will continue to have an effect on the industry in the future. The sport management and sport marketing professional should constantly monitor these factors and others in order to develop educated decisions and strategies.

Questions For Study

1. What is the sport business industry? Give some examples.
2. Describe the size of the sport industry in dollars.
3. What are the many factors that influence the growth and development of the sport industry? Give examples.
4. What is sport management?
5. What is the North American Society for Sport Management?
6. What exists in the sport industry? What are some ways to categorize what exists in the sport industry?

Learning Activities

1. Create a list of sport industry businesses, organizations, clubs, and other enterprises in your city or community. Categorize everything according to the three sport industry segments created by the Pitts, Fielding, & Miller (1994) model: sport performance, sport production, and sport promotion.
2. For each item listed in your list, list the jobs within each.
3. For each item listed in your list, list the sport products offered to the consumer.
4. Write to the North American Society for Sport Management and ask for information about the organization.
5. Subscribe to sport management journals, such as the *Journal of Sport Management, Sport Marketing Quarterly, and the Seton Hall Journal of Sport Law.*

References

Ball, A. (November 13, 1989). Here's who's living with whom. *Adweek's Marketing Week*, p. HM 11.

Coe, R. (1986). *A sense of pride: The story of Gay Games II*. San Francisco: Pride Publications.

Comte, E., & Stogel, C. (1990, January 1). Sports: A $63.1 billion industry. *The Sporting News*, pp. 60-6

Marks, J. (Sept. 30, 1986). Gay Games IV. *The Advocate*, 42-49, 108-10.

Miller, L.K., Fielding, L.W., & Pitts, B.G. (1993). The impact of the Americans with Disabilities Act of 1990. *Clinical Kinesiology, 47*(3), 63-70.

NASPE-NASSM Joint Task Force on Sport Management Curriculum and Accreditation (1993). Standards for curriculum and voluntary accreditation of sport management programs. *Journal of Sport Management, 7*(2), 159-170.

Parks, J.B., & Zanger, B.R.K. (1990). Definition and direction. In J.B. Parks & B.R.K. Zanger (Eds.), *Sport & fitness management: Career strategies and professional content* (pp. 1-14). Champaign, IL: Human Kinetics Books.

Pitts, B.G. (1989). Beyond the bars: The development of leisure activity management in the lesbian and gay population in America. *Leisure Information Quarterly, 15*(3), 4-6.

Pitts, B.G. (1993, September). *The development of sport marketing theory and the sport industry in the United States*. Paper presented at the Fourth International Conference on Management Development in Sport and Recreation, Johannesburg, Durban, Port Elizabeth, and Capetown, South Africa.

Pitts, B.G. (1994, June). *Leagues of their own: Growth and development of lesbian and gay sport in America.* Paper presented at the First International Gay Games Conference, New York, NY.

Pitts, B.G., & Fielding, L.W. (1991). Strategic sport marketing: Case analysis. In B. Parkhouse (Ed.) *The Management of Sport: Its Foundation and Application* (pp. 333-346). St. Louis, MO: Mosby Year Book, Inc.

Pitts, B.G., Fielding, L.W., & Miller, L.K. (1994). Industry segmentation theory and the sport industry: Developing a sport industry segment model. *Sport Marketing Quarterly, 3*(1), 15-24.

Porter, M.E. (1985). *Competitive advantage: Creating and sustaining superior performance.* New York: the Free Press.

Sandomir, R. (1988). The $50-Billion sports industry. *Sports Inc, 1*(43), 14-23.

Schaap, D. (July 27, 1987). The death of an athlete. *Sports Illustrated*, 26-28, 31-32.

The Global Market for the Sport Industry

Globalization is not coming, it is here. The NBA, NFL, Nike and nearly every major sport enterprise in the United States are doing business in a global environment. The purpose of this chapter is to enable sport marketers to think in international and global terms. It is not intended to provide the framework for billion-dollar multinational corporations. Although many of the lessons and examples may be from such companies, you do not have to play in their league to learn from their experiences. Therefore, this chapter has been written with the following objectives in mind: (a) to provide information about the global marketplace for the sport marketer, (b) to identify information and knowledge necessary for entry into a global market, and (c) to present a context for thinking about marketing internationally.

According to Tuller (1991), fewer than 1% of small-to-midsize companies participate in global marketing and trade. It seems only natural then that many businesses have little knowledge of international trade. This information void may contribute to a reluctance to begin examining global aspects of the sport industry.

Traditional concepts of import and export arise when international markets are mentioned; yet, these are not the only factors in a global approach. It will become increasingly necessary to view all of the corporate resources finance, manufacturing, distribution, retailing, and human resource management from a global perspective. As Americans have experienced, much of our sport equipment is manufactured abroad, but have we truly examined foreign markets for the sale of our products and services? Are there markets where our products or services could dominate? Could mergers and cooperative agreements provide increased revenue and markets for U.S. and foreign companies?

With these questions in mind, it becomes necessary to investigate the global market in more detail. Although the global marketplace is ever-changing, the areas presented below may provide some knowledge and insight for international market exploration.

The Global Business Structure

The structure of the international business environment is complex. Business schools offer complete courses in international business, and some graduate programs are designed with international commerce as a focus of study. Following is an overview for the sport marketing professional of the key topics in the area.

International Economics and Finance

Gaining a working understanding of world banking and finance is essential for sport marketers. Most Americans are used to dealing with commercial banks through such services as deposits, loans, and checking accounts. In the United States, commercial banks are widespread and need only a license to operate. However, most industrialized nations have a system controlled by a central national bank. For the sport entrepreneur, two choices exist: You can deal with the central bank of the host country, or you can deal with a foreign branch of an American bank.

American banks may have familiar-sounding names and executives who understand the American way, but overall, foreign banks have fewer restrictions and regulation than do American banks. As such, "foreign banks are generally easier to deal with, cheaper, and less inclined to hassle the customer, than their American counterparts" (Tuller, 1991, p. 214).

In selecting a bank for foreign business activities, the size of the bank is not as important as the services it can provide. Managers should look specifically for banking institutions that can:

1. Move money from banks in one country to banks in another through wire transfer.
2. Handle export financing through personnel in their internal department.
3. Arrange for collections and payments in various currencies.
4. Process foreign currency through exchange conversion at the lowest possible rate.
5. Issue and process letters of credit to guarantee payments and collections from clients.

A common nightmare for sport marketers is foreign currency. If the only experience you have in dealing with foreign currency is at the bank on your Mexican vacation exchanging your dollars for pesos, you are in for an education. Not all international monetary units are the same with regard to exchange and convertibility. The term hard currency has generally been defined as a unit of monetary value readily convertible to other units. In international business transactions, the U.S. dollar, the German mark, the Japanese yen, the English pound, and the French franc are all convertible with one another at established rates of exchange. However, because of fluctuating exchange rates, variance in financial backing, and government stability, not all world currencies are equally acceptable.

Problems can easily result in situations where the standard payment method has not been well conceived. Suppose you closed a deal to provide 100,000 baseball bats at 675 Venezuelan Bolivars each. Once the shipment arrived, payment was required within 30 days. However, because of inflation within the country, the value of the payment is less than expected at the time of delivery to your account in Caracas. Secondly, the international monetary system may have devalued the Bolivar against the dollar. The result could be that you would actually lose money on your deal.

This same situation can also wreak havoc with international employees. If agreements for salary were negotiated in local currency, employees might find that their standard of living deteriorated considerably with inflation or devaluation. On the other hand, if they contracted to be paid in U.S. dollars and the local currency decreased in its value against the dollar, they could expand their buying power immensely. Most international corporations have contractual language that addresses this issue. When possible, avoid taking foreign currency in payment for an account.

In dealing with the problems of international currency, many companies use countertrade agreements. These agreements are similar to bartering, where products and services are exchanged for other products or services that can be resold to another party for hard currency. According to Tuller (1991), "countertrade is probably the best guarded secret in international trade" (p. 263).

One multinational sport corporation, ProServ, encountered a situation such as this in negotiating with Eastern European backers for a professional tennis tournament. Although the promoters wanted television production and coverage of the event, they did not have any hard currency with which to pay. However, a German firm was located that needed to make a series of payments for their employees in the local currency, and ProServ agreed to make the payment for the German firm, which would in turn, pay ProServ in deutsche Marks (Briner, 1992).

Finally, Tuller (1991) recommends the following guidelines for using the global banking system:

1. The education process. Get up to speed in internal finance as soon as possible. Take a college course in internal finance. Spend some time with the head of the international department of a regional bank.
2. Read, read, read. The fastest way to learn about global banking and to develop a global financial mentality is to read everything available on the subject.

3. Choosing a commercial bank. Determine which local bank has an international department. Interview the department manager.
4. Experiment. Open a foreign bank account. Transfer small amounts back and forth Incorporate exchange rate variances in forecasts, even if you have to use fictitious entries.
5. Conquer the "big boy" syndrome. The more a person investigates global banking the more one realizes it is not just for the "big boys" (p. 221).

Trade Regulations

Since the industrialization that occurred after World War II, much of international trade has been governed by the General Agreement on Tariffs and Trade (GATT). Through this accord, member nations agreed to certain practices involving international commerce. Although it may be beneficial for sport marketers to review this agreement, few of the member countries actually follow its bylaws. Most countries in the world establish and enforce trade agreements and tariffs that protect their products and restrict competition (Tuller, 1991).

Examples of trade regulation affecting sports organizations are numerous. In 1989, the United States and Canada entered into a free trade agreement that reduced and eliminated many previously imposed tariffs. If you had been contemplating creating a product to compete with a Canadian firm, the price differentials pre- and post-legislation could have been substantially impacted. At the time of this writing, similar free trade regulations were being developed between the United States and Mexico, where the costs of labor have traditionally been much lower. In the manufacture of sporting goods, this labor market may prove attractive in business relocation. This could also have an impact on the export of products where previous tariffs may have priced U.S. goods too high for some consumers, thus opening additional markets for U.S. sporting goods and equipment companies.

Free trade agreements could also impact sport-related corporations in terms of liability costs. In the last 20 years, many sporting goods corporations relocated to foreign countries because of the growing cost of equipment-related liability in the United States. If import tariffs were eliminated between the United States and the manufacturer's host country, some corporations might be able to realize greater profit margins by relocating to a foreign manufacturing site.

Specifically in Europe, the formation and liberalization that took place with the European Community (EC) in 1992 brought many challenges and opportunities in sport. This event had dramatic effects on the sport industry. Prior to the unification of the EC, sport marketers who desired to do business in Europe had a multitude of rules and regulations specific to each country. However, with consolidation in many key business areas, the bureaucracy of transacting business in Europe has been standardized, if not reduced.

In sport marketing, we must be careful not to become too restricted in our perceptions. Although EC regulations may allow for more standardized products to be sold, the sport marketer should not automatically conclude that European consumers have homogeneous needs and desires. Specific demographic and psychographic research will continue to be required. As an example, the spread of income across the richest EC member nations to the poorest was 138% in 1987. EC markets have become more accessible, but as yet, not more similar (Quelch, Buzzell, & Salama, 1990).

A primary concern for professional sport organizations is the free movement of labor. Both the Single Europe Act of 1986 and Article 48 of the 1957 Treaty of Rome stated that members of States have the right to work and live in member States and that a free movement of goods, services, persons, and capital would be ensured. In European sports, this meant a free and open market for all athletes within the sports teams of the EC. The general effect of free trade in professional sports remains unclear. Meetings of the EC Committee for the Development of Sport in 1992 produced legislation that limited the number of "foreign" players to three per team (*Sports Information Bulletin*, 1992). It may be that bidding wars for the top players will cause salaries to escalate substantially or, quite possibly, supply and demand may equalize player earnings across Europe.

Another area of concern has been in sports equipment. Manufacturers in England had previously been required to follow one set of product safety codes whereas those in France have had another. These and other issues related to sport and commerce are continually being clarified.

The general strategy predicted for companies in the EC will be that as new markets open, price-cutting is likely to be a popular move to increase initial market share. New products will also be utilized as development will have been made less costly through standardization. New products will also help attract consumers who may have been previously unfamiliar with a company's product line. Experts have also postulated that distribution of goods will be facilitated because rules and regulations covering truck transport (accounting for 80% of EC goods) will be reduced, and border clearances will be considerably faster (Quelch, et al., 1990). The EC unification, therefore, brought serious issues to light for sports professionals and sporting goods companies.

The United States Sports Academy (USSA), an American college located in Mobile, Alabama, has conducted business affairs in Saudi Arabia since the mid 1970s. At one point, the USSA had over 500 employees in the region. However, with changing regulations in the 1980s, the Saudi government changed the rules for calculating taxes and income for foreign corporations. Excellent planning by the CEO of USSA provided for the formation of a locally held corporation to take over the sport and recreation services once provided by the United States Sports Academy. By seeking local executives and changing the business structure of the venture, the United States Sports Academy was able to continue effectively to do business with the country.

Free Trade zones also provide interesting opportunities for sport marketers. These Zones are regulated by government agencies in host countries. In the United States they allow for the manufacture and/or assembly for goods that are not intended for national consumption. As such, you could import parts for gymnastics equipment from Asia, assemble them in a Colorado Free Trade Zone, and ship them to Europe without paying customs duties. Similar situations have also been developed in foreign nations. On a recent trip to Taiwan, a sport executive planned to purchase a high-quality set of golf clubs that he had discovered were manufactured in Taiwan. Figuring that he could find a great bargain, he began to search for his prized clubs. Much to his surprise, he learned that they were manufactured in Taiwan, but they were produced for "export only." Yes, they could be purchased in Taiwan, but only when re-imported from the United States. Needless to say that with twice the shipping expense, the clubs were less expensive in the United States.

International Marketing Structure

The structure of international marketing, in contrast to that of domestic sport enterprises, contains more similarities than differences. Tuller (1991) reports that the main concepts of selling directly to consumers or selling through agents are indeed the same. Other traditional marketing activities contained in this book are also required in global marketing efforts. The process is similar, but the information and sources will be significantly different.

Differences come in the format that facilitates transactions. Terms such as *foreign trading corporations* and *export management companies* are unique to international business. Sport marketers who choose to compete in the global market will invariably learn to deal with these terms and to work effectively with foreign distributors.

Probably the most difficult aspect of foreign trade is customs. If you are dealing in sporting goods, negotiating the customs system will be a key to your success. If you are importing into the United States goods that have been manufactured overseas, you will be required to clear the goods through customs at their port of entry. In the United States there are four steps in the customs process: "1) filing appropriate entry documents, 2) inspection and classification of goods, 3) preliminary declaration of value, 4) final determination of duty and payment" (Tuller, 1991, p. 332).

Kapoor and McKay (1971) also cite factors that differentiate international marketing from domestic. There appears to be greater government regulation in foreign markets and consequently a greater need for feedback and control. In addition, more data are needed for marketing decisions because of the cultural differences that exist. Many marketing decisions are made in U.S. sport organizations because of a knowledge of sport in our societal context. This knowledge simply does not exist for U.S. sport managers making decisions in foreign countries. To offset this problem, most organizations will enlist the assistance of national experts from the target nation.

These experts can also be helpful in communicating value differences between cultures. For example, U.S. and German executives typically value punctuality and promptness, whereas in other cultures a 10:00 a.m. meeting simply means sometime in the morning. It is not that they are being rude; punctuality is just not important in their value system. International managers must learn to respect the value systems of others, not merely tolerate them.

Another difference in international marketing is that in many countries government-owned businesses can compete with privately held companies. For instance, you may own a sport concession management business similar to Ogden-Allied in the United States. Ogden-Allied has a variety of contracts with professional and collegiate stadiums around the country to supply concession and management services. However, in some foreign countries, government-owned corporations may be granted exclusive rights to public stadiums. Another complication could be government subsidies to local corporations. Either of these practices would severely restrict the ability of a successful U.S. company from competing in that market.

The Global Sports Structure

A precursor to involvement in international sport management is a thorough understanding of the global sport environment. The best source for a study of this topic is Thoma and Chalip's book in this series entitled *Sport Governance in the Global Community* (in press). The framework for comprehension begins in the United States with the recognition that the United States Olympic Committee (USOC) is chartered by Congress to oversee amateur sport in the country. The charter encompasses all sports that are in the Olympic and Pan-American Games. Sports that fall outside those parameters may hold membership with the USOC but are not governed by them. Professional and collegiate sports in the United States are self-governing through private voluntary associations, such as the major league offices and the National Collegiate Athletic Association.

In the international sports environment, the International Olympic Committee (IOC) maintains authority over the Olympic Games and regional Olympic-style competitions (Pan-American Games, Asian Games, etc.). It is only these multisport competitions where the IOC retains control.

Each specific sport is governed by an International Federation for that sport. Track and field is a member of the International Amateur Athletic Federation; basketball has its International Amateur Basketball Federation; and each sport maintains an affiliation with its International Federation (IF). These federations work very closely with the IOC in staging the Olympics but have as their main purpose setting rules and regulations for their sports and conducting the world championships in their sport on a yearly basis.

The organizations are also linked through National Governing Bodies (NGB). Each IF designates an NGB in each country to organize and govern a specific sport within national borders. This NGB must be recognized by its National Olympic Committee (i.e., USOC). As such, the NGBs work with the IFs for rules and regulations within a one-sport setting; yet, for Olympic competition, the NGBs work with their National Olympic Committee to ensure participation in the Olympic Games.

Becoming active within these organizations can be advantageous to the sport marketer. One example may well support this contention. The IOC has a single licensing agency for marketing the Olympic Games, ISL Marketing of Switzerland, a company created by Adidas magnate Horst Dassler. ISL is also the marketing agency used by FIFA, the international federation for soccer, the largest and most popular sport in the world. As a sport marketer, it is imperative that you become well versed in the relationships between each of these groups and tune into the political dynamics of the world sport community.

Global Market Selection and Identification

Global markets can seem overwhelming if viewed as a whole. Only when they are dissected and analyzed individually can the sport marketer make wise marketing decisions. Fortunately for the sport marketer, there are a variety of ways to investigate foreign markets.

Contrary to what you may think, your tax dollars really do provide service for American citizens. The U.S. government is one of the best sources for information on foreign markets. The United States Information Agency (Sports America Desk) has contacts worldwide in the area of sport. For decades its programs have sent U.S. sport experts throughout the world presenting seminars and sport training information. Information and contacts obtained through USIA offices can be invaluable in developing a network of sport professionals.

As an example, the U.S. Information Agency managed the U.S. Pavilion at the 1992 World Expo in Seville, Spain. During the run of the Expo, one American sport or fitness activity was presented every day for the 50,000 (per day) visitors. This created excellent opportunities for American firms to demonstrate their products and services to worldwide consumers.

Other government offices in the Department of State also have reams of information about foreign economies, information that is available at little or no cost. Consideration also should be given to contacting the U.S. Agency for International Development, which has as its main purpose improving trade with developing countries.

Interestingly, most foreign governments are also attempting to attract U.S. business and have personnel at their embassy to accommodate your needs. Brief meetings or telephone conversations with their staff are often excellent during the early stages of project development. Other sources for international marketing contacts can be made through international trade associations, economic development councils at the state or local level, and international trade shows. With a little digging, even small sport companies can obtain quality information for entering the global market place.

Key issues, according to Tuller (1991), include whether a market economy exists or one that is government controlled, the existing market demand, growth, competitive forces, U.S. government trade policies, and the local government policies toward trade with the United States. Each factor should be evaluated, and the decision regarding market entry should be based on a thorough analysis.

Considerable attention over the past 15 years has been focused in varying degrees on Japan, the Pacific Rim, Europe, South America, and developing nations throughout the world. In no particular order, a discussion of several of these markets follows.

Japan and Asia

Why, you might ask, has this section been divided as Japan and Asia? Isn't Japan part of Asia? Yes, from a geographical perspective, but no, from a marketing point of view. Japan has for many years presented an obstacle to American sport marketers. With the endless debate over Japan's high tariffs, complex system of distribution and sales, and governmental reluctance to encourage foreign business activity, sport marketers have not generally been successful. The climate has appeared positive for them with a stable hard currency and an attractive market size. Yet, many have taken the approach of trying to sell the Japanese on American products. Sport marketers may find better results if they would concentrate more on the needs of the consumer rather than the products and services their company needs to sell.

In his paper *Development and Structural Changes in Sport Business in Japan*, Harada (1993) indicated that the sport market in Japan rose from $25 billion in 1982 to $50 billion in 1992. As with the general economy in Japan in the early 1990s, some slow growth was seen as a result of the recession. "Nevertheless, as lifestyles change in Japan, people should be showing greater interest in lifetime sports activities and thus sports business on the whole should see an increase in market scale" (Harada, 1993, p. 4).

Asia, as a geographic and social region, is extremely diverse. Social and political conditions affecting sport vary considerably from predominantly Muslim nations, such as Malaysia, to the communist ideology in the People's Republic of China. Some of the nations are newly industrialized (Singapore, South Korea, Taiwan) and can provide active, growing markets for both consumption and production of sports products. Other nations are still in the stages of economic development. Entry into the sports markets of Japan and Asia will demand considerable study and analysis, but the rewards can be immense.

Eastern and Western Europe

Considerable attention has already been given to Western Europe. The dynamic changes with the formation of the European Economic Community will in some ways help sport marketers and in other ways hinder their success. A unified Western European market will allow a much freer access to markets than was previously available, yet the increased competitiveness of EC companies will also increase competition. The generally held view is that in most sport industry segments, the opportunities will be limited and extremely competitive.

Eastern Europe, on the other hand, may provide more opportunities. With pent-up consumer demand and a reduction of government controls, sport purchasing and sponsorship avenues may proliferate. However, some of the problems that sport marketers will encounter include the lack of hard currency and unstable governments. It is also important to realize that sport expenditures are often considered as luxuries and are made with discretionary funds. These funds may be limited in the Eastern European communities well into the next decade.

The situation in Hungary was reported by Dénes and Misovicz (1993). Their research indicated several phenomena that may be similar in other parts of Eastern Europe. In Hungary, the demise of socialist rule in the early 1990s meant that the sport economy changed as well. Previously, the government had subsidized sports, yet with the political changes, governmental resources were allocated to other parts of the economy. Ticket prices for sports events rose with inflation that impacted the economy; however, few citizens could afford to attend, instead diverting their income to cover the costs of food and shelter. In addition, many workers took on second jobs to generate funds necessary for maintaining an acceptable lifestyle. The market for leisure sports products, once supplied by the government, had all but disappeared (Dénes & Misovicz,1993).

The Caribbean, Central and South America

In 1983 the U.S. government passed a law that made trade with the Caribbean nations both more accessible and more lucrative. The Caribbean Basin Initiative (CBI) was designed to increase trade and assist in the economic development of this region. The 1989 report indicated that recreational items and sporting goods were some of the products that had benefited the most from this legislation (Tuller, 1991). The business climate in the area has been enhanced through this Act, and sport marketers should examine the possibility of taking advantage of the benefits extended through the CBI Act. These include tax breaks and the elimination of reduction of import duties. In addition, special financing programs are available for start-up companies. Of special note is the fact that many of these nations also have special agreements with European nations for importing and exporting goods and services. Therefore, it may behoove the sport marketer to investigate the range of possibilities of operating out of the Caribbean.

Central America presents several points of interest. With the previously discussed free trade possibilities, manufacturing potential exists in the sports goods industry. Depending on the economic and political fortunes of the area, additional consumer demand for both goods and services may also exist.

South America has been under the shadow of its severe debt crisis for the past two decades. As mentioned in the section on international economics and finance, triple-digit inflation and hard currency issues will hamper sports entrepreneurs in South America. The sport marketer should realize that the public interest in sport is considerably high in much of the region and that considerable potential exists in numerous market segments.

Conducting business in the Caribbean, Central and South America has positive attributes, but only if the sport marketer is able to cope effectively with the business and political idiosyncrasies of the region.

Africa

As diverse as Central and South America, the African market is understood by few American companies (Tuller, 1991). Generally, the continent consists of Muslim North Africa, Central, East and West Africa, with South Africa presenting a special case. Sports activities in North Africa are in line with traditional Muslim view, predominantly male and rooted in tradition. For American sport managers to conduct business there demands an understanding of the culture and the emphasis on sport. Within that context, the markets are available to U.S. representatives.

West Africa has, for the most part, put political upheaval behind and is entering an era in which sport market development is possible. Of specific importance will be sport equipment and supplies as well as sport services in coaching and sport management. As recent as 1990, the product advertised in the window of a sporting goods store was a pair of Adidas Rome running shoes, popular in the United States in the early 1970s. Central Africa has yet to achieve the stability conducive to market entry. This will of course be an area to watch for future grow and development in sport.

In South Africa, enough wealth exists for any multinational corporation to flourish. However, because of past economic and political practices, a two-tiered economic market exists. For the sport marketer, both segments offer possibilities. With the political changes in the country in the early 1990s, the lower class was provided greater access to sport and recreational facilities. This created immense demand for sports equipment. Corporate sponsorship and financing for sport activities also created an atmosphere conducive for a growth market. Another factor in favor of expansion into South Africa is the abundance of well-educated and effective sport management personnel.

As with other regions in the world, the problems of soft currency and political instability will restrict many sport marketing opportunities. Yet, with attention to these factors and a careful study of the market, sport marketers can be successful in meeting the demands of these consumers.

International Sport Marketing Personnel

The selection of well-trained and experienced personnel is essential. Tuller (1991) indicated that trying to enter global markets without the expertise of someone experienced in international trade is a common error made by American executives. "To try to arrange financing, market products, or negotiate contracts with foreign customers without assistance from internationally experienced management personnel will always lead to disaster" (Tuller, 1991, p. 12).

The selection of personnel for managing foreign markets or for directing foreign units is impacted by several criteria. Among those found to be most important were proven domestic marketing ability, foreign national status, prior international training, and a strong desire for global involvement (Kapoor & McKay, 1971).

Personnel training can occur through a variety of different methods. Some corporations conduct in-house training sessions using the expertise and experience of their existing staff. Some corporations handle the training through their foreign offices. Both of these methods have proven to be successful in the sports environment. Outside resources have also been retained for the training process. This method is often expensive, but without internal expertise, is essential.

Kapoor & McKay (1971) indicated that the main difficulty experienced by foreign market managers was adapting to cultural diversity. Therefore, it is imperative that personnel be educated for cultural sensitivity prior to their involvement in international affairs. Research has indicated that adaptability to foreign cultures is equal in importance to marketing skills developed in a domestic position.

Adapting to Cultural Diversity

Sport business personnel have a common bond with sport executives in other nations through their athletic experiences; however, culture variations on appropriate business and sport etiquette can sabotage chances for success. The successful sport marketer needs to have a clear understanding of the "dos and don'ts" of foreign culture. What follows are some national and international customs in business relations. Before traveling and dealing with international executives, be sure to review the special characteristics of your host nation.

Touching. In much of North America, touching is acceptable between friends, but overt touching of casual acquaintances in a business setting is not tolerated. The local custom in many Latin countries allows for hugs following an introduction. In the Middle East, on the other hand, you may find two men walking down the street holding hands to signify their friendship (Axtell, 1991).

Women in sport business and other nations. Women have for many years played increasing roles in the conduct of sport business in the United States. Many women serve as CEOs of major sport corporations, sport marketing firms, and professional team franchises. Yet, in other parts of the world, women may not be accepted in business meetings. Because we believe in equality of the sexes does not mean that everyone in the world does. Your firm must make a decision whether to do business with countries that have different beliefs about the role of women in business relations and follow a strategy that will produce the best business results.

Alcohol. The easiest rule for alcohol is to follow the lead of the host. If the host orders a drink, you are welcome to imbibe. Be cautious about bringing alcoholic gifts for your host. Possession of a fifth of Southern Comfort will land you in prison in almost any Islamic East nation. On the opposite end of the spectrum, refusing a glass of wine in France or a cup of saki in Japan will be considered rude. At the International Olympic Academy in Greece, the Russian delegations' vodka was one of the most cherished barter items between participants being worth at least five Olympic pins.

Gifts. Exchanging gifts is a custom that is more prevalent in other countries than it is in the United States. In fact, in the 1970s the U.S. government passed the Foreign Corrupt Practices Act to curtail bribes and kickbacks (Tuller, 1991). The line between "payoffs" and "generous gifts" is unclear. Most sport marketers will face difficulty in this area. Try to learn ahead of time from a confidante or friend the tradition and local custom. A good practice is to carry small company pins or souvenirs and to graciously accept similar extensions from your host.

Time and schedules. In many parts of the world, time is a relative concept. This is especially true in many Latin countries and in the Middle East. Both authors of this text have conducted sport marketing seminars around the globe and can attest to this phenomenon. In Malaysia, an 8:00 a.m. meeting means in the morning, yet just across the bridge in Singapore, you had better be there at 7:30 to get a seat. One is not better than the other; they are just different. It is also important that everyone be clear on how dates are written. The U.S. military writes dates with the day first, then the month and year (i.e., 7 June 1992). This does not create confusion until it appears as 7/6/92. Much of the world follows the U.S. military style, so when placing the order for the delivery of your tennis rackets, be specific.

Business Etiquette. Every country will have its unique protocol for conducting business. In England, you should wear a jacket and tie for your initial business meeting; however, in Manila such apparel is inappropriate and uncomfortable because of the heat. The mix of business attire and casual sports clothing is something that should be explored carefully; it never hurts to ask. Careful determination should also be made in deciding when and where to talk business. In England, work is work and play is play; don't confuse the two. However, in many other countries, the best deals are put together on the golf course. You should also be perceptive about special interrelationships. In England, you seat the most important person to your right, according to British military custom. In South Africa, you rise to greet your Afrikaner guest, but remain seated when meeting a Zulu guest; rising is considered confrontational by tribal custom. In South Africa and other parts of southern Africa, sport marketers and event organizers have experienced problems from a simple question, "Do you understand this proposal?" When the answer was "yes," all matters seemed settled. Only later was it determined that all was not well. The polite answer to the question was "yes." To answer "no" would imply that you had not explained it well and be considered insulting. Better initial questions would have been, "What is your understanding?" or "Do we have an agreement on these points?" (Axtell, 1991; McGarvey, 1992; Tuller, 1991).

The integration of international marketing into the domestic corporate culture is also of great importance. Depending on the size and nature of the international versus the domestic market, jealousies and conflicts can arise if executives are not adamant in clarifying the priority of both global and national marketing activities (Tuller, 1991). The selection and training of international sport executives encompasses many different considerations. They involve often difficult and awkward adaptations to normal business practices. However, if you invest the time, the results can be rewarding.

Specifics of International Sport Marketing

The expansion of professional and amateur sports internationally has been well recognized in the sport marketing arena. "Faced with a maturing U.S. sports market, the [professional] leagues have looked overseas" (Ozanian & Taub, 1992, p. 49). One of the first professional sport organizations to recognize the global demand for its product was the National Basketball Association. From an historical standpoint, professional boxing has had worldwide events for many years, but these have been primarily single events. Professional baseball had early opportunities to restructure and include demand in Asia and Latin America but decided that such a move was not in its best interests. The NBA, on the other hand, has viewed international markets in an entirely different perspective.

In recognition of the 200 million people around the world who participate in basketball, the NBA embarked on a global marketing campaign in 1989. Games played in Europe and Asia spawned a growth in NBA television rights of 30% per year with the sales of licensed goods growing at twice that rate. With the success of the 1992 U.S. Olympic basketball team, a team comprised of NBA players, the NBA commissioner commented that he recognized the global nature of basketball and was positioning the league to capitalize on the phenomenon (Ober, 1992).

As the NBA has stressed global marketing, basketball equipment manufacturers have followed suit. Nike, Reebok, Converse, and Spalding all saw tremendous growth in global sales of basketballs and basketball shoes in conjunction with NBA positioning. In the early 1990s shoe sales were in the neighborhood of $40 million per company, an increase of 300% from the mid-1980s (Stotlar, 1989). In Europe alone, NBA licensing revenues climbed from $15 million in 1991 to $45 million in 1992 (Ozanian & Taub, 1992).

It should also be noted that global demographics are significantly different from those in the United States. The United States has an aging population; yet, in much of the developing world, the population is considerably younger and becoming even younger. An amazing 70% of the world's consumers abide in developing countries. With respect to the example above, children tend to buy shoes more frequently than adults do, which contributes to many of the marketing decisions for sporting goods manufacturers.

The international reach of the fitness business is also noteworthy. "Overseas clubs call on U.S. fitness experts to fashion American-style clubs that meet the demands of style-conscious clientele" (Holland, 1992, p. 41). The depth of the market is such that IDEA: the Association for Fitness Professionals has representatives in 69 foreign countries.

World tournaments and international events are at the center of many international marketing activities. The recognition and value of international events grew considerably in the 1980s and early 1990s. Consequently, most television agreements, sponsorship contracts, and licensing programs have necessarily become international. Without attention to these details, sport marketers could find themselves in the same situation as Nike during the 1992 Olympic Games. At that time, the word "Nike" had been registered by another company in Spain, complicating the U.S. firm's marketing efforts.

Television agreements must also be constructed with international marketing as a key ingredient. The situation of the 1987 America's Cup races in Australia presented an interesting problem. For decades, the races had been conducted in the United States, but after a defeat of the American team in 1983, the races moved to Perth, Australia. Previous television and marketing arrangements had always been made with the holders of the Cup, the New York Yacht Club. However, the New York Yacht Club refused to give up or assign its trademark and licensing rights to the Cup to the Royal Perth Yacht Club. Needless to say, lawyers on both sides prepared for battle. It was the plan of IMG Chairman Mark McCormack to interject a marketing decision, not a legal maneuver to solve the problem. Because the holder of the Cup (Royal Perth Yacht Club) could dictate the rules of competition, a clause was added stating that anyone interfering with the marketing of the race (i. e., New York Yacht Club) would be barred from the competition (McCormack, 1987).

Trends for the Future

As the United States and many leading economic powers evolve as information societies and reduce their strength in manufacturing, the licensing of sport manufacturing technology and professional services will be a major growth area in the sport industry. Sporting goods companies and sport consultants will protect products through extensive licensing and manufacturing agreements and will issue "covenants not to compete" to ensure the protection of their intellectual properties. The result will be a greater emphasis on strategic alliances, mergers, and joint ventures than has existed in the past.

Sport marketers will begin to think more of international demographics in the development of products and services in the sport industry. Pan-European consumers will begin to develop more similarities than differences as the EC matures (Quelch et al., 1990) and the newly industrialized nations will begin to demand more sport-related products and services. Friction between the countries in which costs of labor are inexpensive for sporting goods production and those countries that consume the products will probably continue.

Companies that can communicate their concern for global problems through the delivery of the sport products and services will be more highly valued than will those who ignore this social component. Cause-related sport marketing will also make favorable impressions on consumers. These humanistic trends must be incorporated in the operation of all sport organizations in the global environment.

With the developments outlined in this chapter and evidence in the professional literature, there will undoubtedly be a greater need for internationally trained and educated sport managers. Professionals in the area and aspiring sport managers should become well versed in international sports affairs. This training will open a vast new job market and should provide an array of exciting experiences.

Chapter Summary

The purpose of this chapter was to provide information about the global marketplace for the sport marketer. It is clear that sport is a major component in the global economy and that sport marketers must be prepared to work in this environment. Specific skills and knowledge regarding the international banking system, world sport structure, and the application of marketing principles in specific cultural contexts are necessary to succeed in international markets. Sport marketers must obtain the requisite training. The global sport marketplace provides a wealth of opportunities for corporations and organizations that commit to spending the time for market research and flexibility in market perception.

Questions for Study

1. Diagram the relationship of the International Olympic Committee to a specific International Federation. Include a discussion of how each functions with the United States Olympic Committee and a National Governing Body in the United States.
2. What are the keys to successful banking in international sport marketing?
3. How does marketing a sport product internationally differ from marketing the same product in the United States?

Learning Activities

1. Investigate opening a Swiss bank account. It could be a lot of fun and a great conversation topic among friends.
2. How would you handle the following situation? You just completed a consulting project negotiating sponsorship deals for the Lithuanian National Basketball team and are due to be paid $10,000 in U.S. dollars. At the last minute, you have been informed that they will pay you only in the local currency. What is that currency? How much of it would you get? Would you accept payment in that form, and if not, what would be an alternative?

Professional Associations and Organizations

United States Information Agency
Sports America Desk
301 4th Street SW
Washington, DC 20547

International Events Group
213 West Institute Place, Suite 303
Chicago, IL 60610

Suggested Readings

Axtell, R. E. (1991). *The do's and taboos of body language around the world.* New York: John Wiley & Sons.

Thoma, J. & Chalip, L. (in press). *Sport governance in the global community.* Morgantown, WV: Fitness Information Technology.

Tuller, L. W. (1991). *Going global.* Homewood, IL: Business One Irwin.

References

Axtell, R. E. (1991). *The do's and taboos of body language around the world.* New York: John Wiley & Sons.

Briner, R. A. (1992, April 9). *European sports business opportunities.* Paper presented at the International Conference on Sport Business. Columbia, SC.

Dénes, F. & Misovicz, (1993, October). *Changes and contradictions: Sport market in Hungary.* Paper presented at the International Conference on Sport Business, Paris, France.

Harada M. (1993, October). *Development and structural changes in sport business in Japan.* Paper presented at the International Conference on Sport Business, Paris, France.

Holland, M. (1992, May). International opportunities. *Fitness Management, 8,* 39-43.

Kapoor, A., & McKay, R. J. (1971). *Managing international markets.* Princeton, NJ: The Darwin Press.

McCormack, M. H. (1987). *The terrible truth about lawyers.* New York: Beech Tree Books.

McGarvey, R. (1992, June). Foreign exchange. *USAir Magazine, 7,* 58-65.

Ober, E. (1992, Aug. 5). Interview with David Stern, Commissioner NBA. New York: CBS Evening News.

Ozanian, M. K., & Taub, S. (1992, July 7). Big leagues, bad business. *Financial World, 24,* 34-51.

Quelch, J. A., Buzzell, R. D., & Salama, E. R. (1990). *The marketing challenge of 1992.* New York: Addison-Wesley.

Sports information bulletin. (1992, June). Brussels: Sport for All Clearing House.

Stotlar, D. K. (1989). *Successful sport marketing and sponsorship plans.* Dubuque, IA: Wm. C. Brown.

Thoma, J. & Chalip, L. (in press). *Sport governance in the global community.* Morgantown, WV: Fitness Information Technology, Inc.

Tuller, L. W. (1991). *Going global.* Homewood, IL: Business One Irwin.

CHAPTER 3

HISTORICAL ERAS IN SPORT MARKETING

Lawrence W. Fielding, Ph.D. and Lori K. Miller, Ed.D.
University of Louisville

Hillerich & Bradsby's Marketing Plan

In 1921 Hillerich & Bradsby (H&B), producers of the Louisville Slugger baseball bat, became the industrial leader in baseball bat production. H&B's market position resulted from the implementation of a market plan. The market plan included an analysis of external forces (macromarketing) that were beyond the control of H&B. H&B's reaction to these external forces resulted in decisions about their product, place, price, and promotion (micromarketing). An analysis of H&B's market plan will inform readers about the elements of sport marketing and functions as an introduction to sport marketing's historical development.

External Forces (Macromarketing)

Ten external forces influenced H&B's market decisions. These forces are briefly outlined below.

1. Increased market size. (a) Growth of the youth baseball bat market beginning in 1912 and rapidly expanding after 1919; (b) Expansion of adult baseball bat market after World War I.
2. Market growth rate. Increase after 1919 because of youth market expansion and return of soldiers from World War I.
3. Industrial profitability. The sporting goods industry in general and the baseball bat industry in particular experienced high profits in the years immediately before and following World War I. This led to the emergence of new entrants, like Hilton Collins and Wilson Sporting Goods.
4. Government policy change. Beginning in 1919 the U.S. government imposed a 10% tax on all sporting goods sales. The tax gave buyers

greater power over producers. Some manufacturers elected to absorb the tax, not wishing to lose sales. Other companies attached the extra 10% cost to selling price and attempted to maintain sales through advertising and promotions. Overall, the 10% tax increased competition among baseball bat producers.

5. Resource availability. Between 1919 and 1923 there was a shortage of second-growth ash wood. This caused baseball bat manufacturers to scramble to line up supplies. It also influenced a search for alternative material to make baseball bats.

6. Technological change. The cork-centered baseball, introduced by Reach & Co. in 1909, gradually changed the emphasis in baseball from base hits to home runs. With the advent of home-run hitters like Babe Ruth, the emphasis on bat weights changed from heavy to light. The problem with lightweight ash bats was breakage. Technological innovations in the early 1920s made lightweight bats stronger and more resistant to breaking. Successful companies used warranties to alert buyers about their new break-resistant bats.

7. Economies of scope. Strategic fits among related businesses offered competitive advantages. The amalgamation of Wright & Ditson with Victor Sporting Goods and the acquisition of Chicago Sporting Goods and Sell Sporting Goods by Thomas E. Wilson Company allowed these companies to reduce costs and gain competitive advantage. Much of the competitive advantage was gained through market-related fits. Wilson Company, for example, combined sales forces, used the same brand names, advertised related products in the same advertisements, and coordinated delivery and shipping. Operating and management benefits were also realized by Wilson.

8. Economies of scale. Economies of scale existed in bat production, in distribution, and in raw material purchase.

9. Buyer preferences for differentiated products. Baseball bat purchasers wanted special bats, bats that increased prowess or linked the buyer to a special player.

10. National economy. A depression swept through the American economy during 1920 and 1921. Sporting goods manufacturers believed that the depression actually increased sales because of forced leisure.

Internal Responses (Micromarketing)

H&B's response to the external forces listed above involved micromarketing decisions about product, place, price, and promotion. External forces influenced more than one micro decision area. H&B's micromarketing decisions are briefly outlined below.

1. Product. Product development at H&B was a response to market size and growth. H&B's first autograph-model Louisville Slugger was introduced in 1905. It was an exact replica of the bat used by Honus Wagner and was intended only for the adult market. With the growth and expansion of the youth market, H&B introduced the autograph-model junior slugger in 1915. The large market growth rate that occurred after 1919 induced H&B to produce a variety of autograph models in a variety of lengths and weights to appeal to different segments of the baseball bat market. This decision was also influenced by changes in buyer preferences. Customers wanted autograph models of their favorite players. The technological changes that brought about the "lively ball" also influenced H&B. In 1921 H&B introduced the new "powerized" Louisville Slugger, a lighter, stronger bat that resisted breakage. The "powerized" bat was marketed with warranties and appealed to the new class of baseball home-run hitters. During this same period H&B became aware of the necessity of economies of scale. Consequently, H&B increased production capacity and efficiency through a series of changes that permitted the company to increase production capacity to 10,000 bats a day by 1923.

2. Place. H&B's largest competitors, Spalding, Wilson, Draper & Maynard, Goldstein, and Rawlings, benefited from economies of scope. Economies of scope permitted better distribution and greater customer contact. To combat these advantages, H&B increased the size of its sales force in order to increase contact with independent retailers. Although H&B continued to sell through jobbers, the company began a direct-sale-to-retailer policy in 1919.

3. Price. H&B's pricing policy was a response to the 10% sporting goods tax, resource availability, and a concern for the continuation of industrial profitability. H&B emphasized vertical price maintenance. They wanted Louisville Slugger bats sold at recommended prices by jobbers and retailers. H&B saw this policy as necessary to maintain profitability in the face of the increased competition from chain stores and mail-order houses. The cost of ash wood and the 10% sales tax also influenced their policy. H&B also considered economies of scale in setting prices. H&B was able to cut production and distribution costs through economies of scale. H&B's pricing policy passed these savings along to customers in the form of lower prices. Buyer preferences for special bats also influenced H&B's pricing policy. H&B realized that customers were willing to pay higher prices for differentiated products like autograph-model baseball bats.

4. Promotion. H&B desired to increase market share in an expanding baseball bat market. The company was also concerned about industry profitability. Promotional decisions were based upon these concerns and were also responses to economies of scope that competitors employed.

> The need to differentiate products to meet buyer preferences further influenced H&B's promotional decisions. H&B expanded advertising and sales promotions. In 1919 the company began an integrated advertising and promotion campaign that included popular and trade magazine advertisements, a promotional pamphlet, and an advertising slogan. These decisions were prompted by a desire to increase market share in an expanding baseball bat market. H&B's advertising and sales promotional decisions were also a method of combating economies of scope employed by larger companies. In addition, H&B's decision to employ economies of scale emphasized the need for a unified promotional campaign. Finally, because customers preferred differentiated products, H&B needed an effective method for informing potential buyers about the special bats produced by the company.

H&B's market plan considered external forces (macromarketing) and developed internal responses (micromarketing) either to utilize or to combat the external forces outlined under macromarketing. H&B's marketing plan was a competitive strategy. The plan utilized H&B's resources to manipulate product, place, price, and promotion in response to influences beyond the company's direct control. These influences were in effect large aggregates that influenced the national economy in general and the baseball bat industry in particular. H&B's marketing plan began with an analysis of the whole industry: market size, market growth rate, industrial profitability, government policy, resource availability, technological change, economies of scope and scale, buyer preferences, and national economy. H&B analyzed how the purposes and resources of the company interacted with the contingencies imposed upon it by external forces. H&B's marketing plan sought to capitalize on the industry's opportunities and the company's strengths while mitigating industry threats and company weaknesses. For example, when H&B developed the autograph-model junior slugger, they assumed the new product would be attractive to members of the growing youth market (Miller, Fielding, & Pitts, 1993).

Historical Eras In Sport Marketing

Sport marketing consists of two interrelated concepts. The first concept considers sport marketing at the macro level. Sport marketing at the macro level considers external forces that affect the industry as a whole. It analyzes these forces in an attempt to develop a competitive advantage. The second concept defines sport marketing at the micro level. It includes a set of activities performed by the company in an attempt to get and to keep customers. Typically, these marketing activities include: anticipating needs, determining what products are to be made, developing and designing products for sale, packaging, pricing, developing credit and collection policies, determining transportation and storage needs, deciding when and how products are to be advertised and sold, and planning after-sale services, warranties, and product disposal (McCarthy &

Perreault, 1984).

Sport marketing evolved over time. Its history is an account of how individuals and companies attempted to solve marketing problems. H&B's marketing plan was an attempt to solve marketing problems. It benefited from techniques, traditions, and knowledge that had developed in sport marketing during the 19th and early 20th centuries. The marketing plan was, of course, solely H&B's. Further, it was positioned in time. The company's macromarketing analysis dealt with external forces that existed in the years immediately following World War I. The company's micromarketing responses depended upon resources and abilities that existed at that same point in time. Later H&B marketing plans and marketing plans developed by other companies were attempts to solve marketing problems that existed at other points in time.

The history of sport marketing is a history of both continuity and change over time. The continuity part involves the linkage of macro opportunities and threats with micro reactions. All companies, regardless of historical date, dealt with external forces and developed internal responses in an attempt to achieve a competitive advantage. Their success or failure depended upon their ability to understand external forces and their ability to use resources to respond effectively. What changed over time was the nature, extent, and power of both external forces and internal resources with which companies responded. The development of sport marketing was influenced by changes in market size, market growth rate, industry profitability, government policy, resource availability, technological change, economies of scope and scale, buyer preferences, and national economy. Company responses to these external forces, the manipulation of product, place, price, and promotion, also influenced the development of sport marketing.

The discussion that follows will develop a brief outline of the history of sport marketing in America. The major focus will be on change over time. However, continuity, the linkage of macro concerns with micro solutions, will form the basic structure of the discussion. The discussion will be limited to only two aspects of the sport industry: spectator sports in the form of college athletics and professional sport and the sporting goods industry.

Based upon historical models developed by Fullerton (1988) and Hardy (1990), the history of American sport marketing will be divided into three broad contrasting periods: (a) The Era of Origins: 1820 - 1880; (b) The Era of Institutional Development: 1880 - 1920; and (c) The Era of Refinement and Formalization: 1920 - 1990 (Figure 3.1). Only the first two of these eras will be discussed at length. The major emphasis will be placed upon the second era, The Era of Institutional Development, because during this era all the elements of modern marketing were developed and refined. The third era, The Era of Refinement and Formalization, will be summarized, highlighting the changes in external forces that influenced refinements in marketing techniques.

The general characteristics of the first two eras will be discussed and examples of sport marketing within each era presented. Within this brief historical outline of sport marketing we contend that all the micro and macro concepts associated

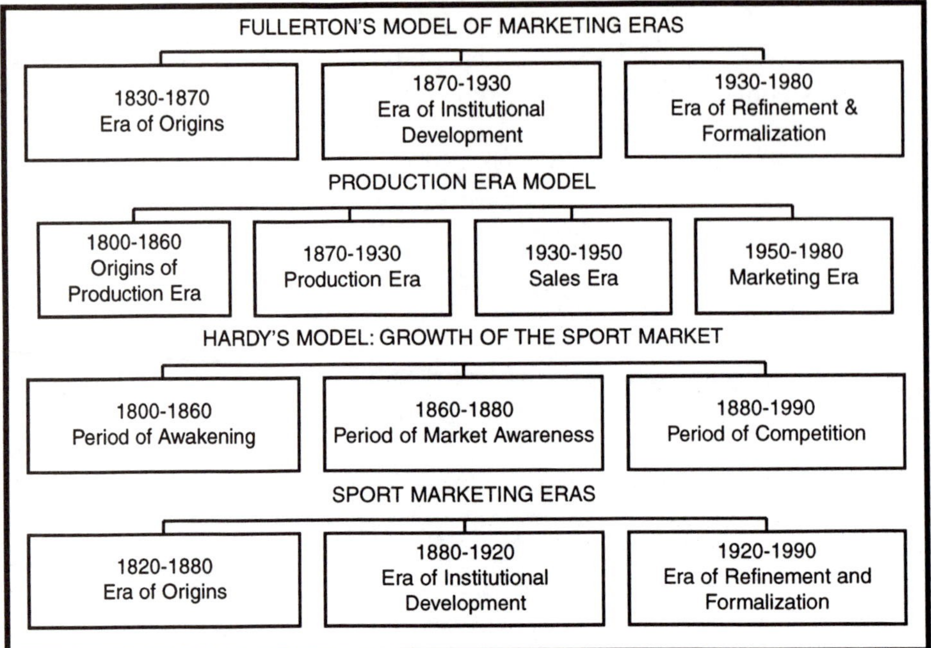

FIGURE 3.1 - Marketing Era Models

with modern sport marketing evolved between the years of 1880 and 1920. During these years micro marketing functions, such as product planning, product development, and product management gradually emerged. Other marketing functions, such as distribution, pricing, and promotion, also evolved. Prior to 1880 product development proceeded with little regard to buyer demand and other marketing elements.

After 1880 marketing considerations influenced product development. Macro marketing considerations evolved with micro concerns. Producers considered competition and demand and were concerned about overproduction. General economic conditions influenced micro decisions about sport contests and sport products. Society's needs, aspirations, and objectives affected the development of sporting goods products as well as influencing decisions about athletic opportunities at the amateur and professional levels.

By 1920 all the fundamentals of modern sport marketing were established. Developments after 1920 were refinements. Sport marketing adjusted to new technologies, such as motion pictures, radio, television, and computers. Sport marketing activities existed before 1880. Attempts to market harness racing, horse racing, pedestrianism, boxing, billiards, baseball, and a variety of sport equipment occurred before 1880. However, sport marketing before 1880 was confined to isolated sport events and local circumstance. Sport entrepreneurs copied marketing techniques that had proven successful in selling other nonsport products or services. Some modern marketing activities were employed, but there was no systematic linkage of activities and no marketing plan.

The Era of Origins: 1820 - 1880

Sport marketing micro activities existed before 1880. William Fuller's tactics in promoting boxing in Charleston, South Carolina, during 1824 are an early example. Fuller enticed paying customers to his "Extravaganza of Fun, Frolic, Fashion, and Flash" through newspaper advertisements and handbills that announced theater plays, boxing, and fireworks (Wignall, 1924, p. 209). Boxing promotions in the 1840s and 1850s followed similar tactics with more elaboration. Although boxing was illegal, individual boxers still promoted bouts through newspapers, issuing challenges and setting stakes. Newspapers reported the local and ethnic rivalries that added meaning and increased interest in the fight. Estimates of the amount of money wagered on the outcome both measured and increased interest. To avoid police interference, newspapers seldom informed readers about exact fight locations. Instead, fans were directed to a meeting place or a transportation site. Excursion tickets were purchased, and fans traveled by boat or rail to the secret fight site. Word of mouth was also used to direct customers to the fight location (Adelman, 1986; Gorn, 1986; Riess, 1989).

Michael Phelan's promotion of billiards and billiard tables during the 1850s and 1860s marked a significant advance over earlier boxing promotions. Phelan began his billiard career in 1846 as the proprietor of the Arcade Billiard Saloon in New York City. Like earlier boxing promoters, Phelan used the *Spirit of the Times,* a national circulation newspaper, to challenge British champion John Roberts to a $500-per-match, home-and-home series in 1850.

Phelan's challenge served two promotional functions. First, it helped to promote Phelan's book, *Billiards Without Masters* (1850). Phelan included in the challenge the fact that he was writing a book about billiards. Second, the challenge functioned to promote Phelan as America's foremost billiard player (Adelman, 1986). When Phelan went into business with Hugh Collender to produce billiard tables in 1854, he promoted himself as the American champion who manufactured billiard tables. Phelan promoted business by suggesting that an American championship tournament be organized among the leading billiard players. In 1856 Phelan began publication of the *Billiard Cue*, the first billiard periodical in America (Adelman, 1986).[1] He also played in several challenge matches defeating opponents and proclaiming the merits of his billiard tables. Phelan's challenges were published in newspapers and contained specifications about the equipment to be used. "The balls to be played with are to be 2 3/8 in. in diameter, and the game to be played on a true and correct cushion table" (Betts, 1974, p. 42). A true and correct cushion table could mean only a Phelan table since Phelan held the patent for the India rubber cushion (Betts, 1974).[2] Phelan retired from active challenge play in 1863 but remained the sport's leading figure. In 1865 he helped organize the American Billiard Players Association. Throughout his career Phelan used his influence and reputation to advance the sale of his billiard equipment. Phelan and Collender were the leading manufacturers of billiard tables until Collender joined with Brunswick and Blake in 1884 (Adelman, 1986).

Although the examples of Fuller and Phelan have much in common, there are important differences. The differences link the development of sport and the development of sport marketing. Fuller attempted to sell boxing along with other forms of entertainment. In 1824 boxing was not only illegal but also not very popular. Boxing became more popular during the 1840s and 1850s. During these decades large numbers of Irish immigrants came to American cities like New York and Boston. They became part of what Polsky (1969), Somers (1972), Adelman (1986), Riess (1989), and Rader (1990) have termed the male bachelor subculture. This bachelor subculture formed the basis of the sporting fraternity (Riess, 1989). In 1824 when Fuller attempted to sell boxing in Charleston, South Carolina, this sporting fraternity did not exist in large numbers. Only 5% of the total population lived in cities (Chudacoff, 1981). Fuller and other early boxing promoters marketed a varied product (excursions, trips, and frolics). Price was unannounced or part of a package (transportation or in Fuller's case, theater plays and fireworks). Place was hidden or hard to reach. Promotions included newspapers and handbills but relied heavily upon word of mouth among a small sporting fraternity whose membership was, quite possibly, unknown to Fuller.

In contrast, Phelan was very much aware of the male bachelor subculture that existed in 1850. The sporting fraternity had grown considerably between 1820 and 1850. This was particularly true of billiard players. In the 1820s only 16 tables existed in all of New York City. By 1850 the number of tables had increased to over 400 (Phelan, 1850). By the late 1840s the poolroom had emerged as the major locus of the bachelor subculture (Polsky, 1969). Urban population growth, particularly in respect to males between the ages of 18 and 35, provided recruits for the sporting fraternity in cities like New York, Boston, Chicago, Philadelphia, New Orleans, and Detroit. Phelan attempted to market billiard equipment to a growing sporting fraternity and the proprietors of poolrooms and taverns who catered to this fraternity.

Phelan either knew or assumed that the market for billiard equipment extended beyond New York City to other large cities. His hyped challenges to other billiard players, his attempts to organize national tournaments, his attempts to be declared national champion, his publication of the *Billiard Cue,* and his leadership in the organization of the American Billiard Players Association all helped extend the popularity of billiards (Adelman, 1986). They were also marketing tools that functioned in two important ways. First, they helped connect Phelan's name with the billiard equipment he and his partner Hugh Collender produced. The basic message was that Michael Phelan, the best billiard player in America, made the best billiard equipment (Adelman, 1986).[3]

Phelan and Collender were not the only billiard manufacturers in America. There were at least four others in New York City. More important, Phelan and Collender were contending with two very successful Cincinnati companies. Julius Blake's Great Western Billiard Manufactory was well established by 1854 when Phelan and Collender began production. Brunswick had been producing billiard tables in Cincinnati since 1845 and had established a second factory in Chicago by 1848. By 1854 when Phelan and Collender began production, Brunswick had established a branch office in New Orleans. By the middle 1860s Brunswick had sales offices in 10 cities in the United States and Canada (Kogan, 1985).

Phelan and Collender needed name recognition in order to contend with these larger, more successful companies. Second, Phelan and Collender needed the name recognition to contend with newer companies entering the field. Because of the growing popularity of billiards, other manufacturing companies began to produce billiard equipment. Phelan used his influence and well-established reputation as a billiard player to block the entry of these new companies. By 1869 the fight for the biggest share of the billiard market was down to three companies: Brunswick, Blake (Great Western Billiard Manufactory), and Phelan & Collender (Kogan, 1985).

External forces limited Fuller's success in marketing boxing but aided Phelan's marketing of billiard equipment. As already noted Phelan dealt with a much larger market than Fuller did and had the additional advantage of large market growth.[4] Phelan had several other advantages. First, unlike boxing in the 1820s, there was no government policy against billiards.[5] Second, technological changes influenced billiard table production. The development of the band power saw for cutting slate increased resource availability and made large production of slate-bed tables possible. Phelan's patent on the India rubber cushion improved billiard tables, allowing for a more exciting style of play (Adelman, 1986; Kogan, 1985). These technological changes, combined with Phelan's influence through rule committees on the standardization of billiard equipment, permitted Phelan to influence buyer preferences for differentiated products.[6]

Whether or not Phelan can be classified as a key innovator in sport marketing, particularly in the sense that Hardy (1986) intended in his ground-breaking essay, "Entrepreneurs, Organizations, and the Sport Marketplace: Subjects in Search of Historians," is debatable. However, Phelan's actions were a prelude to a more thorough development of micromarketing techniques during the 1865-to-1870 baseball fad.

The commercialization of baseball began with the charging of an admission fee for a series of all-star matches between New York and Brooklyn played at the Fashion Course in 1858 (Goldstein, 1989). After this example, clubs charged occasional admission fees under the guise of prize matches, "benefits" for players, and to raise money for charities (Goldstein, 1989). By 1862 the charging of admission had become firmly established as a method to meet expenses and to pay players (Rader, 1990). By the end of the Civil War, baseball players demanded a share of the gate receipts and baseball became openly professional (Adelman, 1986; Kirsch, 1989; Seymour, 1989; Voigt, 1983).

The commercialization of baseball brought with it a more thorough development of micromarketing techniques. Descriptions of baseball as a product were designed to attract customers. Baseball was entertainment. It was skilled action, filled with drama and excitement. Baseball was scientific play by popular players and stars. Teams represented towns, neighborhoods, and cities. Games were intensely competitive rivalries or championships in which victory meant supremacy and bragging rights. These elements describe the baseball product that appeared in newspapers, weekly journals, and special baseball publications (Adelman, 1986; Goldstein, 1989; Kirsch, 1989).

The micromarketing elements of place and price were influenced by macro elements including the emergence of large commercial and industrial cities. The commercialization of baseball began in New York City. It spread to other large urban, industrial cities: Boston, Philadelphia, Baltimore, and Washington on the East Coast; Chicago, Detroit, and St. Louis in the Midwest; New Orleans in the South, and San Francisco on the West Coast. These urban centers shared common features that influenced the marketing of baseball. The economic impact was most important. White collar, middle-class citizens experienced improved standards of living and more discretionary time. There was a concomitant growth in the popularity of baseball (Adelman, 1986; Freedman, 1978; Goldstein, 1989; Kirsch, 1989). Industrialization gave rise to a growing pool of semiskilled and unskilled workers who worked long hours at low pay. The physical growth of cities and the increase in population influenced land use. Inner-city play space declined; baseball fields moved outside of the urban core either near middle class neighborhoods or along transportation routes (Hardy, 1982; Riess, 1989).

In 1862 baseball clubs charged 10 cents admission. By 1865 this had been raised to 50 cents. Some promoters argued that the increase was necessary to support a higher level of play. Other promoters argued that the increase was necessary in order to keep rowdies out (Adelman, 1986). Both explanations are plausible. Baseball micromarketers catered to a middle-class audience.

Baseball promotions involved a variety of techniques between 1865 and 1870. Tours functioned in two ways. First, they expanded the market by further popularizing the game. Second, tours served to increase the recognition and prestige of particular teams. The Cincinnati Red Stockings' 1869 tour, for example, accelerated the growth of baseball but also brought fame to the Red Stockings as they completed an undefeated season with lopsided victories in the San Francisco area (Barney, 1978; Kirsch, 1989). Baseball tournaments and championships relied upon urban boosterism and resulted in similar though not always positive publicity. Most championship matches were contrived. They consisted of a three-game series with the winner claiming to be champion. Players from both teams received a share of the gate receipts. Rumors of second games being lost on purpose to permit a third game and larger gate receipts were common (Adelman, 1986; Kirsch, 1989).

Local newspapers, national sporting journals (*Wilkes' Spirit of the Times* and *The New York Clipper*), and special baseball publications (*Beadle's Dime Baseball Player* and *The Ball Player's Chronicle*) promoted baseball in a number of ways. They announced baseball games, tours, tournaments, all-star contests, and championship games. They also provided statistical reviews of games and seasons.

Writers emphasized baseball's drama and excitement. Newspapers promoted the representational nature of baseball teams, linking victory to local prestige and superiority, connecting team success to local pride (Adelman, 1986; Kirsch, 1989). By stressing the health and moral aspects of baseball, local and national writers also helped legitimate the game (Adelman, 1986).[7] Baseball's propagandists further promoted baseball by declaring it America's national pastime (Kirsch, 1989).

During the Era of Origins (1820 - 1880) micromarketing decisions gradually became more sophisticated in response to the growth and greater impact of external forces. The examples of William Fuller, Michael Phelan, and the baseball promoters during the late 1860s demonstrate the evolution of sport marketing in respect to micro decisions and macro forces as well as the continuity of the interaction of external forces with internal marketing decisions.[8] Fuller's decisions about product, price, place, and promotion were framed by external forces that he could not manipulate or use to gain much of a competitive advantage. Fuller, of course, had few competitors. Phelan faced heavy competition. His micromarketing decisions attempted to manipulate external forces, such as market size, market growth, and technology, to gain a competitive advantage over other billiard equipment manufacturers.

Like Phelan, early baseball promoters made decisions about product, price, place, and promotion based upon market size and market growth. Baseball promoters took advantage of the increase in per capita and discretionary time. Micromarketing decisions in baseball also took advantage of technological advances in transportation, communication, and publishing. Fuller's micromarketing decisions were fairly simple. He had few competitors, and the external forces he dealt with were few and local. Forty years later baseball promoters faced a more complex market. There were many more competitors. External forces were greater in number and far more extensive. Micromarketing decisions were more sophisticated because they had to be. During the next 60 years, external forces would continue to expand, and micromarketing responses would become more complex.

The Era of Institutionalized Development: 1880 - 1920

The Era of Institutionalized Development built upon the Era of Origins. Micromarketing functions expanded to combat or take advantage of new and more powerful external forces. Product considerations, little more than reactions to anticipated demand during the period of Origins, expanded to include strategic planning, development, and management. During the period of Institutionalized Development, sport products were branded and trademarked. Packaging to identify brand and enhance appeal became a standard practice. Sport products were graded in an attempt to expand demand by segmenting products by price ranges and by allowing consumers to better judge quality from grade. Many products also became standardized to meet the requirements of sport governing bodies and rules committees. Sport products were designed by experts to improve performance, autographed by renowned players to signify quality, and styled by shape, color, and texture to enhance appeal. Market analysis to determine customer needs, estimate market potential, and study competition began at the turn of the century. By 1920 large companies like A.G. Spalding & Brothers and Thomas E. Wilson had their own marketing departments.[9]

Distribution activities and initiatives changed between 1880 and 1920. Producer-owned "branch houses," begun in the 1860s by companies like Brunswick, became widespread after 1900 as companies took over wholesale and retail functions in order to circumvent antitrust laws and control distribution.[10] Many sporting goods companies used historical inventory trends to guide ordering and developed connections between inventory and market analysis. Sporting goods manufacturers also increased contact with independent retailers and chain stores. In order to compete with other manufacturers, a manufacturer was required to provide financial assistance to retailers in the areas of advertising, market research, window displays, and equipment demonstration (Fullerton, 1988).

During the Era of Institutional Development, price became an important part of the marketing plan. Before 1880 pricing had been largely a matter of guesswork or negotiation. It was not a major factor in the marketing plan. After 1880 sporting goods manufacturers and sport promoters began to see the relationships between product quality and price and market segmentation and sales. Sporting goods manufacturers, for example, advocated vertical price maintenance for two reasons. First, it was a way to control perceived consumer quality. Second, it was a way to enlarge distribution channels by allowing the small retailer to compete with the large distributor who was engaged in significant price gouging. Manufacturers believed that price was too important a part of marketing to be left outside the control of the producer. Without vertical price maintenance, marketing plans that relied upon grading or market-plus pricing (pricing that reflected the psychic value of trademark) were worthless (Fullerton, 1988).

Promotional activities expanded in volume and intensity between 1880 and 1920 and became more highly organized. Prior to 1880, Phelan and the early baseball promoters demonstrated how to use newspapers, journals, special publications, tours, championships, and popular players to induce customers to buy tickets and products. These kinds of activities increased after 1880. Advertising, for example, expanded enormously. During the 1890s many sporting goods manufacturers hired professional advertising agencies to handle ad campaigns, and at least four sporting goods manufacturers were among the top 25 national advertisers. Before 1920 all the larger sporting goods manufacturers had marketing departments responsible for developing and integrating promotional campaigns. Sporting goods producers assumed the role of communicating with customers and attempted to build awareness and appeal for their products. Company sales forces became an integral part of promotions during the period. Equipped with displays, advertising, direct mail follow-ups, advertising and sales advice, and technical knowledge about products company representatives visited jobbers and retailers to promote company products. By 1920 nearly all medium and large firms had their own sales forces (Fullerton, 1988).

External forces made the above changes in marketing necessary. Market growth in terms of increased population was tremendous between 1880 and 1920. During each decade between 1880 and 1920 the population increased by more than 10 million. Annual immigration reached peaks of over 800,000 in the early 1880s and in 1910, and it seldom fell below 200,000 annually (Higgs, 1971). The population increased from slightly over 50 million in 1880 to well over 100 million by 1920 (U.S. Department of Commerce, 1924). The increased population was marked by two important trends. The first trend was a migration from the settled areas in the east to the less populated sections of the west (Paulin, 1932). The second trend was a steady movement from rural to urban areas. In 1880, 28% of the American population lived in cities of 2,500 or over. By 1920 this figure had climbed to 51% (Legergott, 1946; U.S. Department of Commerce, 1976). Considered together, the two trends describe a market that was continually expanding and, at the same time, a market that was becoming more and more concentrated within urban environments as it spread west.

Population expansion and concentration were accompanied by a significant increase in discretionary money. With the exception of the depression years during the 1890s, yearly earnings of nonfarm employees increased at a rapid rate between 1880 and 1920. The cost of living decreased during the 1880s and 1890s. The increase in the cost of living during the first decade of the 20th century was overshadowed by a much larger increase in yearly earnings. Only during the latter part of the second decade, when the impact of the European War began to be felt, were cost of living increases greater than increases in yearly income.

As Table 3.2 demonstrates, Americans had more money to spend during the period between 1880 and 1920 (Borden, 1942; Legergott, 1946). Indeed, as Murphy and Zellner (1959) have argued, during the three decades preceding World War I, the levels of income for various sectors of the work force, "did not deviate greatly from those to which they aspired" (Murphy & Zellner, 1959, p. 402). According to Norris (1990), much of the public complaint against the rising cost of living near the end of the second decade of the 20th century was "conditioned by the experience of over two generations with a rising standard of living" (Norris, 1990, pp. 10-11).

Sport benefited from these developments. Industry profitability increased during each decade between 1880 and 1920. Numerous studies document the increased popularity of sport (Betts, 1974; Lucas & Smith, 1978; Mrozek, 1983; Rader, 1990). To meet the demand for sporting goods products, established companies in related industries began to produce sporting goods products while new manufacturing companies also evolved.

Table 3.3 documents the growth of new companies. In 1879 only 86 companies manufactured goods categorized as sporting and athletic goods.[11] By 1921 the number of manufacturing companies had risen to 152. During this same period of time the aggregate value of manufactured products increased from

TABLE 3.2 - Comparison of Annual Earnings and Consumer Price Index

	Yearly Earnings	% Increase/ Decrease	CPI	% Increase/ Decrease	Difference YE-CPI
1880	386		97.8		
1890	475	+23.0%	91.5	-6.0%	+29.0%
1900	483	+1.7%	84.3	-7.9%	+9.6%
1910	634	+31.0%	94.7	+12.3%	+18.7%
1912	657	+3.6%	97.2	+2.6%	+1.0%
1914	696	+5.9%	100.0	+2.9%	+3.0%
1916	706	+1.4%	108.7	+8.7%	-7.3%
1917	805	+14.0%	127.7	+17.0%	-3.0%
1918	1041	+29.0%	150.0	+17.0%	+12.0%
1919	1174	+12.8%	172.5	+15.0%	-2.2%
1920	1343	+14.2%	199.7	+15.8%	-1.6%

Source: Davis, L.E., Easterlin, R.A., and Parker, W.N. (Eds.). (1972). *American economic growth.* Harper & Row: New York. p. 212.

slightly over $1.5 million in 1879 to over $34.7 million in 1921 (U.S. Department of Commerce, 1924).

Technological changes influenced the distribution and the production of sporting goods. The railroad brought about a revolution in distribution. By 1880 over 70,000 miles of railroad track were in operation. The overland transport network, including both east-west and north-south trunk lines, was completed during the 1880s. By 1900 over 200,000 miles of track were in use. This increased to over 250,000 by 1920. Most small cities, villages, and even hamlets in the nation had railroad service by 1920 (Chandler, 1977). Increased mileage meant increased service. The railroad provided fast, dependable, and inexpensive transportation for manufactured products. It made possible economies of scale in regard to distribution (Chandler, 1977). One reflection of the increased importance of the railroad in distribution was the rise in tons of freight shipped. Freight carried by the railroad increased from 338 million tons in 1880 to 2,002 million tons in 1914 (Frickey, 1947). Sporting goods were a part of the freight transported by rail.

The revolution in distribution made possible by the railroad also was influenced by the telegraph and the telephone. The telegraph followed the railroad, relying upon the same right of way. Where the railroad provided fast, regular, dependable, all-weather transportation, the telegraph made possible fast, regular, dependable, all-weather communication (Chandler, 1977). The railroad and the telegraph combined made the traveling salesperson not only possible but, also essential. Increased competition influenced manufacturing companies, jobbers, and wholesalers to communicate directly with retailers in an attempt to gain a competitive advantage. This was particularly true for bicycle manufacturers during the 1890s and sporting goods and athletic goods manufacturers after the turn of the century. The telephone began commercial operations in the 1880s.

Initially, it was used almost totally for local communication. With the development of long-distance lines in the 1890s, faster, almost instantaneous communication became possible, and the telephone emerged as an important business tool (Chandler, 1977).

Technological changes influenced the production of certain kinds of sporting goods. Most sport equipment manufactured during the Era of Institutional Development was labor intensive. The prerequisites for mass production of sporting equipment did not exist (Hounshell, 1984). However, some progress towards mass production was made in certain segments of the industry. Bicycle manufacturers developed and applied techniques such as drop forging, straight-machining, nickel plating, brazing, and sheet-steel stamping to bicycle production. Bicycle manufacturers like the Pope Manufacturing Company and the Western Wheel Works used quantitative models, gauging systems, rational jigs, fixtures, special purpose machines, and sequencing to improve the quality and the quantity of bicycle production. Assembly was the greatest production problem. Despite improvements in all other areas of production, assembly

TABLE 3.3 - Sporting and Athletic Goods Manufacturers

	Number of Manufacturers	Number of Workers Employed	Value of Product
1879	86	1401	1,556,258
1889	136	2008	2,709,449
1899	143	2225	3,628,496
1909	180	5321	11,291,552[1]
1919	188	6412	25,335,063[1]
1921	152	7063	34,711,174[1]

[1]includes production values of establishment in other industries that produced sport equipment.

Source: Department of Commerce: Bureau of Census. (1921). *Biennial Census of Manufacturers.* p. 1242.

remained very labor intensive (Hounshell, 1984). Producers of golf and tennis balls, like B.F. Goodrich, used technology to improve products and speed production.[12] A. J. Reach used sequenced machines to produce baseballs during the late 1890s ("How Base Balls Are Made," 1899). The automatic lathe and the automatic sander speeded up the production of baseball bats ("Baseball Bats," 1906). In each of the above examples, technology improved quality and permitted larger product quantities. However, none of the above examples eliminated the need for extensive labor in the production of sport equipment.

The advent of the 10-cent magazine between 1885 and 1905 added another external force for sport marketers to utilize and contend with. Lower priced magazines were made possible by technological improvements in the printing press (Isaacs, 1931) and by an increased use of advertising to lower cost to readers (Norris, 1990). The passage of the Postal Act of 1879, which granted favorable mailing rates and privileges to journals and magazines, helped to increase market size (Norris, 1990). In 1885 only four general magazines with a circulation of over 1,000 existed. Each was priced at either 25 cents or 35 cents per copy. By 1905 there were 20 general-purpose magazines catering to a middle-class market. All but four of these magazines sold for 10 or 15 cents. The aggregate circulation of these middle class magazines was over 5 and 1/2 million (Mott, 1957).

Cheaper prices recruited millions of new readers and advertising dollars. The new magazines were intended to make money primarily from advertising (Norris, 1990). The formula for success of these magazines — mass circulation, low unit cost of production, aimed at the growing middle class — proved attractive to advertisers. The *Saturday Evening Post* is a good example. The *Post* was taken over by Louisa Knapp Curtis in 1897 when it was almost defunct. Advertising revenue during the first 2 years was low. By 1900 advertising revenue reached $159,300. By 1905 advertising revenues were greater than $1 million. Advertising revenues were $5 million in 1910 when circulation reached one million. In 1917 the *Post's* circulation exceeded 1.8 million and advertising revenues were over $16 million (Wood, 1949). Sporting goods manufacturers were very much a part of the advertising revolution. By 1898, 11 of the top 150 national advertisers were sporting goods firms, and sporting goods advertising made up 10% of all national advertising (Presbrey, 1929). Sporting goods manufacturers continued to emphasize advertising throughout the Era of Institutional Development.[13]

The increased production capacity of manufacturers, the revolution in distribution and communication, and the revolution in advertising made economies of scale possible and necessary. High-volume producers achieved competitive advantage by lowering the cost of per-unit production (Hounshell, 1984). High-volume distribution extended the advantage by lowering the cost per unit for shipping goods (Bucklin, 1972). High-volume advertising lowered the cost per ad and influenced wholesale and retail turnover rates (Norris, 1990). Sporting goods manufacturers expanded plant size and updated equipment, beginning in the 1890s and continuing for the next three decades, in an attempt to achieve economies of scale.[14]

Economies of scale influenced economies of scope and vice versa. Once a firm had reached sufficient size to engage in economies of scale, it often found that it could not simply produce goods and achieve competitive advantage. Economies of scope became an attractive alternative. Companies achieved economies of scope in one of two ways. First, some companies pursued economies of scope through vertical growth. This vertical integration strategy was usually forward into marketing, but some companies integrated backward into owning their own raw materials. Second, an alternative strategy involved horizontal growth. Horizontal integration was achieved when companies that produced similar products or product lines joined together to form a combination of their interests. Occasionally, horizontal integration led to vertical integration. Economies of scope provided strategic benefits. They permitted greater utilization of economies of scale in production, distribution, and advertising.

With few exceptions, sporting goods manufacturers were not involved in economies of scope until after the first decade of the 20th century. The sport industry was not part of what Porter (1973), *The Rise of Big Business*, has termed the "Great Merger Wave," which took place between 1895 and 1905. A.G. Spalding and Brothers began vertical integration in the late 1870s with the acquisition of Wilkins Manufacturing Company (Levine, 1985). A decade later Spalding initiated a horizontal integration strategy with the acquisition of Peck and Snyder and in the early 1890s acquired Wright & Ditson and A.J. Reach and Company (Van Pelt, 1946). As the 20th century opened, several sporting goods companies chose not to engage in economies of scope but joined together to enact barriers to entry and control the market, achieving advantages related to economies of scope. These amalgamations included the Bicycle Trust (1899), the Ammunition Trust (1901), and the Bicycle Bell Trust (1904).[15]

Economies of scope became common after the creation of Thomas E. Wilson Company in 1913. The Wilson Company, bolstered by an enormous amount of money from its meat-packing business, moved quickly into both horizontal and vertical integration in an attempt to gain a competitive advantage over A.G. Spalding and Brothers ("Ashland Personnel," 1916).[16] Spalding responded by purchasing the Victor Sporting Goods Company through its subsidiary, Wright & Ditson ("Wright & Ditson and Victor Consolidate," 1918).[17] The period ended with a flurry of amalgamations as other sporting goods companies attempted to compete.

Successful sporting goods companies during the Era of Institutional Development reacted to and utilized external forces to achieve a competitive advantage. In this process of reaction and utilization, sporting goods companies relied upon internal resources to manipulate micromarketing techniques (promotion, product, place, and price) to gain competitive advantage. The best single example of how successful companies utilized internal resources to combat or manipulate external forces to achieve a competitive advantage is the A.G. Spalding and Brothers Company. Spalding began in 1876 with a capital of $3,800. Profits for the first 10 months amounted to $1,083.[18] In 1920 Spalding's net income was $1,172,910, and the company was capitalized at $7 million ("Spalding Increases Capital Stock," 1922).

In November of 1915 the leaders of A.G. Spalding and Brothers discussed the reasons for their success with the editorial staff of the *Sporting Goods Dealer* ("Reasons for Spalding Success," 1915). First, Spalding resources, "great aggregations of capital," allowed the company to operate economies of scale and scope ("Reasons for Spalding Success," 1915, p.41). Spalding operated 15 large factories in the United States. The Chicopee plant, for example, had 4 1/2 acres of floor space ("Spalding's Chicopee Plant," 1911). Spalding manufactured on a large scale. Spalding also operated 35 branch stores that performed retail and wholesale functions ("New Spalding Store Acme of Perfection," 1918). Spalding's vertical integration was considered a second major factor influencing company success. A third reason was Spalding's organizational structure and management.

Marketing decisions, for example, were made and coordinated by top management. These decisions were passed on to factories and branch stores by vice presidents. Factories and branch stores followed these directives but were operated as separate units by career oriented middle managers. The marketing strategy functioned to coordinate production, distribution, and sales. Spalding recruited and trained middle managers and provided career-ladder opportunities for advancement within the organization. Top management visited branch stores and factories to provide direction and ideas. In the words of one Spalding manager, "it is the system that works" ("Reasons for Spalding Success," 1915, p. 49). The system provided for a "uniformity and regularity of everything," a fourth reason cited for Spalding success. A fifth reason given for Spalding success was the variety of merchandise sold under the Spalding brand name ("Reasons for Spalding Success," 1915).

The expansion of the Spalding product line took place gradually and was a reaction to external forces. Spalding began as a small retail store in 1876. The company sold only baseball equipment and their largest customer was the Chicago White Sox Baseball Club ("J. Walter Spalding Original Ledger," 1947; "Have Had Remarkable Growth," 1908).[19] Encouraged by the growing market for other forms of athletic goods, Spalding expanded his product line in 1878 ("Spalding Re-establishes Downtown Store," 1907). A year later Spalding purchased an interest in the Wilkins Manufacturing Company, which produced ice skates, fishing equipment, baseball bats, and croquet equipment (Levine, 1985). To "insure the quality of goods," Spalding bought out Wilkins in 1881 and established the policy of manufacturing all Spalding trade-mark goods (Levine, 1985; "Have Had Remarkable Growth," 1908, p. 11).

Throughout the 1880s Spalding responded to market opportunities by expanding the products manufactured by the company. In 1886, for example, Spalding began manufacturing footballs because the market growth of football in colleges and high schools insured financial success (Levine, 1985; "Spalding Football Gear," 1906).[20] Product expansion continued in the 1890s with the acquisition of A. J. Reach & Co. (1889), Peck and Snyder (1889), Wright & Ditson (1891), Lamb Manufacturing Company (1893), St. Lawrence River Skiff and Canoe Company (1895), and the George Barnard Company (1896) (Levine, 1985; Van Pelt, 1946).

These purchases permitted Spalding and Brothers to expand their policy of insuring quality by producing their own trademark goods ("Andrew Peck, Pioneer," 1916; Levine, 1985; Van Pelt, 1946).[21] The new acquisitions also allowed Spalding and Brothers to more effectively tap into expanding markets in baseball, ice skating, tennis, bicycles, golf, boating, and athletic wear. By the turn of the century, Spalding was manufacturing bowling balls, protective football equipment, tackling dummies, bathing suits, table tennis equipment, and gymnasium lockers, all to meet the growing market demand for sporting goods products (*Sporting Goods Dealer*, 1900a,b,c,; 1902a,b).

Spalding continued to expand their product lines throughout the period. By

1920 the company owned 15 factories in the United States, 4 in England, and 2 in Canada ("New Spalding Store Acme of Perfection," 1918). A. G. Spalding and Brothers produced a greater variety of products than did any other company in the United States. The gradual expansion of product lines was a reaction to opportunities created by market growth.

Spalding reacted to opportunities created by market growth with promotions that targeted specific populations. Promotional efforts began as soon as the company was formed. Spalding spent $483.51 on advertising over the first 10 months, approximately 4% of the company's total sales.[22] Spalding acquired the right to publish the "official" book for the National League. At the same time he published *Spalding's Official Baseball Guide*. Both books promoted the Spalding name and advertised Spalding products (Hardy, 1990; Levine, 1985).[23] Both books promoted baseball. *Spalding's Official Baseball Guide*, for example, included league rules and constitution, records, descriptions of the past season's play, playing instructions, and history (Hardy, 1990). As early as 1878, Spalding held a contract to provide the National League with the Official Ball. Spalding had wrestled the contract away from L. H. Mann of Boston by agreeing to pay the National League a dollar a dozen for the privilege of supplying free balls (Hardy, 1990; Levine, 1985). Official guides and official balls were great promotional tools. Spalding knew that his target audience would never play major league ball. He understood that his audience desired to use what the professionals used because in their minds it signified the best (Levine, 1985). Spalding marketed other "official balls" for football, basketball, polo, soccer, and volleyball as well as "official" boxing gloves and the "official" discus (*Sporting Goods Dealer*, 1900d; "Spalding Football Gear," 1906). Spalding added guides for a variety of other sports when the market appeared favorable (*Sporting Goods Dealer*, 1899a,b). A. G. Spalding and Brothers was among the first companies to promote sales through packaging. They were among the first to develop general catalogs and to use seasonal catalogs. It was among the first to develop a national sales force. It was among the first to target specific markets through the use of grading techniques (*Sporting Goods Dealer*, 1899a,b). It was among the first companies to target the youth market (*Sporting Goods Dealer*, 1901a; "How The Boy As An Asset Helped Build The Gigantic Spalding Business," 1923).[24]

Spalding not only reacted to opportunities created by market growth; the company also influenced market growth (Hardy, 1990; Levine, 1985; Porter, 1985). A. G. Spalding realized that the key to market growth was increased sport participation. Spalding's promotional efforts were designed not just to sell Spalding products but to expand the sport market by enlisting new participants. The Spalding Library of American Sports, inaugurated in 1885, was designed to educate future participants (Levine, 1985). Changed to "Spalding's Athletic Library" when James E. Sullivan became managing editor in 1892, by the turn of the century the Athletic Library contained over 300 separate titles on sport and physical activity. By 1916 the series listed 16 separate groups of activities arranged by activity. Spalding claimed that it was "the greatest educational series on athletic and physical training subjects that has ever been compiled" (Levine, 1985, pp. 82, 162).[25] The Spalding Athletic Library taught readers about sport, provided instruction from experts, presented the benefits of participation, and encouraged activity. Spalding also promoted sport by organizing tours, organizing contests, donating trophies, participating in sport shows, establishing instructional schools, sponsoring professional teams, supporting the Olympic movement, and providing expert advice for facility construction (Levine, 1985; *Sporting Goods Dealer*, 1899b; 1901a; 1902a; 1905; 1927). These activities promoted sport participation, which influenced market growth and also helped to sell Spalding products.

Spalding's product development and product diversity and Spalding's promotional efforts were key factors in the company's success ("Have Had Remarkable Growth," 1908). Equally important was Spalding's vertical integration into wholesale and the expansion of its retail operation into a national system of branch stores ("New Spalding Store Acme of Perfection," 1918). Backward integration into distribution began in 1884 when Spalding opened a wholesale store in New York City. Expansion to New York was prompted by two considerations. First, establishing a wholesale house in New York would more effectively serve east coast retailers. The move meant that Spalding products could be displayed in a place far more accessible to eastern retailers (Carney, 1928; "New Gotham," 1924).[26] Second, the New York operation was also a distribution center. Spalding goods were displayed on the first floor, and products were stored on the remaining four floors. This permitted Spalding to ship goods to eastern retailers far more effectively (Carney, 1928).[27] Spalding continued the policy of creating wholesale/distribution centers during the next 2 1/2 decades. By 1908 the company had 20 such centers in the United States and one each in Canada and England ("Have Had Remarkable Growth," 1908).

Spalding's development of retail branch stores occurred much more slowly. Spalding opened a retail store in New York in 1885. Boston and Philadelphia stores were opened in the early 1890s. The push for retail outlets occurred after the turn of the century (Meek, 1927). Three divisions were formed, one in the East, another in the West, and later one on the Pacific Coast to coordinate activities and services (Meek, 1927). The development of retail branch stores was prompted by three considerations. First, Spalding saw the opportunity to increase sales. Company stores would sell all kinds of equipment manufactured by other companies but would more effectively push Spalding products ("Spalding To Open Branch Stores," 1902). The Spalding name and trademark would be displayed on the storefront, and Spalding products could be seen in the store windows. Second, the company believed that it could more effectively serve its customers by establishing a retail chain (Carney, 1928). Company leaders believed that branch stores would ensure quick shipment of goods. Store managers would be more aware of customer needs and alert Spalding distribution centers about those needs in a timely fashion.

Finally, it appears that Spalding was concerned about price maintenance. In

1899 Spalding established a policy of dealing directly with retailers. Spalding would sell to everyone at the same price in exchange for the assurance that the retailer would sell Spalding products at prices determined by the firm (Levine, 1985). According to Levine, Spalding thought the policy would "increase business, stabilize market situations and eliminate price-cutting" (p. 83). The policy appeared to be a huge success. Six months after its inception Walter Spalding "told a *Sporting News* reporter that 'there had been a wonderful increase in their athletic business' and that price-cutting had virtually ended" (cited in Levine, 1985, p. 84).

The movement into retail branch stores 3 years later was prompted, at least in part, by the success of the 1899 policy. It appears that Spalding Company leaders, like Julian Curtiss and C.S. Lincoln, believed that retail store owners were maintaining Spalding prices but were discounting comparable goods of other sporting goods manufacturers. This practice hurt the sale of top grade Spalding products ("How The Boy As An Asset Helped Build The Gigantic Spalding Business," 1923).[28] The only way to combat such practices was to control the retail outlets where the goods were sold (Van Pelt, 1946).[29] Spalding moved into the development of retail branch stores so that they could control prices at those stores.[30]

Very little is known about Spalding and Brothers' price policies. The company began in 1876 with a cash sales policy (Hardy, 1990). This was continued until 1893. During that year Spalding established a credit policy to improve bicycle sales. There is no evidence that Spalding extended the credit policy to other Spalding products until after the turn of the century. Spalding advertisements to dealers are silent about the possibilities for discounts or terms. These matters could have been handled by Spalding's traveling sales representatives. When Spalding moved into the mass market during 1884, they established a grading policy. A decade later they advertised 18 different grades of bats and 15 grades of baseball. Prices for baseballs ranged from 5 cents to $1.25 (Levine, 1985; *Sporting Goods Dealer*, 1901a). Spalding adjusted prices on high-quality goods for the youth market, claiming that the company actually lost money on these products ("How The Boy As An Asset Helped Build The Gigantic Spalding Business," 1923). Spalding and Brothers' concern for price maintenance, discussed briefly above, continued throughout the period of Institutional Development. Other than the 1899 sales policy and the suggested connection between retail branch stores and price maintenance, little is known about Spalding pricing policies.

A. G. Spalding and Brothers was not the only sporting goods manufacturer to apply micromarketing techniques as a response to external forces. Spalding's attempts to achieve a competitive advantage were copied by other companies. Table 3.4 documents the use of micromarketing techniques by a large number of sporting goods manufacturers to gain a competitive advantage or to establish a barrier to entry.

Table 3.4 is an adaptation of Fullerton's (1988), "How Modern is Modern Marketing." The left-hand column lists 14 producer activities. These producer

TABLE 3.4 - Sporting Goods Industry 1899-1905 (*N*=516)

Producer Activities	Yes	Percent	No	Percent	Undetermined	Percent
Trademarks	430	84%	86	16%		
Packaging	293	57%	223	43%		
Grading and Standardization	325	63%	191	37%		
Segmentation (By Price)	235	45%	281	55%		
Market Analysis	94	18%	181	35%	241	47%
Product Design	353	68%	160	31%	3	1%
Producer Owned Branch House	45	9%	471	91%		
Producer Owned Retail Stores	19	4%	497	96%		
Direct Sales to Consumer	191	37%	325	63%		
Cooperation with Independent Retailer	288	56%	228	44%		
Price Maintenance	71	14%	445	86%		
Co. Sales Force	317	61%	199	39%		
National Advertising	335	65%	181	35%		
Advertising Agency	102	20%	221	43%	193	37%

activities correspond to specific micromarketing functions. Trademarks, packaging, grading and standardization, segmentation, market analysis, and product design are product micromarketing activities. Producer-owned branch houses, producer-owned retail stores, direct sales to customers, and contacting independent retailers are distribution functions. Price maintenance is a price micromarketing activity. Company sales forces and national advertising are promotional activities (Fullerton, 1988). The "Yes" column in Table 3.4 lists the number of sporting goods companies that employed the technique. This column is followed by a percentage column. The "No" column in Table 3.4 lists the number of companies that did not use the micromarketing technique. This column is followed by a percentage. For example, 430 sporting goods producers, which constituted 84% of the sample, used trademarks. Eighty-six sporting goods producers, which constitutes 16% of the sample, did not use trademarks. The "Undetermined" column in Table 3.4 lists the number of companies in the sample for which data about the marketing activity do not exist. This column is followed by a percentage. For example, under number 5, "market analysis," there were 241 companies in the sample for which we could not determine whether market analysis was applied or not. This constituted 47% of the total sample.

Table 3.5 divides the sample into specific categories of sporting goods manufacturers. The data for Tables 3.4 and 3.5 were gathered from company histories, trade magazines, and advertisements and include only those companies that existed between 1899 and 1905. The sample included 516 companies that manufactured products for the sporting goods market. Some companies made products for other markets. For example, many companies classified under Arms and Ammo also manufactured products for the military. Twenty-eight companies produced a variety of sporting products. To avoid confusion, these companies are classified as General Manufacturers. A. G. Spalding and Brothers, for example, manufactured a variety of sport equipment products. Rather than list the Spalding company several times under each separate heading, it is listed only once, under General Manufacturers.

TABLE 3.5 - Categories of Sporting Goods Manufactuers

Category	Number
General Manufacturer	28
Arms and Ammo	104
Bicycles	138
Fishing Equipment	60
Boats and Equipment	43
Skating	13
Golf	41
Gymnastics and Exercise	13
Billiards and Bowling	11
Uniforms and Spt. Clothing	27
Boxing	15
Tennis	8
Baseball	25
Basketball	3
Football	13

Table 3.6 illustrates the extremes within the sport industry. It follows an abbreviated format of Table 3.4 and adds some key examples. Table 3.6 suggests that certain categories of sporting goods manufacturers were far more advanced in the use of micromarketing techniques than were others. As Table 3.6 documents, general manufacturers of sporting goods and arms and ammo producers used micromarketing techniques to a greater extent than did golf and tennis equipment manufacturers.

The two extremes portrayed in Table 3.6 have two important implications for the development of sport marketing. First, participation in tennis and golf was not

TABLE 3.6 - Extremes within the Industry: 1899-1905

PRODUCER ACTIVITIES	GENERAL MFG Sp.Good		ARM & AMMO		GOLF		TENNIS		KEY EXAMPLES
	Yes	No	Yes	No	Yes	No	Yes	No	
1. Trademarks	24	4	70	0	16	25	6	2	Chicago Sporting Goods Peter's Cartridge
2. Packaging	18	10	69	1	12	29	6	2	Spalding & Bros. Peter's Cartridge
3. Grading & Standardization	27	1	68	2	22	19	5	3	Remington Arms Co. A. J. Reach
4. Segmentation	25	3	58	12	6	35	2	6	A. J. Reach Daisy Mfg. Remington
5. Market Analysis	14	2	38	12	5	28	2	1	D & M McClean Arms Co. Wright & Division
6. Product Designed by Specialist	25	3	70	0	16	25	4	4	Goldsmith & Sons Ted Kennedy
7. Producer Owned Branch Houses	11	17	20	50	2	39	1	7	Spalding Hazard Powder B. F. Goodrich
8. Producer Owned Retail Stores	13	15	0	70	1	40	0	8	Spalding & Bros. BGI
9. Direct Sale to Consumer	20	8	32	38	5	36	0	8	Patrick Bros. Crandel & Stone
10. Contact Independent Retailer-Chain Store	21	7	65	5	10	31	8	0	BGI Winchester
11. Price Maintenance	7	4	26	7	0	41	0	8	Spalding & Bros. Iver Johnson
12. Company Sales Force	20	8	68	2	12	29	8	0	Wright & Ditson A. J. Reach
13. National Advertising	21	3	67	3	11	30	5	3	Winchester Rawlings Goldsmith
14. Advertising Agency or Specialist	19	5	31	7	4	32	2	1	Chicago Sport Goods Spalding & Bros. D&M

as great as participation in hunting. The market was not as large. Competition was not as keen, and barriers to entry were not as great. There were many more manufacturers of arms and ammo than there were of golf or tennis. Manufacturers of golf and tennis equipment did not need to rely upon micromarketing techniques to the same extent that producers of arms and ammo did. Second, the general manufacturers of sporting goods and the arms and ammo producers were much larger companies than were the producers of golf and tennis equipment. In each instance, the key examples listed in the right-hand column of Table 3.6 were large companies. They had the internal resources to combat or utilize external forces through micromarketing activities.

During the Era of Institutional Development (1880-1920) sporting goods manufacturers developed and refined micromarketing techniques in response to new and powerful external forces. Innovators like A. G. Spalding and Brothers introduced new micromarketing activities to the sporting goods industry. Other companies copied and further refined these techniques. By 1920 all the elements of what Fullerton (1988) has called modern marketing existed in the sporting goods industry. What followed during the Era of Refinement and Formalization (1930-1990) was refinement, further development, and formalization of already-established micromarketing techniques as sporting goods companies reacted to new opportunities and challenges made possible by external forces.

The Era of Refinement and Formalization: 1920-1990

During the last 70 years, sport marketing has continued to develop along lines established during the Era of Institutional Development. External forces have played important roles in this development. The increased popularity and diversification of sport interests have increased market size. Sport fads have periodically increased market growth rates. Industry profitability has fluctuated through turbulent periods like the depressions of 1930s and the early 1990s and the prosperous times of the 1950s and 1960s.

Government policies have also influenced sport marketing. The National Industrial Recovery Act (1933) placed restrictions on sporting goods manufacturers but also influenced the development of fair trade practices, particularly when connected to the Robinson Packman Act of 1936. The Miller Tydings Act (1937) and the Consumer Goods Pricing Act (1975) influenced the pricing practices of sporting goods companies. More recently the North American Free Trade Agreement (1993) and the Brady Bill (1994) will influence how sporting goods companies do business.

Technological changes have influenced both how and from what materials sporting goods are made. New materials, such as plastics, fiberglass, aluminum alloys, spandex fibers, and graphite have improved athletic performances and altered athletic styles. At the same time these new materials have made possible the development of special machines to mass produce sport equipment. Economies of scale have been made possible by new materials and new manufacturing techniques, new and more economic forms of transportation, and new and more effective forms of communication.

Modern marketers have the use of many specialized trade journals, radio, television, computers, and fax machines to convey and receive information. The increased opportunities for economies of scale have influenced preferences for economies of scope. Prior to 1920 economies of scope led to amalgamation and consolidation within a domestic sport industry. Today economies of scope include leveraged buy-outs, global competition, and off shore industries.

Questions for Study

1. Identify three ways in which sport marketers contributed to a growing sport market between 1820 and 1880.
2. What problems did Fuller encounter when attempting to market boxing in the early 1820s?
3. Were advertisements used to market the game of baseball in the 1860s significantly different than the modern advertisements used to market baseball?
4. List 10 characteristics associated with the Era of Institutionalized Development and elaborate on their significance.
5. By what year did almost all medium and large sporting goods companies have their own sales force?
6. What stage of the product life-cycle does the sporting goods industry occupy between 1880 and 1920? Defend your answer.
7. Elaborate on the contribution the railroad, telegraph, and telephone provided to sport marketing.
8. Elaborate on the impact of technology during the Era of Institutional Development.
9. How does a competitor's advertising help to sell sport? Elaborate.
10. Elaborate on how both economies of scale and economies of scope can facilitate marketing efforts.
11. How did vertical integration facilitate Spalding's marketing efforts?
12. Identify the five reasons attributed to Spalding's success in the 1920s. Why were these factors important to Spalding's success?
13. Spalding has a significant learning curve advantage. Explain.

References

Adelman, M. L. (1981). The first modern sport in America: Harness racing in New York City, 1825-1870. *Journal of Sport History,* 8(3), 5-32.

Adelman, M. L. (1986). *A sporting time: New York City and the rise of modern athletics, 1820-1870.* Urbana, IL: University of Illinois Press.

Andrew Peck, pioneer (1916). *Sporting Goods Dealer,* 34(4), 55-56.

Ashland personnel (1916). *Sporting Goods Dealer,* 34(1), 78-81.

B. F. Meeks and Sons: Blue grass reel (1911). *Sporting Goods Dealer,* 24(6),10, 11.

Barney, R. K. (1978). Of rails and red stockings: Episodes in the expansion of the national pastime in the American West. *Sport and Recreation in the West,* 61-70.

Baseball Bats (1906). *Sporting Goods Dealer,* 14(6), 6-8.

Betts, J. R. (1974). *America's sporting heritage, 1850-1950.* Reading, MA: Addison-Wesley Publishing Company.

Borden, N. (1942). *The economic effects of advertising.* Chicago, IL: Irwin, Inc.

Bucklin, L. P. (1972). *Competition and evolution in the distributive trades.* Englewood Cliffs, NJ: Prentice-Hall, Inc.

Carney, P. P. (1928). Julian W. Curtis: Master of arts in sports goods merchandising. *Sporting Goods Dealer,* 57(5), 139.

Chandler, A. D., Jr. (1977). *The visible hand: The managerial revolution in American business.* Cambridge, MA: Harvard University Press.

Chudacoff, H. P. (1981). *The evolution of American urban society.* Englewood Cliffs, NJ: Prentice-Hall.

Dewing, A. S. (1924). *Corporate promotion and reorganization.* Cambridge, MA: Harvard University Press.

Freedman, S. (1978). The baseball fad in Chicago. *Journal of Sport History,* 5(1), 42-64.

Frickey, E. (1947). *Production in the United States, 1860-1914.* Cambridge, MA: Harvard University Press.

Fullerton, R. A. (1988). How modern is modern marketing? Marketing's evolution and the myth of the production era. *Journal of Marketing,* 52(1), 108-125.

Goldstein, W. (1989). *Playing for keeps: A history of early baseball.* Ithaca, NY: Cornell University Press.

Gorn, E. J. (1986). *The manly art: Bare-Knuckle prize fighting in America.* Ithaca, NY: Cornell University Press.

Hardy, S. (1982). *How Boston played: Sport, recreation, and community, 1865-1915.* Boston, MA: Northeastern University Press.

Hardy, S. (1986). Entrepreneurs, organizations, and the sport marketplace: Subjects in search of historians. *Journal of Sport History, 13*(1), 21.

Hardy, S. (1990). Adopted by all the leading clubs: Sporting goods and the shaping of leisure, 1800-1900. In Richard Butsch (Ed.), *For fun and profit: The transformation of leisure into consumption* (pp. 71-101). Philadelphia, PA: Temple University Press.

Have had remarkable growth (1908). *Sporting Goods Dealer, 18*(5), 11.

Higgs, R. (1971). *The transformation of American economy, 1865-1914: An essay in interpretation.* New York, NY: Cambridge University Press.

Hounshell, D. A. (1984). *From the American system to mass production, 1800-1932.* Baltimore, MD: The Johns Hopkins University Press.

How base balls are made (1899). *Sporting Goods Dealer, 1*(1), 4-6.

How the boy as an asset helped build the gigantic Spalding business (1923). *Sporting Goods Dealer,* 48(2), 78-82.

Isaacs, G. A. (1931). *The story of the newspaper printing press.* London: Cooperative Printing Society.

J. Walter Spalding original ledger (1947). *Sporting Goods Dealer,* 96(3), 128-129.

Kirsch, G. B. (1989). *The creation of American team sports: Baseball & cricket, 1838-1872.* Urbana, IL: University of Illinois Press.

Kogan, R. (1985). *Brunswick: The story of an American company from 1845 to 1985.* Skokie, IL: Brunswick Corp.

Legergott, S. (1946). *Manpower in economic growth: The American record since 1800.* New York, NY: McGraw-Hill Publishing.

Levine, P. (1985). A. G. *Spalding and the rise of baseball: The promise of American sport.* New York, NY: Oxford University Press.

Lucas, J. A., & Smith, R. A. (1978). *Saga of American sport.* Philadelphia, PA: Lee and Febiger.

McCarthy, E. J. and Perreault, W. D., Jr. (1984). *Basic marketing: A managerial approach.* Homewood, IL: Irwin, Inc.

Meek, J. T. (1927). Spalding spreads out in Chicago. *Sporting Goods Dealer,* 56(2), 88-89.

Miller, L. K., Fielding, L. W. and Pitts, B. G. (1993). The rise of the Louisville Slugger in the mass market. *Sport Marketing Quarterly, 2*(3), 9-16.

Mott, F. L. (1957). *A history of American magazines, 1885-1905.* Cambridge, MA: Harvard University Press.

Mrozek, D. J. (1983). *Sport and American mentality, 1880-1910.* Knoxville, TN: The University of Tennessee Press.

Murphy, G. G. S. & Zellner, A. (1959). Sequential growth, the labor safety-valve doctrine, and the development of American unionism. *Journal of Economic History, 19*(3), 402-419.

Nation's oldest sporting goods house. (1911, February). *Sporting Goods Dealer, 11*(5), 12-14.

Nation's oldest sporting goods house. (1911, March). *Sporting Goods Dealer, 11*(6), 13-15, 67.

New Gotham headquarters opened by A. G. Spalding & Bros. (1924). *Sporting Goods Dealer, 50*(4), 85-87.

New Spalding store acme of perfection. (1918). *Sporting Goods Dealer, 38*(6), 30-33.

Norris, J. D. (1990). *Advertising and the transformation of American society, 1865-1920.* New York, NY: Greenwood Press.

Oriard, M. (1993). *Reading football: How the popular press created an American spectacle.* Chapel Hill, NC: University of North Carolina Press.

Paulin, C. O. (1932). *Atlas of the historical geography of the United States.* Washington, DC: Carnegie Institution.

Phelan, M. (1850). *Billiards without masters.* New York, NY: D. D. Winant.

Polsky, N. (1969). *Hustlers, beats, and others.* New York, NY: Anchor Books.

Porter, G. (1973). *The rise of big business, 1860-1910.* Arlington Heights, IL: Harlan Davidson, Inc.

Porter, M. (1985). *Competitive advantage.* New York, NY: The Free Press.

Presbrey, F. (1929). *The history and development of advertising.* Garden City, NY: Doubleday, Doran & Company, Inc.

Rader, B. G. (1990). *American sports: From the age of folk games to the age of televised sports.* Englewood Cliffs, NJ: Prentice Hall.

Reasons for Spalding success (1915). *Sporting Goods Dealer, 32*(2), 40-49.

Riess, S. A. (1989). *City games: The evolution of American urban society and the rise of sports.* Urbana, IL: University of Illinois Press.

Seymour, H. (1989). *Baseball - the early years.* New York, NY: Oxford University Press.

Somers, D. A. (1972). *The rise of sports in New Orleans, 1850-1900.* Baton Rouge, LA: Louisiana State University Press.

Spalding's Chicopee plant (1911). *Sporting Goods Dealer, 24*(5), 15-17.

Spalding football gear (1906). *Sporting Goods Dealer, 14*(6), 40-43.

Spalding increases capital stock (1922). *Sporting Goods Dealer, 46*(1), 176.

Spalding re-establishes downtown store (1907). *Sporting Goods Dealer 16*(2), 22.

Spalding to open branch stores (1902). *Sporting Goods Dealer,* 6(1), 45.

Sporting Goods Dealer (1899a), *1*(1), 10.

Sporting Goods Dealer (1899b), *1*(2), 10.

Sporting Goods Dealer (1900a), *2*(5), 12.

Sporting Goods Dealer (1900b), *2*(6), 15.

Sporting Goods Dealer (1900c), *2*(1), 27.

Sporting Goods Dealer (1900d), *2*(5), 4.

Sporting Goods Dealer (1901a), *4*(6), 9.

Sporting Goods Dealer (1902a), 6(1), 23.

Sporting Goods Dealer (1902b), 6(2), 16.

Sporting Goods Dealer (1905), *12*(3), 22.

Sporting Goods Dealer (1927), *56*(6), 115-16.

Struna, N. (1981). The North-South races: American thoroughbred racing in transition, 1823-1850. *Journal of Sport History,* 8(1), 28-57.

Tryon, G. W. (1909). Oldest house in the trade. *Sporting Goods Dealer, 10*(2), 15-16.

U.S. Department of Commerce, Bureau of Census (1924). *Biennial Census of Manufacturers, 1921.* Washington, DC: Government Printing Office.

U. S. Department of Commerce, Bureau of Census (1976). *Historical statistics of the U.S.: Colonial times to 1970.* Washington, DC: U.S. Department of Commerce, Part I.

Van Pelt, A. (1946). Spalding: By-word in sports since 1876. *Sporting Goods Dealer, 94*(4), 107-110+.

Voigt, D. Q. (1983). *American baseball: From the gentleman's sport to the commissioner system.* University Park, PA: The Pennsylvania State University Press.

Wignall, T. C. (1924). *The story of boxing.* New York, NY: Brentano Publishing.

Wilson: Fifty years of progress with many more to come (1964). *Sporting Goods Dealer, 129*(4), 251-254.

Wood, J. P. (1949). *The story of advertising.* New York, NY: The Roland Press Company.

Wright & Ditson and Victor consolidate (1918). *Sporting Goods Dealer,* 38(4), 64-65.

Endnotes

[1] The *Billiard Cue* was a four-page monthly. It went out of print in 1874. The exact contents of the periodical are unknown. Doubtless, it promoted Phelan and his billiard products.

[2] Phelan developed the india rubber cushion in 1854. Phelan also held a patent on a machine that made standardized balls.

[3] Adelman points out that other manufacturers, who were not "crack players," took issue with Phelan's claim.

[4] Phelan did of course try to increase market size. According to Adelman (1986), he was successful.

[5] Pool rooms, however, were always opposed by middle class morality (Polsky, 1969, pp. 6, 12).

[6] Phelan did not deal with economies of scope or scale. Brunswick's absorption of Blake in 1869 and Phelan and Collender in 1879 are examples of economies of scope.

[7] This relationship is developed extremely well in respect to football in Oriard (1993).

[8] These examples are not meant to be exhaustive. Struna's (1981) development of the North-South horse races is an excellent study. For an excellent study of harness racing see Adelman (1981). Gorn (1986) is the best single source for the study of early boxing promoters. In the sporting goods industry, accounts of the early development of marketing techniques exist for several companies. See for examples "B.F. Meek and Sons - Bluegrass Reel," *Sporting Goods Dealer* (March, 1911); Tryon, 1909; "Nation's Oldest Sporting Goods House," *Sporting Goods Dealer* (February, March 1911).

[9] Our development of this section follows Fullerton (1988) and Hardy (1990).

[10] Branch houses combined warehouses with selling offices allowing a company to sell and distribute its goods directly to retailers.

[11] Sporting goods included the following: fishing equipment, oars and paddles, gun accessories (such as gun cases and shell boxes), toboggans and skis, bows and arrows. The manufacture of firearms and ammunition were classified as separate industries. Athletic goods included baseball equipment, basketball supplies, boxing, bowling, cricket, exercisers, football, golf, gymnasium goods, hockey, skates, tennis, playground apparatus, circus apparatus and similar commodities (U.S. Department of Commerce, 1924).

[12] B.F. Goodrich produced the Haskell Golf Ball. See *Sporting Goods Dealer*

(September, 1927a) for a discussion and description of the manufacturing process.

[13] Presbrey (1929) maintains that companies within the industry continued to advertise at equal or greater rates after 1898, but comparisons between 1891 figures and 1928 figures are impossible due to the tremendous increase in journal advertising space.

[14] The *Sporting Goods Dealer* published announcements by manufacturing companies about plant expansions in nearly every issue from 1898 through 1920. In almost every instance the reason for expansion was to meet the growing demand and to lower costs to customers.

[15] When people spoke of trusts around the turn of the century, they were usually referring to companies that engaged in horizontal integration (Porter, 1973). None of the trusts survived. The Bicycle Trust was bankrupted by 1902 (Dewing, 1924), the Bicycle Bell Trust collapsed in 1906, and the Ammunition Trust was struck down by the courts in 1908.

[16] Wilson purchased Ashland Manufacturing Company (1913), Sell Sporting Goods Company (1917), the Chicago Specialty Shoe Company (1919), Chicago Sporting Goods (1919), National Baseball Manufacturing Company (1922), and Western Sporting Goods Company (1925). In 1917 it opened its first retail store in Chicago. The original name of the sporting goods company was Ashland Manufacturing Company. It was changed to Thomas E. Wilson Company in 1917. Wilson continued to expand by purchasing companies during the 1930s and 1940s ("Wilson: Fifty Years of Progress with Many More to Come," 1964).

[17] This amalgamation also included Roper Brothers Company of Mass. and the Whitney Sporting Goods Company of Denver. Spalding and Brothers was not named in the article.

[18] Levine (1985) reports that $800 came from Harriet Spalding, the mother of A.G. and Walter Spalding. Hardy (1990), using the records of the Dunn Collection, reports the initial capital at $2,500. Our figures are taken from the "J. Walter Spalding Original Ledger," p.5, which shows a $400.00 contribution from each brother and a $3,000 loan. A photostat copy of parts of the ledger can be found in *Sporting Goods Dealer* (June, 1947, pp. 128-129).

[19] J. Walter Spalding, *Original Ledger*, pp. 138, 173, 176, and 203, list accounts for Reach and Johnson, Pop Anson, Field Lieber and Company (later Marshall Fields), Peck and Snyder, Hibbard Spencer and Company, and Good Year.

[20] By 1886 Spalding advertised tennis equipment, baseball equipment, gymnasium supplies, fishing tackle, guns, bicycles, and general athletic furnishings.

[21] A. J. Reach produced Spalding baseballs and gloves, Peck and Snyder produced Spalding ice skates and became a major distribution center for Spalding products in the East. Wright & Ditson produced tennis rackets and the Lamb Manufacturing Company made bicycles. When Spalding began the production of

golf clubs in 1893 and golf balls in 1896, these products were made by the Lamb Manufacturing Company. The St. Lawrence River Skiff and Canoe Company manufactured boats, canoes, and accessories. The George Barnard Company was the largest manufacturer of athletic apparel wear in the world.

[22] "J. Walter Spalding Original Ledger,"(no page number, page labeled "Profit and Loss"). Spalding sold $12,088 during the first 10 months.

[23] Levine documents Spalding's attempts to expand the circulation of *Spalding's Official Baseball Guide*. Spalding claimed a circulation of 40,000 by 1884. Hardy (1986) provides an insightful analysis of Spalding's chicanery in passing off his guide as the "official" National League Guide Book. *Spalding's Official Baseball Guide* especially promoted Spalding products.

[24] C.S. Lincoln claimed that targeting the youth market was one of the reasons for Spalding's success.

[25] Levine reports that Spalding published guides for "every sport imaginable" (Levine, 1985, p. 162). Spalding also published the official publications of the YMCA, the Public School Athletic League, the National Association of Amateur Oarsmen, and other special publications.

[26] Julian Curtiss, Vice President of Spalding and Brothers, believed that the importance of the wholesale operation in New York City was that it cut travel time required of Eastern retailers when they visited Spalding. Curtis believed that the store increased Eastern sales.

[27] Curtiss believed that this created additional sales for Spalding because it allowed goods to reach the customer more quickly and influenced retailers to reorder.

[28] Lincoln, Vice President of Spalding, believed that the policy forced retailers to sell lower priced grades of Spalding goods in order to compete with other companies. This distracted from the sale of high quality Spalding products.

[29] Significantly, Spalding phased out their retail branch stores when it became possible to maintain prices through state legislation in the late 1930s. Another factor that influenced Spalding policy in the late 1930s was the existence of sporting goods trade organizations that helped maintain prices.

[30] Spalding could not, of course, control prices at retail stores that the company did not own.

CHAPTER 4

SPORT MARKETING THEORY

Theory can be defined as "a system of assumptions, accepted principles, and rules of procedure devised to analyze, predict, or explain a set of phenomena" (Webster's, 1978). Theory is built from a foundation of research and knowledge and may be tested through research and application. *Research* can be defined as a systematic and organized investigation. When the research is complete the results may be used in a variety of ways, some of which are to add to one's knowledge or a body of knowledge, to find solutions for problems, and to discover answers to specific questions.

Sport marketing is a new field of study and does not yet contain a substantial body of knowledge when compared to many other fields of study. Sport marketing is very new when compared to fields of study like law, education, management, medicine, or marketing. For example, this textbook about the fundamentals of sport marketing is one of only four textbooks about various aspects of sport marketing. In comparison, there are hundreds of textbooks about management. There is one research journal for sport marketing, the *Sport Marketing Quarterly*, whereas there are hundreds of journals for law. Sport marketing is not yet considered a singular academic discipline. Marketing, on the other hand, has been considered an academic discipline for decades. Thus, there is not yet a conclusive theory of sport marketing.

Academicians have not yet agreed on what sport marketing is. Some believe it includes exclusively the selling of sports events. Some take a broad approach and believe that wherever marketing principles are applied to any product (goods, services, people, places, and ideas) in the sport industry, this is sport marketing. We have taken the broad perspective approach. Some examples of the breadth of sport marketing in the sport industry include the following:

1. Talent Network Inc. is a company that sells the services of well-known sports personalities (Pesmen, 1991a). If a company wants to use sports people in a marketing campaign, Talent Network Inc. will help the company put together the right mixture of promotional tactics, message, and sports person for the company's product.
2. Marriott Corp. hired Sam Huff in 1971 to sell Marriott to sports people (Pesmen, 1991b). There are thousands of sport participants, spectators, fans, and others who travel, and Marriott wanted to compete for that particular consumer market. Mr. Huff's experience gives him the unique edge in understanding this market because he played and coached professional football, which meant traveling extensively. Mr. Huff designed a company program to serve sports people when they travel and to take care of their special needs. For example, all team members stay on the same floor and special meal arrangements are made. Mr. Huff also arranged for media celebrities who were covering the sports event to stay at the Marriott. With the broadcasters came the crews.
3. In his attempts to find a manufacturer and to market a new sport product, a two-wheel-drive bicycle, Bill Becoat finally resorted to licensing (Hiestand, 1993b). MacGregor Sporting Goods has been licensed to market the 2-Bi-2 bicycle that will sell at $135-$235 in the United States and 32 other countries.
4. Audi, faced with declining sales and lawsuits, used sport to help market its product and to restore Audi automobiles to their former status in the "luxury performance" market (Schwartz, 1988). After marketing research revealed that a large percentage of potential buyer types participated in rowing, sailing, equestrian events, motor sports, and skiing, the Audi company began using sport as a promotional tool. As one example, Audi sponsored "Audi Month at Stowe," a ski resort in Stowe, Vermont. Audi placed several cars in the parking lot, gave away Audi hats, headbands, ski-boot holders, and discount coupons on costs at the resort.

Although sport marketing is a developing field of study, this does not mean that marketing has never been used in the sport industry. As pointed out in chapter 3, marketing practices and principles have been used in many segments of the sport industry throughout history and are being used today. Sport marketers have drawn from and continue to draw from a variety of fields of study. In addition, academicians and practitioners are hard at work conducting research in sport marketing as is evidenced by the studies published in a variety of research journals and trade magazines. Further, this book represents an attempt to add to the young but growing body of knowledge in sport marketing. As marketing principles are applied to the sport industry, they are modified as necessary. As marketing strategies and models in the sport industry are studied and research is published, the body of knowledge will be developed. As higher education responds to the needs of the sport industry, textbooks, courses, and curricula in sport marketing will be developed. Each will add to the development of the body of knowledge and to sport marketing as a field of study and will serve as the foundation of a theory of sport marketing.

To study the developing theory of sport marketing, one must study the foundation from which it is being built. Foundation refers to the basis on which something stands or is supported. Foundation is research, fundamentals, principles, and theories. The foundation of sport marketing is being built primarily from four broad fields of study: sport studies, business administration studies, social science studies, and communications (see Figure 4.1). Within each broad field of study there are specific or specialized areas of study from which sport marketing is developing its body of knowledge. Within sport studies, these specializations include sport sociology, sport psychology, sport philosophy,

SPORT MARKETING THEORY

SPORT STUDIES	BUSINESS ADMINISTRATION	COMMUNICATION	SOCIAL SCIENCES
Philosophy of Sport	Marketing	Journalism	Human Relations
Psychology of Sport	Financial Management	Public Relations	Multicultural Studies
Sociology of Sport	Economics	Media Studies	Population Studies
Administration of Physical Education	Business Law	Advertising	Labor Market Studies
Administration of Intramural Sports	Consumer Behavior	Broadcasting	
Leisure Management	Personnel Management		
Administration of Athletics	Management		

FIGURE 4.1 - Sport Marketing Theory
The fields of study of sport, business, communications, and the social sciences are serving as the foundation from which the fundamentals, principles, theory, and research of sport marketing are being built.

administration of physical education, administration of athletics, administration of intramural sports, recreation administration, leisure studies, and ethics in sport. Within business the specializations include marketing, economics, financial management, business law, consumer behavior, personnel management, and management. In communications, the areas include journalism, public relations, media studies, advertising, and broadcasting. The areas in the social sciences include human relations, multicultural issues studies, population studies, and labor market studies.

As an example of how academicians and practitioners in sport marketing are using other fields of study to develop the theories in sport marketing, let us consider how the social sciences may be used. Yiannakis (1989) suggested that sport marketing can be strengthened through the study and application of sport sociology. In a study of sport sociology literature, Yiannakis suggests that sport sociology can make significant contributions to sport marketing and management in the following ways:

(a) the conceptualization, design, and implementation of good market research;

(b) instrument development;

(c) interpretation of the findings by grounding both a priori and post hoc explanations in existing knowledge bases;

(d) advertising effectiveness by providing essential information bases, especially in the area of lifestyle characteristics;

(e) development of a general marketing information base (target market characteristics);

(f) exploration and identification of new markets; and

(g) introduction of social science orientation to the enterprise.

Yiannakis stated that this involves

> an appreciation of the interactive nature of system forces in the marketing environment and their impact on consumer preferences, underlying patterns and trends and their potential impact on consumer buying readiness, cultural differences and their influence on purchasing decisions, and the role that sport plays in society in terms of influencing values and attitudes, shaping tastes, providing role models, creating new fashions and the like. (p. 105)

In other words, one part of sport marketing theory to be built is the study of the consumer in the sport industry. The fields of social science and sport sociology in particular have existed for a very long time. The subject of these fields is the study of human behavior and the relationships between humans and society. Sport sociology is the study of the relationships between humans and sport and sport and society. Therefore, the theories existing in those fields should be applied in sport marketing and the sport industry and should be used in the development of a sport marketing theory.

Marketing

Marketing is a business process that developed along with the development and growth of business. Bartels (1988) wrote that marketing is the element that "revolutionized the economy of the country and gradually affected the whole world" (p. 1).

The elements, functions, principles, and theories of marketing were developed through the study of many factors, such as industrial production expansion, inventions of new products, the study of human behavior (sociology and psychology), population studies, education and income studies, and studies of new and diverse markets. As a response to these and other factors, a market-driven economy developed. This meant that businesses paid increasing amounts of attention to consumers and studied what the consumer needed or wanted (Bartels, 1988).

Today's marketing concepts evolved from a simple to a more complex and broad concept of marketing. Marketing draws from the social sciences and is more than merely a business activity. Businesses exist in a variety of environments, such as political, social, and economic environments, which constantly provide opportunities and threats for a business. The sport marketer or manager must attain the ability to recognize and analyze the environments, to determine their effects on the sport marketer's business, and to make strategic decisions that will enhance the success of the sport business.

Although marketing is a business function and should be a significant part of every business, the functions of marketing should be a critical part of every department within the business. Marketing must be a total company effort. Companies faced with the challenge of achieving profitable growth in an environment of intense competition, product proliferation, and escalating costs must make marketing a priority function throughout the company.

The marketing concept is a philosophy concerning the way a company should be managed. It consists of three requirements (Cravens & Woodruff, 1986):

1. Examine people's needs and wants as the basis of deciding what the business (or economy) will do.
2. Select the best way to meet the consumer's needs that are targeted by the firm.
3. Achieve the organization's performance objectives by meeting the needs satisfactorily.

In short, the company must discover what the consumer wants and provide it. Although this seems like an easy rule to follow, there are many functions that must be performed and receive critical analysis and proper management in order for successful marketing decisions to be developed. It is not an easy task to identify what someone wants or needs and then provide it. The human being is a complex organism affected by a remarkable variety of influencing factors. Although the marketer might discover what the consumer wants today, that may be different tomorrow!

Complicating the task of producing what the consumer wants is the company's capability to manufacture it and offer it. In addition, the company must consider its values and objectives and if it can ethically offer the products. Therefore, careful management of the marketing functions and critical analysis before decision making can increase the company's chances for success. The incorporation of a marketing management strategy is critical.

Sport Marketing

> SPORT MARKETING is the process of designing and implementing activities for the production, pricing, promotion, and distribution of a sport product to satisfy the needs or desires of consumers and to achieve the company's objectives.

Sport marketing has become the most important function of a sport business. This is because the growth of the sport industry has been phenomenal and shows no signs of stopping. Growth means there are increasing numbers of sport companies and products. Each sport product or company is competition. The concept of competition in business is the idea that a sport business is competing against another business to win the consumer's dollar. Winning in business means staying in business at a successful level. Success is defined by the sport company and is usually measured by achieving the company's objectives.

Companies in the sport industry have plenty of competitors today. A sport company today must employ sport marketing as a significant business function of the company to the extent that every facet of the company is guided by the sport marketing concept. It is the function that guides the sport business toward identifying the products that consumers need or desire. It is the function that identifies and analyzes one's competitors. It develops pricing strategies. It develops the promotional strategies to be used for the company's products in order to get the consumer to the product. It is the function that identifies how to get the product to the consumer.

The Sport Marketing Management Model

Marketing is a process. A process is a continuous cycle. Therefore, marketing is a function that never ends. The sport marketing management model should serve as a guide for the marketer for managing the company's marketing functions. Figure 4.2 illustrates the model. The model illustrates the elements of marketing, the succession of elements and functions, the process of managing, and the interdependency of the elements. This chapter will present an overview of the model, sport marketing management, each element, and the process. Subsequent chapters discuss in detail each sport marketing element.

Sport Company Mission and Objectives

Every business exists for a purpose. Each company strives to stay consistent with its purpose in order to greatly enhance its chances for success. The company's purpose may be found in its stated mission. For example, an intercollegiate athletics program's mission may be "to provide athletic participation opportunities for the college student." In another example, a city parks and recreation department's mission might be "to provide the means for leisure pursuit for the city's population." The company will offer products with the

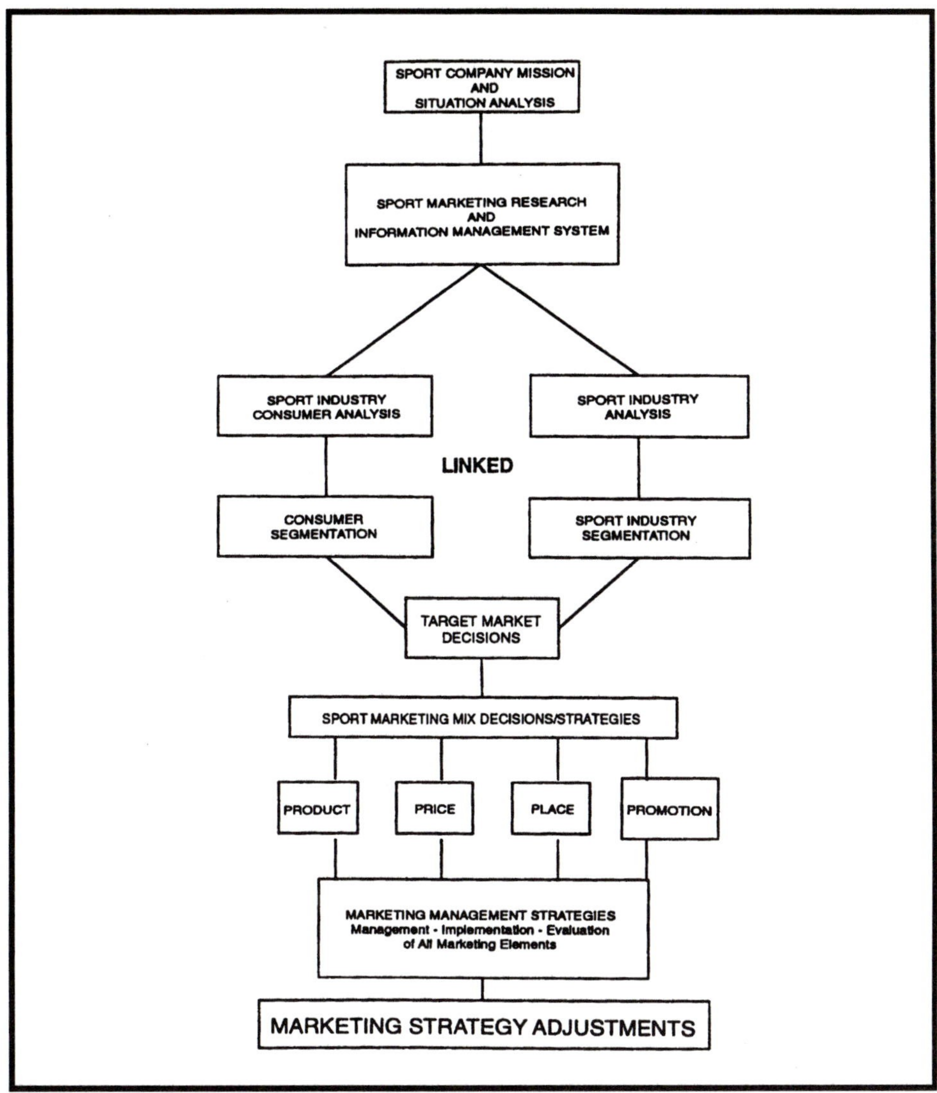

FIGURE 4.2 - The Sport Marketing Management Model

intention of meeting the company's mission. The mission, then, is the reason it exists.

All marketing activities must begin with a clear understanding of the company's mission and the company's current situation. These provide the sport marketer with direction in key decision and strategy formulation. The stated mission must be accompanied by the company's objectives. The objectives provide specific and concrete direction whereas the mission statement often may be broad and ambiguous. The objectives should state the exact directions management wants for the company. For example, whereas the mission of the college athletics department is to provide athletic participation opportunities for the college student, its objectives will be detailed concerning specifically what the athletic department wants to try to achieve within a given period of time. One such objective might be the following: to win a national championship in track and field within 5 years. The direction is established in the objective, and the college will implement programs and strategies that will most likely achieve the stated objective.

In another example, a professional women's basketball league may have an objective to increase consumer awareness of its existence and to increase attendance by 20% by the end of the regular season. The marketer must now make decisions and implement strategies that will take the league toward attaining the stated objective.

Situation Analysis

An important responsibility of management is analyzing the company's situation in relation to its past, present, and future situation. This analysis provides the hard data concerning where the company has been, where it is now, and where it wants to be in the future.

The situation analysis may be divided into six areas (Tarpey, Donnelly, & Peter, 1979): (a) the cooperative environment, (b) the competitive environment, (c) the economic environment, (d) the social environment, (e) the political environment, and (f) the legal environment. Within an analysis of each of these, the sport marketer must determine how each affects the company and the opportunities and threats within each area for the company.

The cooperative environment. The cooperative environment consists of all individuals and companies who are directly involved with the sport company, in particular, those who have a vested interested in the company. This may include all employees, management, investors, suppliers, resellers, and others. An analysis of the company's cooperative environment might include production efficiency, service quality, financial analysis, availability of supplies and materials, distribution lines, and many other factors.

The competitive environment. The competitive environment involves an analysis of other companies that are in the same business. They are the direct competition. This analysis involves studying trends and company movement, the competition's financial capabilities, marketing tactics, buyouts and takeovers, acquisitions, product development, and many other factors. In brief, you must know the competition as well as you know your company. For example, your company happens to be a private golf club. In the past 3 years, five public golf courses have opened and all are within a 30-minute drive of your course. You have read in the local business paper that a golf course development company is considering building two private courses in the area within the next 3 years. Your study of these competitors should include an analysis of products offered, prices, services, financial capability, target markets, and other factors. You would compare the competitor's situation with your company's situation to determine similarities and differences and to calculate the possible impact on your club.

The economic environment. The state of the economy could impact the sport company. The sport marketer must analyze the current economic situation and determine its effect on the company. There may be opportunities for success and, on the other hand, the possibility for financial disaster for the company. For example, how will the Great Flood of 1993 affect tourism in St. Louis and specifically spectatorship and gate receipt revenue at Major League Baseball games? How much of a financial impact will the flood have on the parks and recreation industry and how will a specific recreation area be affected?

The social environment. Cultural and social traditions and attitudes may affect your company. The sport marketer must grasp the social and cultural structures within which the company exists as well as those that exist within the company and analyze the effects on the company and the effects of the company on society. For example, there is great public pressure today to change the "white-only" membership policy of private golf clubs. A golf club with a "white-only" policy will experience negative public relations consequences. This can include societal charges of racial discrimination. The public opinion can have negative results for the club in many ways. In some instances, "white-only" clubs can lose substantial sponsorship and membership funds. In addition, the club may suffer losing major tournaments of the Ladies Professional Golf Association (LPGA) or the men's Professional Golf Association (PGA) that were going to be held at the club.

The political environment. This consists of individuals and organizations that strive to establish tolerance or nontolerance within the public sphere for specific business practices. For example, those private golf clubs that do not allow women to reserve tee times on Saturday mornings are under pressure to change that practice. In another example, collegiate athletic programs are under pressure to change many aspects concerning women in athletics, such as the number of opportunities to participate, which directly affects the number of sports offered, the number of scholarships offered, and the number of coaching and other staff positions directly involved with the women's athletic program.

The legal environment. When all else fails, sue. This seems to be the most popular way of handling issues today. However, it has resulted in a great variety of local, state, and federal legislation aimed at protecting the consumer and at making the competitive playing field a safe place in which to play. It is important that the sport marketer studies the law, how it applies to specific products or segments of the sport industry, and how legislation may be used to reveal opportunities and threats for the sport business.

The sport marketer needs to study and understand the many environments in which the company exists and how each affects the company. This knowledge will guide the sport marketer in developing marketing decisions and strategies.

Sport Marketing Research and Information Management System

Chapters 5 and 6 cover the aspects of sport marketing research and managing information. Information gained from marketing research is a significant element when forming decisions and strategies for the marketing mix. Research will provide vital information in the two key areas the marketer studies: the consumer and the competitor.

We exist in a world that seems small because communication systems are phenomenal. The amount of information produced and disseminated through these communication systems is massive. In fact, the last decade has been labeled as the "Information Era." The marketer must achieve the ability to conduct research, attain information, analyze the results of research and the data gathered, envision uses for the information, and formulate strategic decisions based on the research and information. In addition, the marketer must have or create a system to manage the information and research.

Marketing research is defined as "the systematic gathering, analysis, and reporting of data to answer manager's questions concerning a specific marketing problem, opportunity, or decision" (Cravens & Woodruff, 1986, p. 179). The sport marketer will need the information gained through research to formulate decisions and strategies concerning every aspect of the company and its marketing plan. Marketing research usually focuses on one problem. At the same time, broad data bases may be established and maintained concerning specific aspects of the company or the company's consumer markets and competitors.

The massive amount of information requires a sophisticated information management system. These are usually called marketing information systems, or MIS. The purpose of the MIS is to collect, store, and retrieve specific information.

An MIS can be as simple as a few index cards or as complex as a state-of-the-art computer system. Some of the determining factors include the company's capability for funding a system, the amount and type of information to manage, and the ways in which the marketer will need to use the information.

Sport Consumer Analysis and Analysis of Sport Industry Competition

The sport marketer needs to know and understand the consumers and potential consumers of its products and potential future products. The marketer also needs to know and understand the competitors and potential competitors. As you will see in chapter 5 there are many categories of consumers in the sport industry, and there are many competitors within the sport industry and outside the sport industry. With this knowledge the marketer may make educated strategic decisions for the company that will position the company for success.

There is a phenomenal array of products in the sport industry (refer to chapter 8), and there is a great variety of groups of consumers of these products. Consumers can be grouped, or segmented, in a variety of ways. The sport marketer must decide how to segment existing consumers and potential consumers. Segmenting should be done in a way that will result in the most benefit for the company. The marketer must constantly study every segment of existing consumers and potential consumers in order to have up-to-the-minute information concerning the consumers. This will afford the sport marketer the knowledge to develop new products, change existing products, set new goals, and make other strategic decisions for the company.

The information about consumers must be analyzed along with information about the competitors. As stated earlier, every business operates in a variety of environments and not in a vacuum. What other businesses are doing will affect your business. The sport marketer must continuously study and analyze the competition to gain an understanding of what competitors are doing, what they are capable of doing, and how these activities might impact upon the business. With this information the marketer will be able to change existing strategies, if needed, and formulate new strategies.

Consumer, Industry, and Product Segmentation

Using the information gained through research concerning consumers and competitors in the sport industry, the sport marketer now needs to make some sense of it. A first step is segmentation. Segmentation is the process of categorizing according to characteristics. There are two broad categories of consumers: final consumers and industrial consumers (also sometimes called business consumers). Final consumers are individuals who are purchasing for personal use. Industrial consumers are usually companies that purchase products for production of other products or for resale.

Characteristics of consumers fall under primarily two broad categories: demographics and psychographics. Demographics are primarily quantitative data such as gender, age, income, and race. Psychographics are primarily psychological characteristics, such as favorite color, favorite food, and emotional health. For example, two consumer segments are formed when using gender as a characteristic: females and males. Any number of demographics and psychographics can be used in the creation of any number of segments. For example, if age and favorite color are used with the gender characteristic, more segments may be formed. In formulating this segment, further decisions about age and color are necessary. How will age be categorized and which colors will be identified? As an example, the marketer may create segments such as the following:

gender: female
age: 21 - 25
favorite color: blue

This segment is now a segment of those females between the ages of 21 and 25 whose favorite color is blue. The addition of other characteristics can divide the segment into two segments or subsegments. For example, separate the females whose favorite participant sport is tennis from those whose favorite participant sport is rugby. This creates the following segments:

> **segment 1:** female, age 21 - 25, whose favorite color is blue and is a tennis player
>
> **segment 2:** female, age 21 - 25, whose favorite color is blue and is a rugby player

Each time a characteristic is added more segments are created.

The sport marketer uses segmentation to organize and manage information regarding consumers. This information is then used to formulate strategic decisions concerning the company's products, prices, distribution, and promotion.

Industry segmentation and product segmentation may be conducted similarly. An industry may be segmented according to homogeneous characteristics (Pitts, Fielding, & Miller, 1994). Some of those segments are college athletics, parks & recreation, sporting goods, and professional sport (Pitts et al., 1994). Further, each of these can be segmented. Professional sport, for example, can be segmented by these characteristics: gender, team sports, individual sports. It could also be segmented by sport: tennis, motor sports, rodeo, boating and water sports, and snow sports. Each of the sports can be segmented. Boating and water sports may be segmented into "water sports with boats" and "water sports without boats." Some examples of "water sports without boats" include surfing, scuba, boogey-boarding, windsurfing, body surfing, swimming, diving, and fishing.

The sport marketer must understand the sport industry as a whole, industry segments, the interrelationships of segments, where the sport marketer's company fits, and the impact of the segments on the company. This knowledge is important to the sport marketer's strategy formulation.

Product segmentation involves categorizing products. The marketer can use any method. The most used method is segmenting products by function and characteristic. Product function is what the product does (the function it serves). For example, someone wants to learn to play tennis. The product offered is tennis education. Tennis education may be offered to the consumer in a number of forms, some of which are individual private lessons, group lessons, a college tennis class, videocassette, books, magazines, and tennis camp. The consumer may learn how to play tennis through one of the products offered or through a combination of the products offered. The product segment may be called tennis education products.

Target Market Decisions

Segmentation is used to identify categories, or markets, of consumers and competitors. There can be many segments. The marketer must direct the company in deciding which segments the company is capable of serving. The segments chosen become the company's target markets. A *target market* is a segment of consumers who are homogeneous, who have purchasing power and the willingness to buy. Target markets should be the basis for all marketing strategies. It is the target market for whom a product is produced and offered, a specific price is determined, where to offer the product is selected, and promotion strategies are formulated. Here are a few examples of target marketing.

1. ESPN started ESPN2 in October, 1993 (Hiestand, 1993a). The target market is young viewers, aged 18 to 25. The product is sports programming on television. Programming will include *SportsSmash, Jock and Roll,* and *Max Out,* covering extreme sports and combining them with music videos in MTV fashion, including using former MTV personality "Downtown Julie Brown" as one of the channel's reporters.
2. The University of San Francisco targeted nonstudents in an effort to increase revenue for the student recreation program (Berg, 1992). The products offered were sport and fitness through facility rental, memberships, programs, and sports camps.
3. In 1989 Missy Parks started Title 9, a mail-order catalog for women's fitness and athletic gear (Strauss, 1993). The target market is women. The product is sports equipment and apparel.
4. The Federation of Gay Games' primary target market is the lesbian and gay population around the world. The product is sports participation. The most recent event was Gay Games IV, which was held June 18 - 24, 1994, in New York City (Hill, 1991, 1993; Pitts, 1989, 1994).

In these examples the products were planned and produced specifically for a particular group of consumers — a target market. It is the target market that informs decisions concerning the marketing process, especially the marketing mix.

Sport Marketing Mix Strategies

The marketing mix is typically called the four Ps of marketing. The four Ps are product, price, place, and promotion. Decisions and strategies for each are important for the marketer. Information for making educated decisions involving the four Ps comes from your marketing research: what you know about consumer segments and what you know about competitors. A critical decision and one of the greatest challenges for the sport marketer is how to combine the strategies of the four Ps to best satisfy the consumer and meet marketing objectives.

Each competitor within a specific product market will make marketing mix decisions in an attempt to affect market position. Market position refers to the way a company uses its marketing mix to influence the consumer's perception of a product. Such moves may influence what the consumer thinks about the product's quality, what the consumer is getting for the money, features not found on another similar product, status, convenience, and many other factors.

Product. The centerpiece of a marketing mix is the product. The product should be understood as a concept and not simply as a singular item. This is explained in detail in chapter 8. The consumer is looking for functions and benefits. The product is the satisfaction agent for those. A sport product is any good, service, person, place, or idea with tangible or intangible attributes that satisfy consumer sport, fitness, or recreation-related needs or desires. The product is something that will satisfy something that the consumer needs or wants. Price, place, and promotion strategies are designed specifically for the product in order to increase the probability that the product will sell.

The sport marketer studies the consumer in order to discover what the consumer wants or needs. The result could be developing a new product or changing an existing product in some way. The sport marketer also uses information concerning the competition in making these decisions. If the mechanic for the sailing club discovers that the sailing club members are not buying sailboat hardware at the club's shop because they cannot get what they need, the prices are higher than at other stores, and the quality is not as good, the mechanic should tell the marketer. The marketer may decide to survey the members to get more information. If the research supports what the mechanic said, the marketer must determine if action is needed. In this case, the marketer should consider further research to determine what hardware the members need, find out what prices the other stores are using and whether higher quality products are available and can be sold at a specific price level.

The sport marketer will make many critical decisions concerning the sport company's products. One such decision involves the number and types of products to offer. This is called product mix, the complete set of all products that the sport company offers. A sport company will determine what is or will be the right combination of products for the company. Product management involves tracking the sales of each product to determine if sales are increasing, maintaining, or decreasing. An analysis will provide the sport marketer with the knowledge to make adjustments to specific products or to terminate a product.

The decisions concerning the company's products are important for the company. The product is the company. Any changes, additions, or deletions will have specific effects on the company. It is the sport marketer's job to try to forecast the effects and initiate only those changes that could have positive results for the company and the consumer.

Price. A consumer's decision to buy is affected by many factors. Some of those factors include what the consumer can afford to pay, if what the consumer gets for the money is of value, if the consumer thinks she or he is getting "a good deal," friends' attitudes, family influences, how the product compares to another similar product in terms of features and other factors, and the product's warranty and extended services.

Making the decision to set the price for a product is very important for the sport marketer because price affects the product's success, status quo for the product, and the consumer's perception of the product. The decision should be based on many factors, such as knowledge of the consumer and what the consumer will pay, cost to the company to produce and offer the product, profit-making strategies of the company, the competition's prices, and supply and demand within the product market. Although chapter 9 is a detailed chapter on price and pricing strategies, we will offer one example of how setting prices works.

In Center City, USA, there exists one indoor soccer complex, Soccer City, Inc. The city's population is 600,000 and soccer leagues, both recreational and in the schools, are full and growing. Soccer City opened 5 years ago and its facility includes one indoor soccer court enclosed by a giant net, a concession bar, and a tiny soccer equipment and apparel store (rented space to a local soccer store). Soccer City enjoys a monopoly on indoor soccer. As the popularity of soccer has grown and proliferated in the city, so has indoor soccer. It offers a place to play soccer during the winter months, which are the off season in all outdoor soccer venues. The demand is high. All leagues offered fill quickly even though the price has gone sky high. The adult league fees are $400 for an 8-week session of 1 game per week. The high school and youth fees are even higher. The fees for these teams are per person. The high school players will pay $75 per person for an 8-week session of 1 game a week. Although most of the players complain of the high fees, leagues are always full.

Within the year a new indoor soccer facility will open, Pele's Palace. The sport marketer at Pele's Palace has a choice to make concerning prices. Pele's Palace could charge lower fees compared to Soccer City and probably win quite a few of Soccer City's customers. A second choice is this: Pele's Palace could charge the same fees as Soccer City because it has been established that those prices are what consumers will pay for indoor soccer. Which would you do? Which is best for the company? Which is best for the consumer? Are there any other pricing strategies you could consider? How much does the product (indoor soccer) cost the company to produce and how will this affect your pricing decisions?

As you can see from the example above, pricing a product is not a simple matter. It involves many factors and critical analysis of those factors before determining marketing mix strategies.

Place. Place is where and how a company gets a product from its production or origination point to a place where the targeted consumer can have access to it. Remember that products include people, places, goods, services, and ideas. Products in the sport industry also include people, places, goods, services, and ideas. Goods that are typically manufactured in a factory must be transported from the factory to the market. Some products such as services must be delivered to the marketplace to the consumer in a different way. Sports activities are very different because a sport game does not exist until a person manufactures it. It is a product, like a play in a theater or a live concert by Tina Turner, that is manufactured and consumed simultaneously. In a sport game, the consumer is the participant. The consumer has paid for the product, softball, for example, but does not take possession of it until the consumer actually creates it, or plays softball. In this example, the consumer will probably have to go to a softball field on a given day at a given time to get what was bought. Getting this type of product to the consumer is different from transporting a good from a factory to the marketplace and requires the sport marketer to make specific decisions.

Place, or distribution as it is also called, requires knowledge of type of product, how best to get that product to the consumer, or how to get the consumer to the product, efficient and effective distribution channels, packaging, and other factors. Analysis will lead to better decisions. Chapter 10 details the marketing mix variable place.

Promotion. Promotion is what the general public thinks is marketing. That is because the promotions are what the public sees. More specifically, promotions are especially designed to get a person's attention. Advertising comes in the forms of TV commercials, radio commercials and announcements, advertisements in magazines, in books, in movie theaters, in video movie rentals, on billboards on every highway, on the sides of buses, trucks and cars, signs on tops and sides of buildings, signs on athletic fields, stadia, arenas, and uniforms. In other words, it is everywhere. People are surrounded by advertising.

People are lured to sporting events by special promotional events. Consider these examples: a Beach Boys concert immediately following a minor league men's professional baseball game; a gift, such as a coffee mug, for the first 2,000 people through the gates; a gift, such as a 45-inch television, given away at the halftime break at the local college women's basketball game; and the appearance of a sport superstar who will sign autographs after the game. These are just a very few of the many promotional methods that sport marketers use to get the attention of the consumer.

It is no wonder, then, that the general public thinks that marketing is promotion and promotion is advertising. Promotion, however, involves more than creating advertisements and inventing special events. As you will see in chapters 11, 12, 13, 14, and 15, promotion is multifaceted.

Promotion is the process of promoting. Promoting means making aware. Therefore, a simple definition of promotion may be making people aware of something. The process may involve a variety of methods of gaining the attention of someone in order to tell them something and to educate the person about something, or both. In addition, once the marketer has the person's attention, the marketer must keep it long enough to get a message across. Usually the message contains information about a product or a business. The marketer's purpose for promotion is to encourage the person to purchase the product. Therefore, the message must be developed in such a way that it does three things: First, it gets the attention of people; second, it gets across a message or educates the people; and third, it tempts the people to purchase the product.

The promotion may be any one or more of a variety of promotional methods and strategies. Some examples of promotional methods are direct mail advertising, special limited-time sales, special financing, special customer services, the use of specific colors on the package of a product or in the product, the use of a concert in conjunction with a sporting event, advertising in the local newspaper or in a nationally circulated magazine, the use of roadside billboards for advertising, offers of a variety of fitness club membership packages at a variety of prices, the giveaway of a car during half-time of the university women's basketball game, and the use of radio and television to advertise. The sport marketer may choose any one or a combination of promotional methods and strategies.

The promotional message and strategies are put together to speak to a specific kind of person—a market segment. The sport marketer uses research data about the consumer and the competition to create strategies and the promotional message.

Marketing Management Strategies

The sport marketer must develop a system for managing the process of sport marketing. This system includes the management, implementation, and evaluation of all sport marketing components. Management will involve setting objectives for the sport marketing strategy, selecting and managing of sport marketing personnel, establishing a financial plan, establishing and managing an organizational structure, establishing and overseeing deadlines and scheduling, acting as the liaison between sport marketing personnel and top management, coordinating all sport marketing functions, and other managerial functions. Implementation will involve establishing a system for planning and managing the implementation of the sport company's marketing strategies. Evaluation will involve establishing a system for analyzing marketing strategies to determine if the strategies are accomplishing the established objectives.

Developing The Sport Marketing Plan

Strategic planning functions to strengthen relationships between sport marketing and other management functional areas in the company. The sport marketing plan is the written established plan of action for the company or for an element (or product) of the company.

The plan contains the marketing objectives, identified target markets, financial strategies, and details of the marketing mix strategies. The marketing plan can be written for a single sport product, a group of products, a new promotional strategy, or the entire sport company.

The sport marketing management model, illustrated in Figure 4.2, is a graphic representation of most of the components of a marketing plan and should be used as a guide in the development of a plan. An outline of a sport marketing plan might look something like this:

(1) description of the sport business or product

(2) objectives of the business; marketing objectives

(3) situational status including financial status of the business

(4) summary of consumer market research

(5) summary of the competitive industry research

(6) final sport marketing mix strategies: product, price, place, promotion

(7) detailed plan of action for operation for a given period of time (example: 1 year; 2 years; 3 years; 5 years; 10 years)

(8) method of evaluation including timelines.

The sport marketing plan should not be taken lightly. It requires time, research, and critical analysis. The plan should be the culmination of this effort during which every possible task, angle, financial analysis, and every function of the company and the product have been thoroughly studied and analyzed. The final plan should reflect informed decision making and strategy formulation.

Chapter Summary

In this chapter we presented the concept of sport marketing theory, defined sport marketing, presented the sport marketing management model, and briefly discussed the components of the model. Subsequent chapters will provide specific details, methods, and strategies of each component. We encourage you to refer to the sport marketing management model (Figure 4.2) from time to time. It will remind you of the total picture of marketing and where each component fits.

Theory is built from a foundation of research and knowledge. Sport marketing theory is in the process of being developed as it is a new field of study when compared to many other fields of study. To study the developing theory of sport marketing, one must study the foundation from which it is being built. The foundation of sport marketing is being built primarily from four fields of study: sport studies, business administration studies, social science studies, and communications.

Sport marketing is the process of designing and implementing activities for producing, pricing, promoting, and distributing a sport product to satisfy the needs or desires of consumers and to achieve the company's objectives. Sport marketing is one of many management functions. It has become, however, one of the most important functions because the sport industry continues to grow at a phenomenal rate. The growth means competition and the sport industry is a highly competitive industry.

The sport marketing management model illustrates the elements of sport marketing, the succession of elements and functions, the process of managing, and the interdependency of the elements. The model should be used as a guide for the sport management or sport marketing professional.

Questions for Study

1. What is theory?
2. What is marketing?
3. What is sport marketing?
4. What is sport marketing theory? Where is the foundation of sport marketing theory coming from?
5. What is the Sport Marketing Management Model? What are the components of the model? Define and describe each.
6. What is the primary research journal for the field of sport marketing?
7. What are the different environments within which a sport business exists? Describe each one and how it affects the business?

Learning Activities

1. Select a list of people who work in the sport industry and a list of professors who teach sport marketing courses at colleges and universities across the United States. Ask them to give you a definition of sport marketing, to describe in depth what sport marketing is, and what their theory of sport marketing is.
2. Go to the university library and check out other textbooks about sport marketing. Look for the definitions of sport marketing. Compare them all.
3. Take this book to some people who work in the industry. Ask them to look at the sport marketing management model and to tell you if it matches the marketing activities they perform (or someone performs) in the company.
4. Develop your own definition of sport marketing based on what you have learned from studying chapters 1, 2, and 3.

References

Bartels, R. (1988). *The history of marketing thought.* Columbus, OH: Publishing Horizons.

Berg, R. (1992). Which way to revenue? *Athletic Business, 16*(3), 22-26.

Cravens, D. W., & Woodruff, R. B. (1986). *Marketing.* Reading, MA: Addison-Wesley Publishing Company.

Hiestand, M. (1993a, July 23). ESPN2 created for younger set. *USA Today,* p. 10C.

Hiestand, M. (1993b, March 4). MacGregor gives bike inventor boost. *USA Today,* p. 6C

Hill, J. (Ed). (1991). *Unity '94, 1*(1).

Hill, J. (Ed.). (1993). *U'94 Brief, 1*(4).

Pesmen, S. (1991a, January). Ernie Banks: The effervescent Mr. Cub goes to bat for marketers on television, in direct mail campaigns, at trade shows or golf outings. *Business Marketing,* p. 26.

Pesmen, S. (1991b, January). Sam Huff: Hall-of-Fame linebacker directs Marriott Corp.'s efforts to tackle professional and collegiate teams' business. *Business Marketing,* p. 27.

Pitts, B. G. (1989, Winter). Beyond the bars: The development of leisure-activity management in the lesbian and gay population in America. *Leisure Information Quarterly,* pp. 4-7.

Pitts, B.G. (1994, June). *Leagues of their own: Growth and development of lesbian and gay sport in America.* Paper presented at the First International Gay Games Conference, New York City.

Pitts, B.G., Fielding, L.F., & Miller, L.K. (1994). Industry segmentation theory and the sport industry: Developing a sport industry segment model. *Sport Marketing Quarterly, 3*(1), 15-24.

Schwartz, J. (1988, October). Audi do. *American Demographics,* pp. 50-51.

Strauss, G. (1993, February 9). Fitness firms catch up to female market. *USA Today,* pp. 1B-2B.

Tarpey, L.X., Donnelly, J.H., Jr., & Peter, J.P. (1979). *A preface to marketing management.* Dallas, TX: Business Publications, Inc.

Webster's II New Riverside Pocket Dictionary (1978). Boston, MA: Houghton Mifflin Company.

Yiannakis, A. (1989). Some contributions of sport sociology to the marketing of sport and leisure organizations. *Journal of Sport Management,* 3, 103-115.

CHAPTER 5

SPORT MARKETING RESEARCH AND SEGMENTATION

As you learned in the sport marketing theory chapter, research is the foundation of all sport marketing activity. In this chapter you will learn what sport marketing research is and how it is used in the analysis and development of marketing decisions in the sport industry. In chapter 6 you will learn about how information gathered through research is stored and managed.

PART ONE: SPORT MARKETING RESEARCH

Sport Marketing Research

Sport marketing research is the process of planning and organizing activity to gain information. The sport company needs information. Information is necessary for formulating decisions concerning the sport company's financial aspects, product development, pricing strategies, distribution strategies, promotional strategies, and all other functions and operations within the company. The information comes from research. Research information consists of a constant analysis of the competition and the consumer, as you will learn in part 2 of this chapter.

Sport marketing research can range from a very simple task to a complex and time-consuming job. Figure 5.1 illustrates the range of sport marketing research. The research conducted is based on what information the sport marketer needs. For example, if the sport marketer of an indoor soccer club needs to know where the current consumers live, the information may be gathered easily from membership application forms. At the other end of the range, if the management of the Ladies Professional Golf Association (LPGA) needs to know how many people are attending each event, who they are and why they attend, a study will need to be designed and conducted over a long period of time in order to collect the appropriate data.

SIMPLE | | COMPLEX

EXAMPLES:

SIMPLE - Reading a newspaper, magazine, or sport management journal. Results: learn about a new sport business opening; a new technology being used in sporting equipment; a study on the demographics of fans of the LPGA.

COMPLEX - The design and conduct of a study that involves, for example, (a) a new metal for a new softball bat, (b) a longitudinal study of children with disabilities in sports activities to determine their sports activity choices in adulthood, or (c) a study of arena advertising to determine its effects on spectators over a long period of time.

FIGURE 5.1 - Sport Marketing Research Continuum

Purposes of Sport Marketing Research

Why do we need to do research? What are the purposes of research? Without research and analysis, all of your decisions are risky. When a decision is not research based, the sport company risks making a wrong decision. Most wrong decisions will adversely affect the company. Sometimes the company will be lucky and a wrong decision will have minimal adverse consequences or someone in the company will detect the error and intervene.

Some of the purposes of sport marketing research can be found in the definition of marketing adopted by the American Marketing Association (AMA). This definition states that

> marketing research links the consumer, customer, and public to the marketer through information—information used to identify and define marketing opportunities and problems; generate, refine, and evaluate marketing actions; monitor marketing performance; and improve understanding of marketing as a process. Marketing research specifies the information required to address these issues; designs the methods for collecting information; manages and implements the data collection process; analyzes the results; and communicates the findings and their implications. ("New Marketing," 1987, p. 1).

Let us apply the AMA definition to the sport industry and identify some of the purposes for sport marketing research.

To form a link between the consumer in the sport industry and the sport company. The marketers and managers within the sport company can use the information about the consumer to get to know existing and potential consumers and what they want. The consumer receives messages from the sport company that it is trying to meet the consumer's needs. The National Handicapped Sports Association (NHS) organized to meet the needs of a growing population who want to be involved in sports activities (National Handicapped Sports, 1993). NHS was established in 1967 and is a "national, nonprofit educational association dedicated to providing year-round sports and recreation activities for people of all ages and abilities, including people with orthopedic, spinal cord, neuromuscular and visual impairments" (p. 4). The organization tracks the numbers of people with disabilities who want sports activities and encourages the development of programs to meet the needs of the consumer. Without the research, NHS would not have the information it needs to understand its consumer or offer to its consumer what the consumer needs.

To identify and define marketing opportunities, problems, and threats. A marketing opportunity is a chance for a sport company to capitalize on a new idea, new product, or move to a new location; obtain a specific consumer market; or take advantage of a financial management technique, or other activity that will most likely prove a positive activity for the company. A marketing problem occurs when something is not quite right in the company. A marketing threat is usually more serious for the company. It means that something will have a very serious adverse affect on the company. It is only through research that the sport marketer will discover opportunities, problems, or threats for the company. Let us consider some examples.

Through interviews and casual conversations, both of which are types of research, a soccer league player, Pam Reeves, discovers there is no summer soccer league for women in Louisville, Kentucky, and that there is a group who want to play in the summer (Pitts, 1993). This is a marketing opportunity: there is a group of consumers who want something that does not exist. In further interviews—more research—Reeves gathers information about what type of league the women would like. Some of the data gathered included the following information:

1. Consumers wanted a shorter than regulation game. A regulation game is two 45-minute halves, or 1 1/2 hours of running. In the summer months in Louisville, the average temperature is hot and the humidity is very high, which makes it very uncomfortable. A game that lasts around an hour with breaks would be desirable.
2. They wanted teams to consist of fewer players than regulation. Regulation requires 11 players on the field. Fewer players would allow the teams to be flexible in recruiting players and not have to worry about getting enough to show up. The summer months are used for holidays and vacations, which means that many players will be absent from games.

It is easier to find 10 players who will commit to a team in the summer than for 16 to 18 players to commit to a game every week.

3. They would like for the game to be fun and not as structured as the highly competitive and structured fall and spring leagues.
4. They would like for the games to be held in the evening when it is not as hot as during the day.

Using the information gathered, Reeves invented a game and started the league. The new game is played on a small field. The new game consists of a field 70 yards long and 40 yards wide, whereas a regulation field is 110 yards long and 60 yards wide. The new game is a 7-on-7 game with a goalie. Hence, Reeves named the league "Seven-Up Soccer." There are actually 8 players, but, "Seven-Up Soccer" is a catchy name! Pam incorporated a "you must have fun" rule to create an atmosphere of lightness and fair play. To keep the price down, Reeves uses no officials. This is probably the most unusual and interesting aspect of the product: There are no officials, hence, every player can officiate! Any player can make a call when there is an infraction of a rule or a foul has occurred. This was the toughest part of the game for the players to get used to because, in a regular game, part of a team's game strategy is to figure out which violations and infractions the official will catch and to work around that. When everyone can officiate, a player can not get away with anything! This results in a very clean and almost foul-free game.

In the first year the league was offered on a Sunday evening. However, teams had problems with players not showing up because they were gone on summer vacation. After more research, the league was offered on a Wednesday evening the following year. Wednesday was selected because it is the night most players were available from other summer activities, such as softball and vacations.

Most of the rules were based on the summer heat factor and included unlimited substitutions at any time, including when play is taking place; and the game consists of four 12-minute quarters with 1 minute between quarters and 2 minutes at halftime. The first rule allows the player to get off the field to rest and cool down at any time during play. The latter rule keeps the game short and includes breaks for rest, water, and cooling.

In the first year of the league there were 3 teams. Four years later, there were 10 teams, and Reeves has plans to extend the league to two women's divisions and is considering offering a coed or a men's division.

Through research, Reeves discovered a marketing opportunity. With continuous research, she changed and molded the product to meet the consumer's needs and has a successful product.

Research will also reveal problems and threats. Let us consider fitness centers as an example. Today there are fitness centers everywhere. During the 1970s and 1980s when the number of fitness centers was growing rapidly, the increase was a problem and a threat to the few existing fitness centers. For example, if the

Downtown Fitness Center (DFC) is the only fitness center within a 10-mile radius, the DFC can enjoy knowing that competition is at least 10 miles away. When the owner of the DFC discovers through research that three companies are making plans to open within the 10-mile radius, the owner must consider this as a threat to the DFC. With this information, the owner is in a position to do something so that the new fitness centers will either have no effect or minimal effect on the DFC's business. Without the research effort, however, the owner of the DFC never would have known that competition was about to increase substantially.

To generate, refine, evaluate, and monitor marketing actions. When the sport marketer has finalized marketing plans and the activities of the plans have begun, it is no time to sit back and do nothing! What if the plans, or a part of the plan, are not working? What if the actions developed to reach an objective are actually creating just the opposite response? How will the sport marketer know? The development and implementation of a marketing plan should never take place without a plan for monitoring and evaluating its effectiveness. The evaluation will inform the sport marketer about the positive or adverse effects of a marketing plan. Thorough research and analysis of each is required for understanding as much as possible about each one as well as how they are interconnected.

To analyze and understand the sport company, its industry, and its competition. Within this purpose should be the typical journalist's questions: who, what, when, where, why, and how? The sport marketer should seek to understand the answers to these questions concerning the sport company, its

TABLE 5.2 - Questions for the Sport Marketer

	CONSUMER	COMPANY	COMPETITOR	CLIMATE
WHO..	... are our consumers? ... consumes the competitor's products? ... could become our next 1,000 consumers?	... works for us? ... is making key decisions?	... is our competitor?	... can influence the economy, law, etc.?
WHAT..	... do our consumers like/dislike? ... are they willing to pay?	... does our company do? ... can our company do? ... is our financial status?	... does our competitor do? ... is their advertising like? ... is their financial status? ... are their prices?	... is the future of our economy? ... are the laws that affect my company?
WHEN..	... does the consumer want this product? ... can the consumer pay? ... should we advertise?	... can our company offer a product? ... does the company need to be paid? ... should the company advertise?	... does the competitor offer its products?	... do the new laws go into effect?
WHERE..	... are our existing consumers? ... are our potential consumers?	... is our company located?	... is the competitor located?	... will the economic set-backs hit hardest?
WHY..	... does the consumer want a product? ... does the consumer want to pay a particular price?	... does our company offer this service? ... doesn't our company offer this service?	... does the competitor offer a particular service?	... is the economy hitting hardest in this area?
HOW..	... can the consumer use this product? ... can the consumer pay for this product?	... can our company offer a product? ... does our company track sales of its products?	... do we compare with our competitor? ... are we different? ... does our competitor offer the product?	... will the economy be in 3 years? ... will the new law affect my company?

consumers, its competitors, and the climate. Examples of questions are shown in Table 5.2. Marketing decisions and strategies should be formulated based on real information and an accurate understanding of the company, the consumer, the competition, and the climate. Again, making uneducated and uninformed decisions is risky.

Types of Sport Marketing Research

Sport marketing research is focused on information needed for planning for the future, attempting to discover a problem or the root of a problem, developing solutions, and informing decisions on product development or improvement, pricing, and promotional strategies. Hence, the type of research designed is based on the information needed.

For example, if management of the company needs to know how many high school girls participate in sports as a means of identifying the teen-age female athlete market, the sport marketer will need to develop a plan to study this. Since there are high schools in all 50 states and the District of Columbia, the marketer will need to decide if the information needed is for all 50 states and the District of Columbia. If not, how many states and where are the states? If the marketer needs information for the southeastern states, the project will focus on those states. The type of research study designed will be specific to the information needed. In this example, the sport marketer could contact state school athletic offices to determine first if the information already exists. If the state offices have the information the sport marketer will arrange to collect it. If the offices do not have it, the marketer must design a method for collecting the information.

In a different example, a sport marketer for a running gear mail-order catalogue wants to know how many runners compete in events of 10K (6-plus miles) and longer and wants to get a mailing list from all of the events in the western half of the United States. First, does the information already exist? Who would have it? If not, the sport marketer must design a method to collect it.

There is another option available for companies: Hire a sport marketing research company to do the research. This can be an expensive endeavor because most marketing companies charge high fees. However, it is sometimes necessary if the sport company does not have the personnel to conduct the research. In other cases, sport companies want an outside company to do the research in order to obtain objective work, or simply because the company doesn't want to spend the time to do the research and can afford to pay the fees.

Primarily, all sport marketing research involves searching for information in four categories: the consumer, the competitor, the company, and the climate. The research will be designed for the category and what the sport marketer needs to know about it. A basic process for conducting research is presented in the next section. Some examples of types of sport marketing research include the following:

1. **information search**: gathers information and other data
2. **surveys**: can be performed by phone, in person, or by mail
3. **interviews**: typically done in person; can be performed by phone
4. **scientific research**: involves, for example, laboratory research for new product development, such as studying and testing new materials for sport apparel; designs to increase the aerodynamics of a racing bike or a racing wheelchair; physiological studies of elite athletes to improve a sport technique for enhancing performance. Some scientific research methods include the following:
   (a) **sampling**: collects data from and about people, events, and places from a sample (a subset). For example, if there are 2 million people in a city limits from which you would like to collect data, you could try to collect the data from all 2 million or select a sample of the population from which to collect. The sample could be 1,000 people of the total population. Sampling can involve surveys, questionnaires, or interviews.
   (b) **observation study**: observes and records people's behavior for analysis. This type of study is usually conducted when the company wants to determine buyer behavior. In most instances, the behavior being studied is purchasing habits.
   (c) **trend analysis**: detects trends, both historically and to predict future trends. An excellent book that looks at trends in the recreation industry is *Recreation Trends: Toward The Year 2000* by John R. Kelly (1987).

The research design selected will provide for collecting the data. The sport marketer must then be able to interpret and analyze the data. The next section presents a basic process for designing research.

A Basic Process for Designing Research

There are some specific models and methods for research design and activity. Figure 5.3 illustrates a basic process for designing sport marketing research. This illustration outlines the process and a series of questions to guide the sport marketer through the process.

The first step is to define the objective of the project. In this step, the sport marketer should ask the question "What do I need to know?" Perhaps what you need to know is "How many competitors do I have and where are they?" Perhaps a second part to that question is "What are their businesses like and are they a threat to my company?" Once you have identified an objective for the research you will be guided by it to develop the research project.

The second step is to determine where you can locate information that will

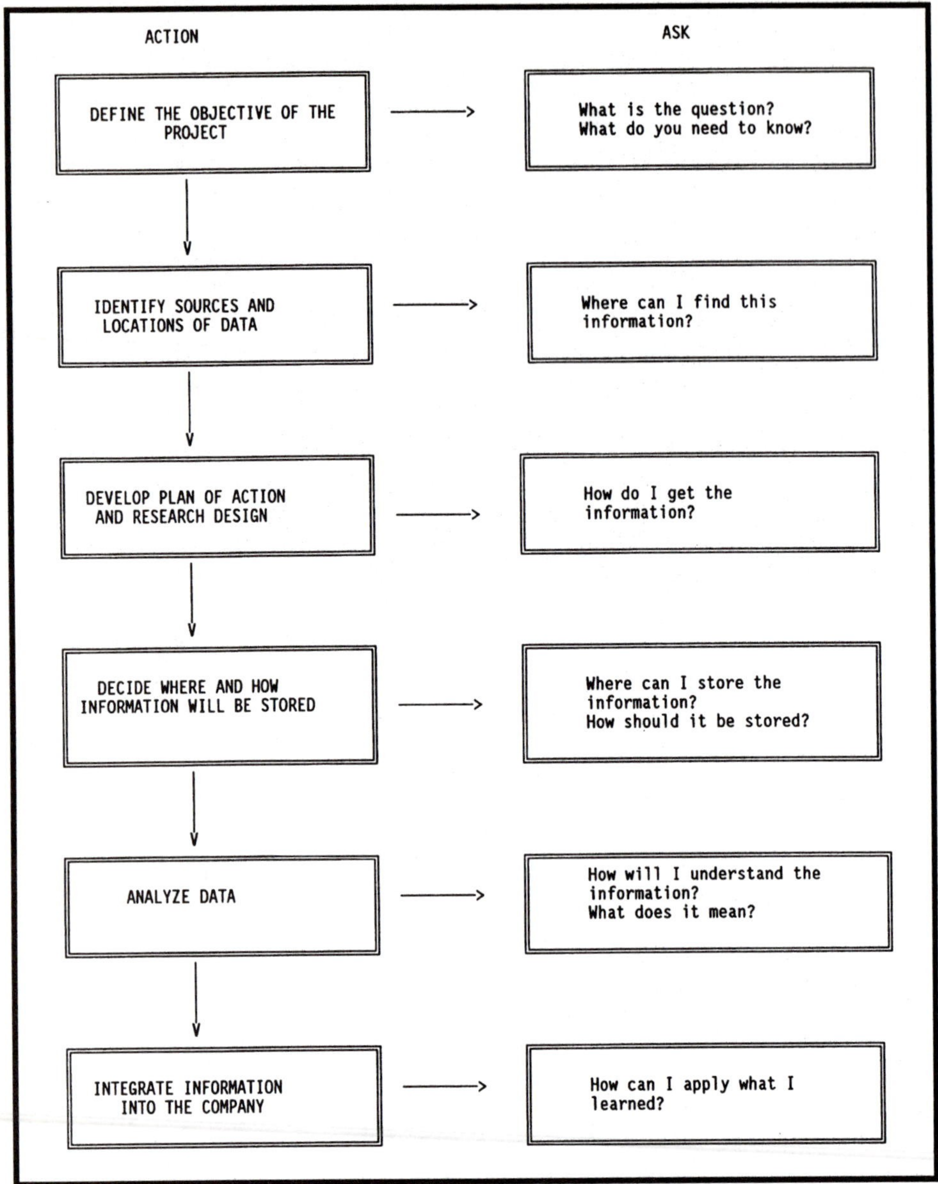

FIGURE 5.3 - A Sport Marketing Research Process

answer your first question. This step involves identifying where you will be able to get the information you need. Typically, information is available in two sources: primary and secondary. Primary sources include those sources from which information is gathered directly. Gathering information about your consumers directly from your consumers is using the primary source—the consumer.

Secondary sources are those that contain information that is already compiled or published. A marketing report purchased from a sport marketing firm is a secondary source. The information comes to you second-hand. There are several secondary sources available to the sport marketer. Refer to the section titled "Sources of Information" for a detailed listing of secondary sources of information.

The third step is to determine how to gather the information. In this step you will design what is called the research methodology—how to perform the study to collect the data. There are many research methodologies—too many to present and discuss in this book. We suggest getting a book on research methods that includes extensive descriptions of the methods and how to conduct them. However, there are some methods commonly used in marketing, as well as other fields, that are presented with a brief description in an earlier section of this chapter "Types of Sport Marketing Research." Refer to that section for some ideas.

The fourth step is to decide on where and how you will store the information gathered. As you will learn in chapter 6, there is a full range of methods available for storing information. The method is dependent on factors including the amount of information to be collected. You may be involved in collecting information on 20 consumers or on 2 million consumers. Certainly, information on 2 million consumers will need a larger storage space than information on 20 consumers. Or will it? Another factor is the type of information and amount of information you will be collecting. If you need entire life information of the 20 people and only the telephone numbers of the 2 million people, you may need a larger storage space for the information gathered on the 20 people.

The fifth step is to analyze the data. In other words, ask the question "What does this information mean?" Interpretation of the data consists of looking at the data over and over and asking many questions. If the data collected are numerical, some simple statistics applied to the data may help. Ask others in the company to study the information and tell you what they see. Compare the information to other similar studies and look for similarities and differences. Another idea is to take the information to a research expert, such as a sport marketing professor who conducts research, a sport marketing research company, or a general marketing research company.

The sixth, and last, step is to determine how you can apply the new knowledge to the business. The information may be used according to why you needed the information in the beginning. Why did you need the information? If you needed the information to understand why your indoor tennis club is losing consumers during the months of June and July, the new information will help you decide what you need to do to retain consumers during June and July. Let us say that the reason the club loses consumers in June and July is that they go to play tennis on outdoor courts so that they can be outside during the summer. What can you do? Your club has no outdoor courts. Can you afford to build outdoor courts? If not, is there another way to compete with the outdoor courts?

Sources of Information

As you have learned, primary information is information collected directly from the consumer via personal interview, phone surveys, or consumer questionnaires. Secondary sources are those sources from which you may collect information that has been published or collected. There are also internal and external sources of information. *Internal sources* are those sources inside the sport company. *External sources* are those sources outside of the sport company. There are primary internal and external sources, and there are secondary internal and external sources. A *primary internal source* is an interview conducted with one of the sport company's employees. A *primary external source* is an interview conducted with consumers. A *secondary internal source* is a report by one of the departments in the company. A *secondary external source* is a report issued by the United States Census Bureau.

Primary sources include your end consumers and business consumers, bank books, mortgage papers, deeds, bills, or other sources from which you can get information. Secondary sources include those reports or information in any form that you collect from a variety of organizations, clubs, agencies, or businesses. The following sections outline some of the many secondary sources available. We recommend an excellent book titled *The Insider's Guide to Demographic Know-How* by Diane Crispell (1993). This book explains how to find demographic information and is a directory of a multitude of local, state, federal, international sources and other categories of sources as well. We have included a short list of those sources in Appendix A at the end of the chapter to get you started.

Here are some ideas on where to find information. You can collect a wide array of information from the local government offices and other nonprofit agencies. Some of these are the local chamber of commerce, department of health, city planning and zoning offices, city census offices, local colleges and universities, and local real estate or homebuilding offices.

Trade- or industry-specific associations can provide information. For almost every career there is a professional association. Many of these associations track demographic and other data concerning their industry. The National Sporting Goods Association, for example, tracks sporting goods sales and sports participation and publishes the information.

Professional associations are another source of information. For example, the American College of Sports Medicine (ACSM) is a professional association for a variety of professionals and practitioners in areas such as sports medicine, athletic training, orthopedic medicine, and exercise physiology. The ACSM tracks and collects information about these areas. There are two outlets for the information: annual conferences and meetings; and newsletters and journals.

Publications are another source of information and consist of magazines, newsletters, newspapers, reports, and journals. Some are available on newstands, some in book stores, some by subscription, and others by membership in an organization. Consider, for example, the many sports magazines. To get an idea of how many there are, walk into any book store and take a look at the magazine section. In many stores, the section will contain over 50% sports and sport-related magazines. Each magazine holds information about that sport and its participants, equipment manufacturers, retailers, and other types of information. Table 5.4 illustrates some data reported in the October 1993 issue of Boating World.

TABLE 5.4 - WATER SPORTS PARTICIPATION IN 1992

	FISHING FRESHWATER	POWER BOATING	FISHING SALTWATER	WATER-SKIING	SAILING
TOTAL (in millions)	41.7	22.3	12.6	7.9	3.5
AGE					
Under 17	22.2%	16.4%	16.7%	20.1	14.7%
18-34	33.8%	37.7%	35.9%	54.5%	33.5%
35-54	32.0%	32.7%	32.4%	22.7%	35.9%
55+	13.0%	13.2%	15.0%	2.7%	1

Source: A demobraphic report in *Boating World*, May (1993).

Primary Areas Of Sport Marketing Research: The Consumer And The Competitor

There are two primary areas of research on which the sport marketer spends the greatest amount of time: the consumer and the competitor. Other areas include the company and the climate. Although you will learn in part 2 of this chapter how research is conducted and used by the sport marketer, a brief description of the area is presented next.

The sport marketer needs information concerning the consumer to make strategic decisions about what the consumer wants, how much a consumer can pay, where the consumer goes to purchase, and which promotional methods and messages will attract the consumer.

The sport marketer needs information concerning the competition and the industry in order to understand the competition's strengths and weaknesses, the realistic capabilities of the competition, and to compare the sport marketer's company with the competition. The information about the competition will help the sport marketer develop strategies based on what the competition is doing. For example, in the 1970s Nike chose to ignore a consumer market of aerobics exercisers. Nike also chose to stand by while Reebok entered into developing a specialized shoe for aerobics exercisers. Aerobics boomed, and Reebok was already positioned with its specialized shoe and cornered the market. Nike then decided it would be a good idea to study the consumer market and the competition and get into the aerobic shoe market.

The sport marketer needs information on the company to understand it. The sport marketer needs to know the company's strengths and weaknesses, its financial capabilities, its physical capabilities, and how it compares to other companies.

The sport marketer should study the climate within which the company operates. This involves studying the political situation, the economic environment, and the legal environment, as well as social and cultural issues that might have an affect on the company. For example, how will the current world recession effect recreational sports participation? How will the American Disabilities Act affect a sport company? What ethical, social, and legal effects will the violent attacks on ice-skating champion Nancy Kerrigan and tennis champion Monica Seles have in the sport industry?

In addition, it is important that the sport marketer study and analyze the interrelationships between the consumer, the competition, the company, and the climate. If the sport marketer studies one area and ignores the others, decisions and strategies will be made that are not research based and well-informed.

PART TWO: SEGMENTATION IN SPORT MARKETING

Segmentation

Segmentation is dividing a whole into parts. In sport business, segmentation involves dividing a population—a market—into market segments or an industry into industry segments. *Sport market segmentation* is the division of total markets into relatively homogeneous segments. *Sport industry segmentation* is the division of the sport industry into relatively homogeneous industry segments.

Sport market segmentation involves consumer analysis. The consumer analysis process involves the study of a total market or population and dividing the population into groups that have similar characteristics. Let us look at an example of sport market segmentation.

According to Barbara Bryant (1987), American adults can be clustered into five segments when it comes to sports and recreation activity seekers:

1. Excitement-Seeking Competitives
2. Get-Away Actives
3. Fitness-Driven
4. Health-Conscious Sociables
5. Unstressed and Unmotivated.

The Excitement-Seeking Competitives are those who feel challenged by sports that are somewhat risky and dangerous. They have a median age of 32, 41% are baby boomers (people born between 1946 and 1961), two-thirds are male. They are upper-middle class and 45% of them are young singles.

The Get-Away Actives are those who want to use sport as a social reason to get away for fun and excitement. Their median age is 35, 48% of them are baby boomers, gender make-up is 50% female and 50% male, and 56% of the group take 4 or 5 mini-vacations a year.

The Fitness-Driven people are those who are motivated almost exclusively by fitness reasons. This group consists of 56% women, 38% are college graduates, and they have a median age of 45.

The Health-Conscious Sociables seek activities that are healthy, but not necessarily exciting and risky. This group makes up about one third of American adults, two-thirds are women, and their median age is 49.

The Unstressed and Unmotivated find no reason to be involved in sports or recreational activities and thus are inactive. Their median age is 49, and this group is equally divided between women and men.

This kind of research is used frequently in the sport industry. Sport companies want to know and understand the people who purchase their products and also about the people who do not purchase their products. These data help the sport marketer make decisions concerning the company's products, prices and promotional strategies. You will learn more about consumer segmentation in the section titled "Consumer Market Segmentation."

Sport industry segmentation involves industry analysis, also called competitive analysis. *Industry segmentation* is the process of studying an industry to divide it into industry segments that have similar characteristics. The sport marketer uses this information to analyze the segments, to analyze which segment the company is in, and to develop decisions and strategies for the sport company based on knowledge of the industry segments. Let us look at some examples of industry segmentation.

DeSensi, Kelley, Blanton, and Beitel (1990) segmented the sport industry into 18 segments. This is presented in Figure 5.5. It is the researchers' contention that all sport businesses may be categorized into one of these segments. The segments are based on the authors' definitions of types of sport businesses.

Pitts, Fielding, and Miller (1994) segmented the sport industry into 3 segments (see Figure 5.6). Their research is based on an industry segmentation model by Porter (1985) and involves segmenting the industry according to product benefits and buyer types. The authors argue that every product in the sport industry may be categorized into one of the three segments.

Parks and Zanger (1990) segmented the sport industry into 14 segments (see Figure 5.7). Their segments are based on career categories.

Other methods include segmenting the industry by product. For example, baseball bat manufacturers study the "baseball bat industry", athletic shoe companies study the "athletic shoe industry", and golf course development and

1. Agencies -- nonprofit
2. Local government agencies (local parks office)
3. Voluntary agencies -- nonprofit -- membership fee supported
4. Corporations, companies, businesses
5. Facilities -- management
6. Hostelries
7. Resort
8. Hotel
9. Intramural sport clubs
10. Private sport clubs
11. Professional sport
12. Retail sales
13. School, college, university athletics
14. Sport businesses
15. Sport management services
16. Sport Marketing merchandizing
17. Sport organizations
18. Travel cruise

FIGURE 5.5 - Sport Industry Segmentation
from DeSensi, Kelley, Blanton, & Beitel (1990)

construction companies study the "golf course industry."

It is important to note here that the terms *market*, *product market*, and *product segment* are often used interchangably. These terms are usually inclusive of the consumers of the products. The "baseball bat market" can be used as the label for the products in this industry and all of the consumer segments of the products offered.

Any method of segmentation can be used by the sport marketer in a number of ways. The industry and industry segment information helps the sport marketer make decisions and plan strategies based on the competition, where the sport marketer's company fits, and how the sport company compares with the competition.

1. **Sport Performance Segment:** sport performance offered to the consumer as a participation or spectatorial product.
2. **Sport Production Segment:** those products needed or desired for the production of or to influence the quality of sport performance.
3. **Sport Promotion Segment:** those products offered as tools to promote the sport product.

FIGURE 5.6 - Sport Industry Segmentation
from Pitts, Fielding and Miller (1994)

1. Intercollegiate Athletics
2. Professional Sport
3. Facility Management
4. Campus Recreation Programs
5. Community-Based Sport
6. Sports Information
7. Sport Marketing
8. Sports Journalism
9. Sports Club Management
10. The Physical Fitness Industry
11. Athletic Training and Sportsmedicine
12. Aquatics Management
13. Consulting
14. Entrepreneurship

FIGURE 5.7 - Sport Industry Segmentation
from Parks & Zanger (1990)

Purposes of Segmentation

The primary purpose of market segmentation is specialization. Using consumer market analysis and segmentation, the sport company can select one or more consumer market segments on which to concentrate and specialize in meeting their needs. Using industry analysis and segmentation, the company can learn how it compares to the competition or determine if it can compete in a particular segment. This allows the company to focus its attention on those segments selected, meet the needs of those segments, limit resources, and concentrate efforts. Products, prices, services, advertising, and other promotional methods are developed for specific consumer market segments and with the competition in mind.

Businesses in the United States have been almost forced to abandon mass marketing. Mass marketing does not involve segmentation. At one time in the United States the population consisted of a group of people very much alike: primarily Caucasian, Christian, married at a young age, with a working husband, a wife not employed outside the home, an average of four children, and other similar characteristics. As the years have gone by in the United States, the population has shifted from one homogeneous population to many different populations. Think about the following statistics from the Institute for Educational Leadership (Hodgkinson, 1992) and *Time* magazine ("The New Face," 1993):

1. In 2010, four states (New York, California, Florida, and Texas) will have approximately one-third of the nation's youth. More than 50% of them will be populations who are today's "minority." This means that the new minority will be white. What will we call minorities when they are more than 50% of the population? (Hodgkinson, 1992)
2. The population of the United States is aging rapidly. In 1992 there were 30 million people over the age of 65. In 2020, that number is expected to be 65 million. Most of them will have one year of retirement for every year of work (Hodgkinson, 1992).
3. Children under the age of 18, who were 34% of the population in 1970, will be only 25% of the population in 2000 (Hodgkinson, 1992).
4. In 1990 the population was: Anglo 76%, Black 12%, Latino 9%, and Asian 3%. By 2050 the breakdown is estimated to be: Anglo 52%, Black 16%, Latino 22%, and Asian 10% ("The New Face," 1993).
5. In 1976 there were 67 Spanish-speaking radio stations. In 1993 there were 311. In addition, there are 3 Spanish-language TV networks and 350 Spanish newspapers ("The New Face," 1993).
6. There are more than 100 languages spoken in the school systems of New York City, Chicago, Los Angeles, and Fairfax County, Virginia ("The New Face," 1993).
7. Ethnic minority shoppers, predominantly African Americans, Asians, and Hispanics, spent $600 billion in 1992. This is an increase of 18% since 1990. By the year 2000, minority populations may account for more than 30% of the economy ("The New Face," 1993).
8. Over 32% of the Asian American households earn an income of $50,000 or more, contrasted with 29% of Caucasian households ("The New Face," 1993).

Businesses are paying attention to the many new population segments. More and more businesses are redesigning their products, prices, and promotional methods for the new markets. In their pursuit, many companies are relying less on traditional forms of mass marketing and more on specialized media (cable-specific television, ethnic-centered magazines, and specific topic magazines) (McCarroll, 1993).

Companies in the sport industry are also paying attention. As pointed out in chapters 1 and 2, there are more sports, events, sporting goods, and other sport products and companies specifically designed for and offering products to the many new markets. Targeting specific populations is the future of marketing in the sport industry (Hiestand, 1993).

As the years have gone by, businesses in the United States have changed.

There are many more industries than ever before and the new ones are different. The newest industries are high technology, such as computers, electronics, cable TV, and space study. Some other new industries are in human services, such as travel agencies, consulting, therapy, management services, and fitness consulting. All are consumer driven: developed to meet the needs of new consumer segments.

The sport industry has grown partially because most of the newest segments, which may also be the fastest growing segments, are also consumer driven. Take, for example, sporting goods and equipment. There is such a variety of people participating in sports activities that equipment is becoming more customized. Golf clubs come in a variety of sizes, weights, materials, colors, and lengths. Tennis rackets are also offered in a variety of sizes, weights, materials, and other factors. Clothing comes in a variety of sizes, styles, and colors. Sport shoes are offered in a variety of sizes, sport specific, and materials. Camping equipment is available in a variety based on consumer preferences and also on geographical and type of camping factors. There is a booming variety of water sports goods and equipment: The air jet engine is revolutionizing the boat industry; and there is a constant new variety of water toys for power boat enthusiasts, such as the knee board, the ski seat, the skurfer, single-, double-, and triple-person tubes, the ski board, and barefoot skiing equipment. It is apparent that the new equipment is popular because any Saturday on any lake reveals that people using the new toys outnumber waterskiers by 4 to 1!

Sports and other activities, sport organizations, and sport businesses developed and designed by and for specific consumer segments are a fast-growing area of the sport industry. As pointed out in chapter 1, many populations in the United States are very busy developing sport organizations, businesses, clubs, leagues, olympics, and facilities specifically for their population.

Consumer Market Segmentation

There are two general categories of consumers: end consumers and business consumers. End consumers are those who want a product for personal or household use, not for business use. Business consumers are those who want a product for a business use, such as manufacturing, wholesale, or resale. Some sport companies sell only to end consumers, some sell only to business consumers, and some sell to both. We will first look at end consumers in the sport industry and then at business consumers.

End consumer market segmentation is based on four types of consumer information: demographics, psychographics, media preferences, and purchase behavior (Crispell, 1993). Figure 5.8 illustrates the four types of consumer information important to the sport marketer. This information is used to gain a more complete picture of the consumer segment and to develop products, prices, and promotional strategies.

Demographics. *Demographics* are primarily quantitative data about a consumer. Age, income, gender, occupation, nationality, geographic location, personal life style information, and education are examples.

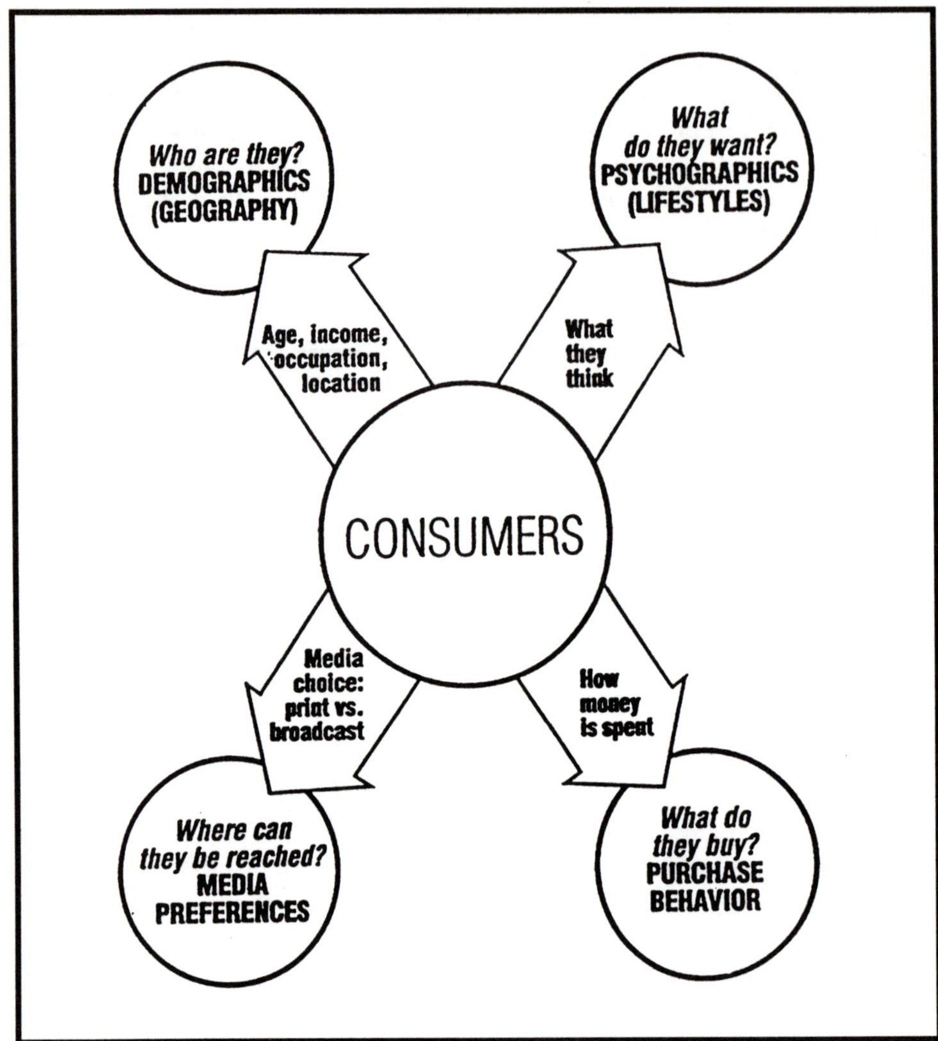

FIGURE 5.8 - The Four Types of Consumer Information
Reprinted with permission from *The Insider's Guide to Demographic Know-How.* 1993. American Demographics, Inc., Ithaca, New York.)

Psychographics. *Psychographics* are primarily psychological data about a consumer. Favorite color, favorite activity, political opinion, personal, vehicle driven, personality type, social class, usage rate, motives, and attitude are examples.

Media Preferences. Media preferences are the information about the consumers concerning what they watch on TV, what they listen to on the radio, and what magazines and newspapers they read.

Purchase Behavior. These data are statistical data concerning the consumer's purchase habits involving what they buy, how often, where they go to buy, how much money they spend, and when they spend it.

These four variables will help the sport marketer piece together a picture of a consumer. The sport marketer can use this information in designing products, and in determining price, promotion, and distribution strategies. Each will be designed specifically for the consumer segment.

Let us use a hypothetical situation to illustrate consumer market possibilities. The Just For Kicks Indoor Soccer Center opened for business 7 years ago. At that time, the manager's indoor soccer consumer analysis and industry analysis revealed the following:

- CONSUMER ANALYSIS: indoor soccer consumer information derived from analysis of membership and league information from the other existing indoor soccer center. Consumer segments included youth categorized as under 10, under 12, under 14, under 16, under 18, and adult. All categories contained girls', boys', women's, men's, and coed groups. Adult groups included skill divisions in women's, men's, and coed: "A" Division for highly skilled; "B" Division for beginners; and others.

  Other potential consumer segments who could possibly be indoor soccer consumers were all outdoor soccer consumers.

- INDUSTRY ANALYSIS: one existing indoor soccer center located in the farthest northeastern part of the city at the edge of the county line in a sparsely populated area. However, this has never hurt participation rates because this center was the only one and every league was always full.

The manager recently conducted another similar study. The results revealed that there are more indoor soccer consumers in all age, gender, and coed groups. The age range of the adult leagues is 19 to 31. The manager was surprised at these data because this was the same age range as 7 years earlier. The manager expected the top end of the range to be at least 38. Upon further study, the manager learned that those consumers were leaving the sport because the younger players were better and faster. They didn't really want to quit. They still wanted to play indoor soccer but didn't want to play against the 19- and 20-year-olds! Based on this information, the manager asked one more question: "If there were a 30-something league, would you play?" The answer was 88% yes. Using what was learned through the study, the manager developed a product specifically for a consumer segment using age: a league for 30-and-over players.

This example of research and segmentation may sound simple, but it is a good example of what takes place in marketing research and segmentation and how the information can be used for the company.

Business consumer segmentation consists of studying and categorizing the many business consumers in the sport industry and other industries. Business consumers include manufacturers, wholesalers, retailers, and government and other nonprofit institutions (Evans & Berman, 1987). They acquire products and services for manufacturing, production, use in operations, enhancing the company's position, or other reasons.

The Hillerich & Bradsby Company, manufacturer of baseball and softball bats, golf clubs, and other sports equipment, sells products to any interested consumer. A large percentage of Hillerich & Bradsby's consumers are retailers, such as sporting goods stores and large national chain department companies. Hillerich & Bradsby also sells to individuals: the professional baseball player. In addition, Hillerich & Bradsby sells bats to companies that will put their company name on the bat for resale.

There are also business consumers that buy for another reason. This reason for purchase may be unique to the sport industry because it involves purchasing something that will not be used in manufacturing and will not be resold. This reason for purchase is for enhancing company position. A company that purchases a skybox (a suite in a stadium or arena) is purchasing it for reasons of entertaining and enhancing the company's position in image. The company will entertain executives from other companies as a way of trying to obtain them as clients or consumers.

In its plan to build a new stadium, the University of Louisville Athletics Department included a variety of box, suite, and other seating arrangements specifically designed for and marketed to businesses. These range from a very plush and roomy suite on the 50-yard line to groups of seats toward the goal lines. Businesses that acquire the suites or boxes will do so to entertain, make deals, and enhance the company's image and position.

Within the same category, sponsorship is a product sold to businesses. A business acquires sponsorship packages for reasons such as advertising because advertising is used to enhance the company's image and position.

Following are some examples of business consumers in the sport industry:

1. Weight-lifting machine and equipment manufacturers sell to fitness centers, colleges, high schools, and retailers;
2. Skyboxes (private company suites) are marketed to corporations;
3. Sportswear and equipment are marketed to college athletic departments and high school departments;
4. Sponsorship is offered to companies as a form of advertising for the company;
5. Advertising, such as signage, is offered to companies;
6. The rights to broadcast a basketball game are sold to television broadcasting companies;
7. The right to sell officially licensed sports gear is sold to companies (mostly retailers); and
8. A softball bat company sells its bats to another company that puts its name on the bat for resale.

Selecting the Target Market(s)

From the segments, the sport marketer will determine which one, or more than one (multiple segmentation), to target. The purpose for selecting a target market is to determine which segment the company will, or is able to, focus on. Although the sport marketer identified all existing consumer segments, the company may not be able to serve all existing consumer segments for a variety of reasons. Therefore, the sport company must select one or more segments to target. Some of the reasons include that the company cannot afford it; there are not enough consumers in a segment to make it profitable; or the company cannot provide the products for a particular consumer segment.

Using the indoor soccer center example, let us say that the manager wants to add the 30-plus league. In order to do that, the company must consider what it must have in order to enter a market or provide a product. In this case, it needs floor space, time, officials, and enough consumers (or enough teams to make a league—usually this number is 4). Upon company analysis, the manager learns that there is no time, not enough officials, and only enough consumers for three teams. With this information, the manager determines that, at this time, the company cannot offer this product. The manager, of course, will keep the idea in mind because the future may bring the opportunity.

Selecting the target market depends primarily on the following factors:

SIZE OF CONSUMER MARKET: Are there enough consumers in the market to meet your purposes?

LOCATION: Are the consumers in the right location?

MEET DEMANDS: Can your company meet the demands—product, price, and other elements—of this segment?

If your answer is no to any one of these questions, you should seriously consider deciding not to target this market currently. There are other factors the company will need to consider specific to the company. Figure 5.9 illustrates the steps that may be taken in the process of selecting a target market.

Competitor Segmentation and Industry Analysis

Competitor segmentation involves industry analysis. The sport marketer needs to know and understand the sport industry. More specifically, the sport marketer needs to study the segments of the sport industry. Industry segmentation may be conducted in a similar manner as consumer segmentation: one whole group divided into categories of smaller groups based on homogeneous characteristics. The primary purpose for industry segmentation is competitive strategy formulation. Other reasons include identifying marketing opportunities and threats within a specific segment, developing an appropriate marketing mix, and informing resource allocation (Pitts et al., 1994).

The sport marketer should study the industry segment in which the sport

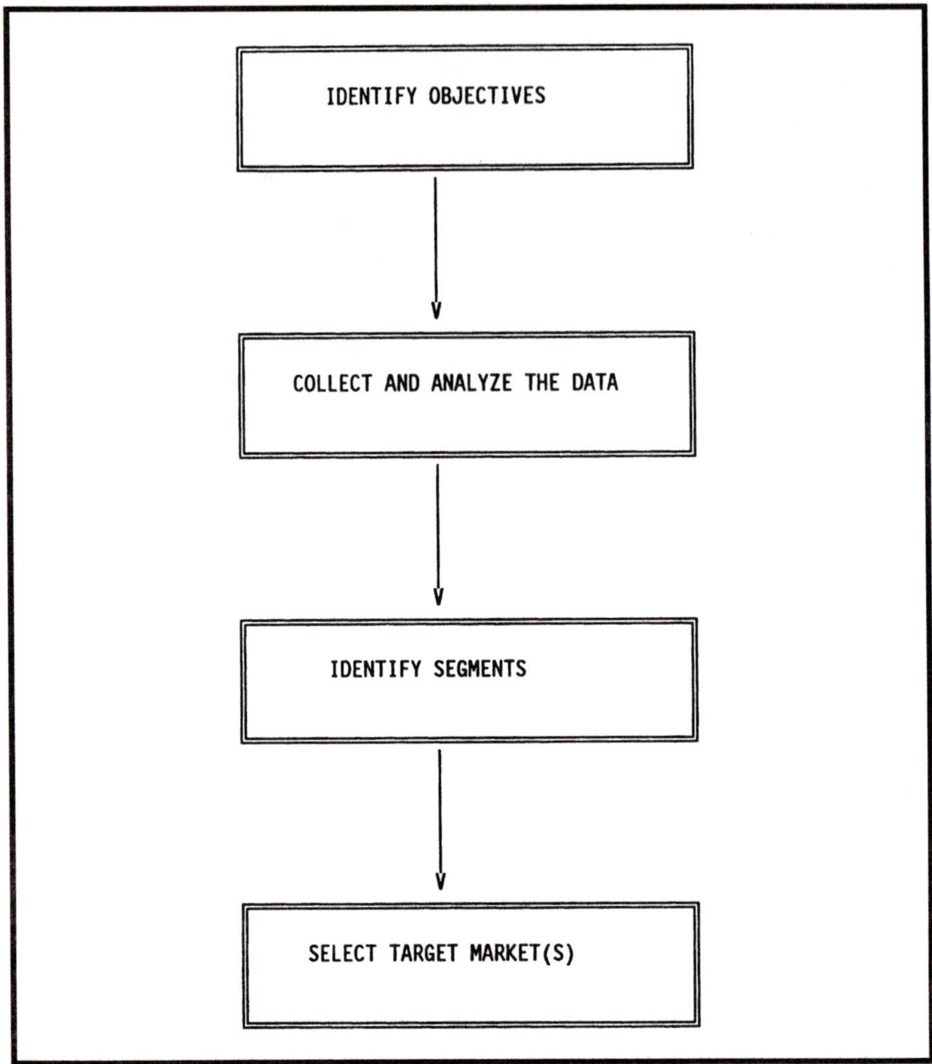

FIGURE 5.9 - Steps in Selection of Target Market(s)

marketer's company exists, industry segments in which the company is considering competing, and other segments.

In the analysis of the industry segment in which the company may be categorized, the sport marketer needs to study its competitors. Knowing and understanding the competition will help in marketing strategy formulation.

The sport marketer should study an industry segment that the company is considering entering. For example, let us say that you own a wheelchair manufacturing company and you are considering the manufacture of sports wheelchairs. You need to study the consumers, the sports wheelchair manufacturing industry, and your company's capabilities for manufacturing sports wheelchairs and competing profitably in this segment. Let us consider specifically what you should study about the industry segment.

What are the companies in this segment? What are their strengths and weaknesses? Where are they located? Who are their consumers? What kind of distribution system do they use? What prices do they charge for their products? What kind of warranties are offered? What kinds of services are offered? What kinds of advertising and other promotional methods do they use? What kinds of wheelchairs are they manufacturing? Are they sport specific or generalized: In other words, are they manufacturing one wheelchair for only one sport, many wheelchairs for many sports, or one wheelchair that can be used for many sports? How many wheelchairs do they sell each year? In which sports are the highest percentage of sales? What are the barriers to entering this segment?

The sport marketer can never know too much about the sport industry, particular industry segments, and specific competitors. The knowledge will help guide the sport marketer in decision-making and strategy formulation.

Chapter Summary

In this chapter we have examined sport marketing research and segmentation. Sport marketing research is the process of planning and organizing activity to gain information: the foundation necessary for formulating decisions within the sport company. Sport marketing research links the sport marketer to the consumer and the industry and helps the sport marketer to identify marketing opportunities, problems, and threats.

The sport marketer needs information concerning the consumer, the competitor, the company, and the climate. These are interrelated factors in the decision-making process. Segmentation is used by the sport marketer to divide a population into consumer markets and to delineate an industry into industry segments. The knowledge gained from the research and analyses helps guide decision making and strategy formulation.

Questions for Study

1. What is sport marketing research? Why is it important?
2. What are the purposes of sport marketing research?
3. List and describe some types of sport marketing research.
4. What are the sources of information? Give examples of each.
5. What are the primary areas of sport marketing research? Give examples of each.
6. What is segmentation?
7. What is sport market segmentation?
8. What is sport industry segmentation?
9. What are the purposes of segmentation? Why is it important to the sport marketer?
10. What are the two broad categories of consumers in the sport industry?
11. Define and give examples of demographics and psychographics.
12. What is a target market? Give an example.
13. Describe the process for selecting the target market.
14. Describe industry analysis and why it is important to the sport marketer.

Learning Activities

1. Interview people in a variety of sport businesses, organizations, or other enterprises in your city or community. Ask them what kind of marketing research they conduct and why.
2. Identify at least 10 different places you could get existing information in your city or community. Go to the places and research the types of information available. Create a notebook of these resources and save this for the future.
3. With a group of other students, develop a research study to determine sponsorship recognition. Conduct the study during a local sports event. Analyze the results and present to the class.
4. Using the list you created in the learning activities in chapter one, categorize the businesses, organizations, or other enterprises by consumer segments. For example, are there businesses, organizations or other enterprises that target the African American population? the Jewish population? the 30-and-over population? or the lesbian and gay population? How many consumer segments can you identify?
5. Select one sport business, organization, or other enterprise from the same list. Complete an industry segmentation and competitor analysis for this business.

References

Boating World. (1993, October).

Bryant, B.E. (1987). Built for excitement. *American Demographics.* 9(3), 38-42.

Crispell, D. (1993). *The insider's guide to demographic know-how.* Chicago, IL: Probus Publishing Company.

DeSensi, J.T., Kelley, D.R., Blanton, M.D., & Beitel, P.A. (1990). Sport management curricular evaluation and needs assessment: A multifaceted approach. *Journal of Sport Management, 4*(1), 31-58.

Evans, J.R., & Berman, B.C. (1987). *Marketing.* New York: Macmillan Publishing Company.

Hiestand, M. (1993, July 23). Targeting demographics: Wave of future. *USA Today,* p. 10C.

Hodgkinson, H.L. (1992, June). *A demographic look at tomorrow.* Washington, DC: Institute for Educational Leadership.

Kelly, J.R. (1987). *Recreation trends: Toward the year 2000.* Champaign, IL: Management Learning Laboratories, Ltd.

McCarroll, T. (1993, Special Issue, Fall). It's a mass market no more. *Time,* pp. 80-81.

National Handicapped Sports. (1993). *Registration pamphlet of the National Handicapped Sports Adaptive Fitness Instructor Workshop.* Rockville, MD: Author.

New marketing research definition approved. (1987, Jan. 2). *Marketing News,* p. 1.

Parks, J.B., & Zanger, B.R.K. (1990). Definition and direction. In J. B. Parks & B. R. K. Zanger (Eds.), *Sport and fitness management: Career strategies and professional content* (pp. 1-14). Champaign, IL: Human Kinetics Books.

Pitts, B.G. (1993). [Interviews with soccer players: The Louisville Women's Soccer Assocation, Inc.]. Unpublished raw data.

Pitts, B.G., Fielding, L.W., & Miller (1994). Industry segmentation theory and the sport industry: Developing a sport industry segment model. *Sport Marketing Quarterly, 3*(1), 15-24.

Porter, M.E. (1985). *Competitive advantage: Creating and sustaining superior performance.* New York: The Free Press.

The new face of America: How immigrants are shaping the face of the world's first multicultural society. *Time, 142*(21).

APPENDIX A

Some Federal Government Sources:

(1) U.S. Bureau of the Census
U.S. Department of Commerce
Washington, DC 20233

TYPES OF INFORMATION: demographic, international, geographic, age research, child care research, crime surveys and research, health research, households research, education research, income research, travel surveys, construction statistics, expenditure data, investment data.

(2) Bureau of Economic Analysis
U.S. Department of Commerce
1401 K Street, NW
Washington, DC 20230

TYPES OF INFORMATION: measures of economic activity at local, regional and national levels, estimates of personal income, demographic and economic characteristics for regions and states.

(3) Immigration and Naturalization Service
425 Eye Street, NW
Room 5020
Washington, DC 20536

TYPES OF INFORMATION: data about immigrants, nonimmigrants, refugees, naturalized citizens, port of entry statistics.

(4) Bureau of Labor Statistics
441 G Street, NW
Washington, DC 20212

TYPES OF INFORMATION: data concerning prices, earnings, employment statistics, unemployment statistics, consumer spending, wages, productivity, population surveys, labor force research, occupational outlook research.

(5) National Park Service
Denver Service Center, T-N-T
P.O. Box 25287
Denver, CO 80225

TYPES OF INFORMATION: data concerning the nation's parks such as public use, recreation visits, camping research, lodging research.

Some Private Sources

(1) Donnelly Marketing Information Services
70 Seaview Avenue
Stamford, CT 06904
TYPES OF INFORMATION: demographic research, retail sales research, product purchases, health care data, and others.

(2) The Wharton Econometric Forecasting Associates
150 Monument Road
Bala Cynwyd, PA 19004
TYPES OF INFORMATION: demographic research, technology development, product-line research, market potential research.

(3) Mediamark Research, Inc.
708 Third Avenue
New York, NY 10017
TYPES OF INFORMATION: demographic and socioeconomic research, media usage, purchase behavior.

(4) American Sports Data, Inc.
234 North Central Avenue
Hartsdale, NY 10530
TYPES OF INFORMATION: annual research on sports and leisure activities.

(5) Simmons Market Research Bureau
420 Lexington Avenue
New York, NY 10017
TYPES OF INFORMATION: demographic data, socioeconomic data, over 800 product/service categories, such as sports and recreation activities.

(6) National Sporting Goods Association
1699 Wall Street
Mt. Prospect, IL 60056
TYPES OF INFORMATION: research on sports participation, sporting goods and equipment purchases, purchases of footwear and other sports apparel, lifestyle data.

CHAPTER 6

MARKETING INFORMATION SYSTEMS

The amount of information that some sport organizations generate daily is staggering. The major problem is that our thinking and skills have not been developed to accommodate this tremendous onslaught of data. It has been estimated that sport executives spend 80% of their time on information transactions. This phenomenon demands the development of systematic methods to process the abundance of information that is available and to use it in marketing our sports products and services.

Marketing Information Systems are about information management. They have been referred to by many names, Marketing Information Systems (MIS), Computer Information Systems (CIS), and Information Asset Management (IAM). Although no one title is singularly appropriate, the importance of developing and utilizing systems that can manage information for your sport organization or company is essential. Mullin (1985) said "the MIS provides the link between the market and the marketer, and it is therefore the lifeline of marketing" (p. 210).

Marketing Information Systems are generally characterized as a collection of data that are utilized by management in the operation and development of marketing programs and market related decisions. In past decades, many sport organizations have been managed by former coaches and athletes. Marketing and management decisions were often made on intuition rather than data. The time has long passed when organizations can remain competitive in today's environment with yesterday's decision-making style. Successful sport marketers must develop skills and abilities to interact with technology in making data-based decisions for marketing their products and services.

Most sport organizations have access to a considerable amount of information on their customers. Some use it, some do not. Mullin (1983) indicated that much of the information available to the sport marketer is "either lost or irretrievable" (p. 76). Therefore, the purpose of this chapter is to assist sport marketers in the development and utilization of an effective Marketing Information System.

Sources of Information

The first step in building an effective marketing information system is to collect or generate useful data. But, you may ask, where do you get the data? Traditionally, sport organizations have not been as sophisticated as many other business operations in collecting and using marketing data, so it is important to improve in this area of operations. Managers of sport organizations receive a variety of information from within their organization and from other sources with which they must interact on an ongoing basis (Stotlar, 1987). These must be clearly identified and will become the main sources for sport marketing data.

Sources of MIS data are typically identified as being either primary or secondary (Mullin, 1983, 1985; Stotlar, 1989). Primary research is research conducted with, or collected directly from, your customers. Sport organizations can, through automation, keep very accurate records of all their clients, all people doing business with the organization. This includes both those who have purchased from the organization and those from whom the organization buys goods and services (Stotlar, 1989).

Health and fitness clubs have access to considerable amounts of information about their clients. They all completed an application form that included not only their name and address, but also typically their occupation and income. Many clubs also have an extended system that can track the programs and equipment used in the club by each member and can generate reports detailing individual and club usage. This information can be quite useful to the market manager in tracking renewals and future marketing campaigns.

The University of Northern Colorado Athletic Department implemented an MIS in 1991 to better track the students attending athletic contests. Prior to implementation, students would just show their ID to access gate entrance; however, with the new system, the ID was scanned at the entry gate. The athletic department now had current and reliable information on student attendance. These data were used successfully to push forward plans to locate a new stadium closer to the main student housing areas. These data could also be cross-referenced with basketball attendance to see if the consumers were the same or different, and appropriate marketing efforts could then be initiated. As a side benefit, former students who had been accustomed to flashing their out-of-date ID and proceeding through the gate could now be stopped and referred to the ticket window.

Another innovative method for collecting marketing and consumer information was introduced at Colorado ski resorts in 1993. Several of the major ski resorts implemented computerized systems by validating and tracking skiers. The systems included scanners located at all lift locations across the resort. When skiers would line up for transport up the mountain, the lift operators would scan their lift ticket or season pass. Information collected through the process could then be analyzed and evaluated by resort managers. Specific information that would be valuable would be the types of terrain skied by the most skiers, the frequency and duration of runs, and the typical ski pattern for the majority of skiers on the mountain. These data could also be tabulated from week to week throughout the season, and individual reports could be generated for season pass holders.

The most popular methods for primary data collection for sports organizations are direct mail surveys, telephone interviews, and personal interviews. Data generated through client questionnaires or surveys can be valuable sources of information about customers' attitudes toward your products and services, as well as short-term demand trends (Stotlar, 1989). Primary data can also enhance a sound quality-control system by eliciting feedback to be used in refining product and service offerings.

Primary data collection can also take the form of pilot testing and product experiments. Those companies that manufacture sporting goods are continuously involved in this type of research, specifically in product development.

Unfortunately, many sport organizations discard valuable consumer information. Mullin (1985), a marketing executive with different Major League Baseball teams, said that some "baseball franchises that make it to the play-offs throw away the names and addresses of unfilled ticket applications, when these individuals clearly should be added to the mailing list" (p. 205).

A similar oversight in many organizations is failure to record information when clients pay by check. These people may not be regular customers and could be included on special mailings designed to attract new business. This technique is often used with fitness clubs when guests of current members register at the front desk. The office staff are trained to enter their names into a "prospects" file that can be used in future marketing activities.

Sport organizations are also consumers; therefore, every supplier to the organization should also be considered as a potential consumer. A wide variety of products and services are purchased by your organization and represent another possible marketing opportunity. These companies could be contacted for ticket purchases, product donations, and sponsorship opportunities (Stotlar, 1989).

Secondary research is characterized by the fact that it is not conducted directly by the sport organization. According to Shaw (1991) "the information-vending business grosses $15 billion in the USA and the fastest growing area of the information business is marketing information" (p. 38).

Several major companies are in the business of market research, including sport market research. A considerable amount of data can be obtained from these organizations, which conduct and publish data about the sport industry.

Probably the most comprehensive data are available through Simmons Market Research Bureau which produces volumes of marketing research for all industries, including sports and fitness. Their data are presented in a variety of areas and an entire volume is devoted to sports and leisure. Sport marketers will be most interested in the data on sports participation, attendance at sporting events, and sports equipments sales. Simmons details consumers by age, income, geographical location, occupation, education, marital status, and size of family. Access to Simmons Market Research Bureau is available at most public libraries.

Professional and trade associations also publish information that is crucial for sport marketers. The Sporting Goods Manufacturers Association conducted a study of 10,000 children aged 10-18 regarding their participation, attitudes, and opinions surrounding sport. These data would be quite valuable in defining both market size and potential for sport retailers. The International Health, Racquet & Sportsclubs Association (IHRSA) (formerly the International Racquet & Sportsclubs Association—IRSA) often conduct a thorough analysis of the fitness and exercise club industry. These data would certainly be helpful to fitness clubs in designing and correctly positioning their products and services.

Manufacturers have become very ingenious in ways to build MIS data. For example, Nike placed a hand-tag on their "Air Jordan" youth apparel. This tag was an application form to join the Air Jordan Flight Club. Membership in the club included a poster, membership card, and special tee shirt, but most important, Nike obtained the name, address, and phone number of a young sports consumer.

The sources for information are almost unlimited, but finding the information takes a little time, imagination, and effort. A national governing body could easily access information from U.S. Olympic Festival managers concerning who purchased tickets to specific competitions. These names could in turn be entered into a database and included in future membership or marketing efforts.

Sport manufacturers and sport organizations must collect market data, and with this abundance of data, the sport marketing professional needs a marketing information system to "provide manager(s) with the necessary data for making intelligent decisions" (Hodgetts, 1975, p. 395). The accuracy and availability of marketing data are vital for sport organizations because their fans, clients, participants, and consumers change rapidly (Mullin, 1983). Therefore, the MIS must be designed to store, retrieve, and assimilate the data in meaningful ways.

Designing Information Systems

The MIS does not make decisions, but merely makes information available quickly, accurately, and in a form that marketers can interpret. Refer to the model of marketing information systems for sport organizations presented in Figure 6.1. It should be noted that although not every MIS is computer-based, the microcomputer and an MIS function well together. The advantages of a microcomputer-based MIS are that information can be retrieved much faster than through traditional methods and that computers are more accurate (Stotlar, 1987).

Marketing Information Systems must be integrated so that fragmented data can be fused into composite pictures of individual consumers and specific sport markets (Shaw, 1991). It is imperative that when sport marketers are required to make decisions, they make informed decisions based on the best and most current

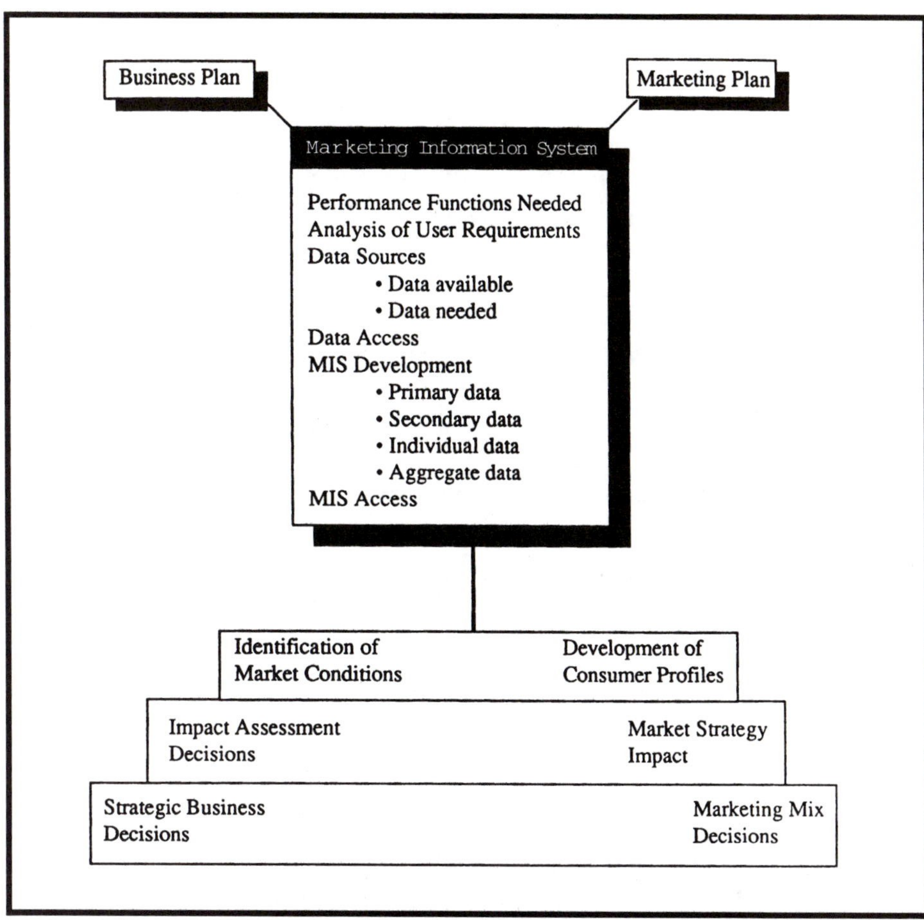

FIGURE 6.1 - Integration of Marketing Information Systems for Sport Organizations

information. All sport marketers can make decisions, but the success of the marketing decision often depends on the quality of the information on which it is based (Stotlar, 1987). It is the function of the MIS to provide that information.

Mullin (1985) indicated that "the full value of an MIS is realized only when data from various sources are integrated into a common database" (p. 207). He describes the essential characteristics of an effective sport marketing database as follows:

1. It must be centralized. An organization needs to have all of its data located in one centralized system.
2. The various databases (consumer files, accounting records, sales records, etc.) need to be fully integrated so that the data from one source can be contrasted and combined with data from another source, or both.
3. The data must be retrievable in a form which the sport marketer can use for decision making (Mullin, 1985, p. 202).

Data Security

Two distinct types of security problems accompany the use of microcomputers. The first problem involves the software used to perform the various tasks. Since the information on the software program and the information that has been entered by the staff are stored on a disk, the characteristics of that disk are important. Almost all microcomputers use combinations of hard drives and magnetic floppy disks. Larger computers will use removable hard drives and tape storage systems. Although storage disks are relatively durable, they can be erased through exposure to any magnetic object. This totally destroys any information on the disk, program and files. Disks have also been known to "crash" on their own. Therefore, one of the most important aspects of data security is "backing up." This involves making a duplicate of all programs and information stored on disks. This may seem like a lot of work, but the penalty for failing to back up work is that someone must reenter all of the information that was lost.

The second problem regarding security involves access to restricted information. Sport organizations consider their marketing information as confidential. It is important that this information be reserved for viewing only by appropriate people. This restricted access is often accomplished through the password system. The user must enter a predetermined password to gain access to MIS files. This process is also quite useful when any unauthorized change could cause severe problems for the organization.

Getting the System to Work

Two common mistakes are often made in the application of computers in sport organizations. First, executives buy a computer with the idea in mind that a job will be found for it to do. Second, the people who will be using the computer are not involved in the testing and purchase of the system (Danziger, 1985; Stotlar, 1987). On many occasions, a well-intentioned administrator has purchased a computer to assist staff, only to discover that the computer will not perform the functions that the staff needs it to perform. The computer and the software should be purchased with specific requirements in mind, and the staff should be involved in the decision for the very beginning of the process.

Two basic types of programs are available, custom programs and commercial "off-the-shelf" business applications. Commercial software packages are readily available to create and manage marketing information and can handle the majority of information storage and retrieval needs of sport marketers. Each program has unique strengths and weaknesses, and many of them will let you create custom forms for storing and retrieving your marketing information. Another advantage is that many office workers will be familiar with the operation of the more famous software programs.

In the event that your organization has special needs, you may need to have a software program written especially for your applications. Although these programs will fit your needs, they are generally expensive, and any future modifications that are required will often mandate hiring the same person (or company) that designed the original program. It goes without saying that this situation would not leave you in the best market position.

A commercial database usually allows for individualized category ("field") names to be developed by the end user. The computer manages pieces of information by these "fields;" therefore, each piece of information by which the marketer may wish to sort, list, or search must have its own field; so it is important for the sport marketer to carefully review the ability of the program to handle files by fields. When considering either a custom-programmed package or a commercial one that allows for individualized fields for each file, the sport marketer must determine the exact information that will be needed for each individual.

Many of the commercial programs have companion software that will allow you to create and move information from one application to another. Thus, a marketing director in a fitness center could have a memo written on the word processor, have the MIS select the addresses of all members who had not been in for a workout in the past month, and merge the mailing list with the memo.

Considerable attention has, thus far, been devoted to the various tasks and programs for the accomplishment of those tasks. One more type of program must be addressed: the integrated database-graphics programs. These programs can also combine word processing, graphics, spreadsheets, databases, and telecommunication. Use of this software facilitates sales reports, market projects, and communication with both clients and staff. This enables the user to purchase one piece of software that will do just about everything. Integrated software is more expensive, but the convenience of a "one-system" package is often worth the expense.

A well-designed database system can also perform many standard business tasks. Some MIS applications can perform accounts-receivable functions, such as preparation of invoices, maintenance of customer accounts, and production of sales and other reports. In sport organizations, this function is often applied to ticket sales or membership payments. The accounts-payable segment of the program would generally enjoy a wider application through the organization detailing all vendors with whom business is transacted. The features that often appear in this function are purchase-order control, invoice processing, check writing and control, cash requirement forecasting, and vendor information analysis (Falk, 1983). Programs may be designed for specific accounting and data management, but a truly integrated MIS can be adapted for a variety of uses in sport marketing activities.

In the sport setting, these features may surpass the needs and desires of the average sport marketer, but they should be fully compatible with the associated needs of the entire sport organization. The business computer industry has expanded so fast in the past decade that it is difficult to believe that a commercially available package cannot be found that could meet all of your MIS needs.

Getting People to Work with the System

It should also be pointed out that an MIS cannot be expected to be used to solve problems efficiently as soon as the computer comes out of the box. It takes about 40 hours for a person to become fully acquainted with the operation of any hardware system and about 20 hours to be become familiar with a specific software package (Danziger, 1985). According to Shaw (1991) an MIS must be designed "with a view to the people who will use them, and with an understanding of how the business in which they work operates. [An MIS] must deliver the the right information to the right people at the right time" (p. 60).

With the right system, access to the information is quick and updating the material is much simpler than with conventional methods. Printouts of data should be available by any combination of factors selected by the sport marketer. This will allow for effective sales and market planning.

Producing Results

The primary purpose of marketing research and data analysis is to better identify segments of the market that are most likely to purchase your goods and services. The individual pieces of data in your MIS can tell you who bought what and when. However important that may be, what you really want to know is who **will** buy what and when. This is the aspect of sport marketing called forecasting. Forecasting is district advantage provided by computerized MIS systems.

Exactly what is forecasting and why is it necessary? Forecasting is the ability of the market manager to see how the future will be affected by anticipated or hypothetical decisions—the playing of "what if?" This can be very beneficial to sport marketers because hypothetical figures can be entered into the MIS for such items as sponsorship revenues, ticket prices, or membership fees. The program could then be manipulated to perform calculations detailing the financial and market consequences of those decisions.

Although MIS information is entered into the system piecemeal, sport marketers need to be able to look at that organization's data in whole. There is a need for aggregate information to develop business and general marketing strategies; yet, there is also a demand for synthesizing data to project individual consumer profiles. Sport marketers must clearly see the macro and micro perspectives of their consumer base. Therefore, both individual and aggregate information is needed for intelligent marketing-mix decisions.

Chapter Summary

All sport organizations deal with consumers, and consumer information is ideally suited to the storage and retrieval capabilities of the MIS. Having discovered the broad range of application for an MIS, it should be clear that Marketing Information Systems will not immediately make a poor sport marketer competent or an inefficient sales person a good one. It is a tool that can be used by skilled employees and managers to assist in the performance of sport marketing tasks and decision making. Typical information contained in MIS files would include the consumer's name, address, age, occupation, and purchasing activity. It is precisely this type of information that is particularly well-suited to MIS and a computer-managed database because of the need to continually update and change entries. Sport marketers can combine these data with other information in the corporation database to facilitate decisions on target markets and consumer profiles. Remember that the quality of one's decisions is reflective of the quality of the information upon which they were based.

Questions for Study

1. What are the essential characteristics of a well-designed Marketing Information System?
2. What MIS sources would be available for an intercollegiate athletic program and how would you go about setting up an MIS?

Learning Activities

1. Select your favorite sport and consult a copy of Simmons Market Research Bureau. See where you fit in the demographic segments presented.
2. Take a trip to your local fitness center or health club and inquire about the types of information they have on their clients. Also look at their application form if they are uncooperative with your first request.

Professional Associations and Organizations

Sporting Goods Manufacturers Association
200 Castlewood Drive
North Palm Beach, FL 33408

Suggested Readings

Poppel, H. L., & Goldstein, B. *Information technology.* New York: McGraw-Hill Book Company.

Shaw, R. (1991). *Computer-aided marketing and selling.* London: Reed International Books.

References

Danziger, G. (1985). Computer applications in sport. In G. Lewis & H. Appenzeller (Eds.), *Successful sport management* (pp. 215-241). Charlottesville, VA: The Michie Company.

Falk, H. (1983). *Handbook of computer applications for the small or medium-sized business*. Radnor, PA: Chilton Book Company.

Hodgetts, R. M. (1975). *Management: Theory, process and practice*. Philadelphia: W. B. Saunders Company.

Mullin, B. J. (1983). *Sports marketing, promotion and public relations*. Amherst: National Sport Management, Inc.

Mullin, B. J. (1985). An information-based approach to marketing sport. In G. Lewis & H. Appenzeller (Eds.), *Successful sport management* (pp. 201-214). Charlottesville, VA: The Michie Company.

Shaw, R. (1991). *Computer-aided marketing and selling*. London: Reed International Books.

Stotlar, D. K. (1987). Managing administrative functions with microcomputers. In J. E. Donnelly (Ed.) *Using microcomputers in physical education and the sport sciences* (pp. 117-132). Champaign, IL: Human Kinetics.

Stotlar, D. K. (1989). *Successful sport marketing and sponsorship plans*. Dubuque, IA: Wm. C. Brown.

Chapter 7

The Marketing Mix and the Sport Industry

Overview

This chapter presents a brief overview of a significant element of the sport marketing management model called the marketing mix. The marketing mix is a crucial element because it defines the sport business, and much of the sport marketer's time is spent on various functions within the marketing mix.

The marketing mix comprises four elements: product, price, place, and promotion. In this chapter we will define the marketing mix, present a description of its place in the sport marketing management model, present a brief description of the elements of the marketing mix, and describe how the elements are combined to create the marketing mix for the sport company.

The Marketing Mix

The marketing mix is the strategic combination (mix) of four elements called the 4 Ps. These are product, price, place, and promotion. Creation of the marketing mix involves the process of discovering or developing the right combination of the elements. At the heart of the decision-making process is the research conducted and knowledge gained about the consumer, the competition, the company, and the climate (see Chapter 5). All factors must be given significant attention. If the sport marketer ignores one or the other, this increases the chances of making wrong decisions (Schnaars, 1991).

The marketing mix involves deciding on the right combination of product, price, promotion, and place. There are many elements of each of these variables that can be manipulated by the sport marketer. They are manipulated in order to meet the consumer's desires or needs, to provide competitive strategy, according to what the company can do, and within ethical, political, economical, and legal constraints. The following are a brief presentation of each of the marketing mix elements and some strategies for manipulation.

Product

The product is what the sport company is trying to sell. The challenge is to produce the right product for the consumer. Products can be goods, services, people, places, and ideas. There are many products in the sport industry. There are many consumers and competitors also. As you learned in chapter 4, "Sport Marketing Theory," and in chapter 5, "Sport Marketing Research and Segmentation," the sport marketer must analyze the consumers in order to understand exactly what the consumer wants and analyze its competitors to learn what already exists in the market. As you will learn in chapter 8, "The Product in the Sport Industry," the process for developing the right product can be very involved.

The product can be manipulated, or differentiated, as it is called in marketing. A tennis racket may be produced with a new shape or a new color. The sport center can offer new divisions in a volleyball league based on age, gender, or skill level. The same sport center could offer a new form of volleyball simply by changing some rules, court size, or number of players. As an example there is now beach volleyball that can be played in a 2-player, 3-player, or 4-player format.

Price

Price is the exchange value of a product. The challenge for the sport marketer is to determine the right price for the consumer. If the consumer believes that a product is overpriced or even underpriced, there is a good chance that the consumer will not purchase the product.

The price of a product can be manipulated many ways. Promotional pricing can be used: 2-for-1 tickets to the game or 2-for-1 memberships to the fitness club; special sale prices on sports clothing for special times such as holidays; special sale prices on sporting goods equipment for seasonal sports; or price breaks as the quantity purchased increases. There are also long term price planning strategies that the sport marketer can use. Refer to chapter 9 for details of price as a marketing mix element.

Place

Place involves the process of getting the sport product to the consumer. It is also called distribution: distributing the sport product to the consumer. The sport marketer will analyze the types of distribution methods available and select those that will deliver the product to the right place. The right place means "where the consumer is, shops, or will travel to." There are two types of distribution in the sport industry because of the types of products offered. Hard goods are those products that must go from a manufacturing plant to a retail outlet and therefore involve the kind of distribution in which moving products is involved. There are products that cannot be moved in the sport industry. For example, a basketball game is not a product that can be moved to a retail outlet and sold. The consumer must go to the place in which the game will be played (manufactured) in order to consume it.

The distribution (place) of a product can be changed. One can now purchase tickets to various sporting events through many different ticket outlets because they are distributed through many outlets. Sport facilities are becoming a one-stop-shopping facility: Many new ones include hotels, shopping malls, and other attractions, including fitness centers and amusement parks. Sport sold as a spectator product can change other factors in the way it is distributed to the consumer. For example, there are over 60 official Kentucky Derby Festival events prior to the actual Derby race that is a sporting event that lasts about 2 minutes! Refer to chapter 10 for the detailed information about distribution.

Promotion

Promotion is the element of marketing that the general public thinks IS marketing. That is because it is the element that the general public sees and relates to as marketing. Promotion includes advertising and other promotional methods. These are designed to attract the consumer's attention. Therefore, the consumer believes that promotion is all that marketing is about.

Promotion is the process of creating interest in a product to bring attention to it with the ultimate goal of creating enough interest that the consumer purchases the product. There are many promotional methods and techniques available for the sport marketer to use, and there are some used in the sport industry that are rarely used in other industries. An extreme example of trying to get the attention of the consumer and the media was associated with the first Super Bowl (at that time it was called the AFL-NFL World Championship Game) of the National Football League (NFL) played in 1966. Organizers were so worried that the event would be ignored by the nation, they planned to create interest by staging a kidnapping of the silver trophy (Carucci, 1994)!

Some promotional methods include television commercials, print advertisements in magazines, direct mail advertising, promotional pricing, "giveaways" at sports events, and press guides. See chapters 11 - 15 for the detailed information concerning promotion in the sport industry.

Manipulating the Elements

All of the marketing mix elements are manipulated by the sport marketer for two reasons: first, to stay in business and, second, to be successful. The only way to do this is to offer products that will sell, at a price that will be paid, offered through a place where they can be bought, and made attractive to the consumer. In other words, the sport marketer needs to develop the right product at the right price offered at the right place and promote it with the right promotional methods.

The sport marketer uses the elements to develop the right combination for target markets and in response to changes in the market. It is the responsibility of the sport marketer to control and manage the marketing mix. Although each of the elements is developed through a specific planning process, they are not planned in a vacuum. The elements are interrelated. As such, all decisions regarding one element must be done in conjunction with decisions regarding all other elements. In addition, decisions concerning the elements in the marketing mix must be made in relation to what the consumer wants, compared to what the competitor has, considered for its fit for the company, and considered against legal, ethical, and political elements.

The Interrelationship Of The Elements

The marketing mix elements are interrelated. This means that each element affects the others. The sport marketer must develop the right combination. Decisions will be made based on the information gained in the marketing research. As you learned in chapter 5, "Sport Marketing Research and Segmentation," research is the foundation upon which all marketing decisions are made.

The consumer is looking for the right product, at just the right price, which can be purchased at the right location. As you will learn in chapter 8, "The Sport Product," the consumer does not buy products: The consumer is looking for something to satisfy a need or desire. From that perspective, the product and everything about the product take on characteristics beyond the intended function of the product. This notion must be understood by the sport marketer and used during the development of a marketing mix. For example, let us look at a consumer who wants a new pair of running shoes.

The consumer's existing shoes are not quite worn out, but this consumer is becoming a serious runner. A serious runner is a different person than a recreational runner and therefore has different characteristics. For example, the shoes must be thought of in the running community as serious runner shoes, price is no factor, and the shoes must look like serious runner shoes. The consumer is looking for a product to create an image and fulfill a desire, and price is no factor. The sport marketer, having studied the serious runner consumer, understands what the consumer wants. Therefore, the sport marketer will produce a serious runner shoe, and most likely, price will be no factor! The shoe will be advertised in serious runner publications only, and the advertisements will carry the message and image that this shoe is only for the serious runner. In addition, the shoe will be sold only through serious runner stores. This will add to the idea that the shoes are for serious runners only.

In this example, the sport marketer studies and understands this particular consumer. A product is produced specifically for this consumer; the price is set at what the consumer is willing to pay; the promotional methods imply the type of product for this particular type of consumer; and the product is offered for sale in specific places. This process and the decisions on the combination of the four elements are indicative of the interrelationship and impact of the elements.

Marketing Mix Strategy In The Sport Industry

The primary strategy for the sport marketer in designing a marketing mix is to customize the marketing mix for a specific consumer market. As the sport marketer identifies consumer market segments and selects target markets, the marketing mix elements are designed specifically for the consumer. For example, the sport marketer determines from research that the typical consumer of memberships in fitness centers is female, age between 28 to 46, single, has 1 child, an income range of $32,000 to $98,000, an education level of at least a bachelor's degree, and whose favorite sport and fitness activities are weight training, working out on the stair machine, aerobics, tennis, and volleyball. Using this information, the sport marketer can design the product—a fitness and sport center—for the consumer, price it for the consumer, develop promotional methods designed to attract the consumer, and place the facility in an area of the city in which a high percentage of those types of consumers live.

Also affecting the decision to open a fitness center is information concerning the industry and the competition. For example, if a fitness center already exists that offers exactly what the consumer wants, at the desired price, and in the right location, the sport marketer must determine if it will be feasible to open a fitness center. If reports of the fitness industry nationwide show that fitness center membership purchase is increasing, how does this compare to the local fitness industry?

In addition, the marketing mix should change as markets change. You have learned in this chapter that the product, price, place, and promotional methods can be manipulated. Here is where the constant research is needed. If it has been 8 years since your company conducted any marketing research, the decisions and strategies are riskier as every year goes by. The information gained from research should be current. Therefore, research should be an ongoing process within the company. With a flow of current and accurate information, the sport marketer's decisions and strategies for the marketing mix can be much more successful.

Chapter Summary

The marketing mix is the strategic combination of four elements: product, price, place, and promotion. It is the component of the sport marketing management model on which the sport marketer will spend a great percentage of time. It is a crucial element because it involves decisions and strategies concerning the product, price, place, and promotion. The marketing mix is designed based on information concerning the consumer, the competition, the company, and the climate. Chapters 8 through 15 are devoted to the 4 Ps and detail the intricate functions within each element.

References

Carucci, V. (1994). Touchdown south: Super Bowl XXVIII in Atlanta. *Sky Magazine, 23*(1), 36-40, 43-44, 46.

Schnaars, S.P. (1991). *Marketing strategy: A consumer-driven approach.* New York: The Free Press.

CHAPTER 8

THE PRODUCT IN THE SPORT INDUSTRY

What Is A Product?

People seek goods or services to satisfy needs or desires. Products perform as the satisfaction agent. Consider the following examples:

1. A softball player wants to improve hitting and enhance batting average. The player will search for the product that will fulfill those desires—the right bat. What the person wants is to hit better and to attain a better batting average. The bat is the implement that might meet the consumer's desires.
2. Someone wants to lose weight and get into shape. This person decides that the product to fulfill those desires is a fitness center. In order to get into the fitness center, the individual must purchase the opportunity to do so: a fitness center membership. The fitness center is offered as the opportunity for the person to fulfill those desires: the place to exercise.
3. While playing tennis, the strings of an individual's tennis racket snap. This person wants to continue playing tennis. In order to fulfill that desire, the racket's strings must be replaced. The service of stringing the racket provides the opportunity for the racket to be repaired so that the individual can fulfill the desire to play tennis once again.

These examples serve to partially explain why and how a person purchases a product: The person is actually purchasing functions and benefits. The product is the satisfaction agent for those functions and benefits.

A definition of product should represent the breadth of the term. Therefore, *product* needs to be understood as a **concept** and must be used as an umbrella term that includes goods, services, people, places, and ideas with tangible or intangible attributes (Stanton, Etzel, & Walker, 1991). The softball player wants the softball bat for what it will do, the function it will fulfill, and not because it is simply a softball bat. A sport marketer should strive to understand exactly what the consumer wants in order to make that the product offered.

Products provide benefits and fulfill functions. The fitness-center product is a "place" that provides the opportunity to fulfill desires for fitness, weight loss, socializing, fun, relaxation, and other benefits. The National Collegiate Athletic Association (NCAA) provides an "idea" and a "service." The idea is that participation in collegiate athletics builds character and is good for a person. The service is the government of collegiate athletics. The NCAA offers sports events, such as the women's and men's basketball chanpionships. In the example of replacing the broken tennis racket strings, the consumer gets both a "good" and a "service"—new string and the job (service) of putting the strings on the racket.

Benefits of products include intangibles, such as guarantee of quality. The consumer purchases a product with the company's promise of "satisfaction or your money back." The seller is promising that the product will meet with satisfaction the consumer's desires or needs. If satisfaction is not realized, whether real or perceived, the consumer may return the product to the seller, who will give the consumer a refund or satisfy the consumer in some other way. For example, the tennis racket stringing was guaranteed. If the strings were to break, the consumer might return the racket to the company, which would resolve the situation.

The fitness center example is somewhat different. The fitness center may guarantee satisfaction. In this case, satisfaction may be measurable only by the consumer's perception. This is different from the tennis racket stringing. If the strings break, the materials or the service was faulty. If the fitness center consumer is not losing weight and getting into shape, at least according to the consumer's definitions, where does the fault lie—with the consumer or the center? In this situation, the consumer must perform—exercise—in order for the product—weight loss and fitness—to work. The fitness center can only provide the opportunity—the place and the means (exercising equipment, classes, and other). Hence, if the consumer does not perform, there will most likely be no weight loss or fitness gain. In this case, is there an obvious opportunity for consumer satisfaction and a money-back guarantee? One fitness center in Arizona offers a 30-day money-back guarantee (Feld, 1988). However, it is based on an agreement between the club and the consumer: The consumer promises to attend three times a week for a 4-week period, and the agreement includes fitness goals. This resulted in only 3 of 3,000 members asking for a refund.

Toward developing an understanding of a concept of product, let us first consider some definitions of product:

> "A product is everything, both favorable and unfavorable, that one receives in an exchange. It is a complexity of tangible and intangible attributes, including functional, social, and psychological utilities or benefits" (Pride & Ferrell,

1991, p. 240).

"A product is a bundle of physical, service, and symbolic attributes designed to enhance consumer want satisfaction" (Boone & Kurtz, 1989, p. 271).

"A product is a set of tangible and intangible attributes, including packaging, color, price, quality, and brand, plus the services and reputation of the seller. A product may be a tangible good, service, place, person, or idea" (Stanton et al., 1991, pp. 168-169).

A product is "the sum of the physical, psychological, and sociological satisfactions that the buyer derives from purchase, ownership, and consumption" and includes "accessories, packaging, and service" (Tarpey, Donnelly, & Peter, 1979).

There are words common to most of these definitions. It is important in reaching an understanding of the concept of product to first understand these terms.

Tangible and intangible. A *tangible product* is something that is concrete, definite, discernible, and material. It is a physical object. A softball bat is a tangible product. It physically exists. An *intangible product* is something that is indefinite, indiscernible, indistinguishable, and imperceptible. It is not a physical object. When the broken tennis racket strings need to be repaired, the task of replacing the strings is an intangible product; in this example, a service. Further, a tangible object is involved in this purchase. The consumer gets new strings, a tangible product, and the broken strings are replaced, an intangible product.

Professional sport events provide us with examples of intangible products. A professional men's basketball game is an intangible product. One can only watch the game. Benefits realized include entertainment, socializing, fun, and a number of other personal satisfactions.

It is important that sport marketing decision makers understand the concepts of tangible and intangible. This knowledge guides decisions concerning product strategies and influences other marketing variables as well.

Utility and benefits. Stanton et al. (1991) provide a very good definition of utility: "Utility may be defined as the attribute in an item that makes it capable of satisfying human wants" (p. 16). There are four types of utility: form, time, place, and ownership (possession) (Boone & Kurtz, 1989). *Form utility* is the production of a product—using raw materials to create finished products (Boone & Kurtz, 1989). *Time utility* means getting a product to the consumer **when** the consumer wants it (Boone & Kurtz, 1989). *Place utility* is getting the product to the consumer **where** the consumer shops (Boone & Kurtz, 1989). *Possession utility* is the ability to transfer ownership or possession of a product from seller to buyer (Boone & Kurtz, 1989).

Using our previous examples, let us consider utility. The consumer who wants a specific softball bat (form utility) to improve batting average wants the bat *before* the softball season begins (time utility), *from* a reputable sporting goods store *close to* where the consumer lives (ownership and place utilities). The sport marketer's job is to produce the bat from specific raw materials (form utility), get it on the market in advance of softball season (time utility), and in reputable sporting goods stores and other outlets (ownership and place utilities). It is only when the sport marketer completely understands the consumer's specific needs—what, when, how, why—that the marketer may make informed decisions concerning form, time, place, and ownership utilities.

The *benefits of a product* are everything the consumer derives from the product. In other words, benefits may include functions of the product and intangible benefits, such as status, quality, durability, cost effectiveness, and others. For example, the consumer who wants to improve batting average expects that the selected bat will improve her or his batting average. The sport marketer, based on an understanding of what the softball player wants, promotes the bat as a bat that will give the consumer a better batting average. Promotion messages, such as "this bat has a bigger sweet spot," "the only bat for champions," or "the home-run hitter's dream bat," are strong suggestions to the consumer that this bat will give the consumer what he or she wants, a better batting average.

You should now have a good understanding of product. It is not simply a good or a service. It is something that functions in some capacity for the consumer and fulfills a desire or need for the consumer. The sport marketer must know what the consumer wants the product to do—benefits—and guide the company toward meeting those demands—utility. The sport company produces a product **after** learning what the consumer wants.

What Is A Sport Product?

There is a vast array of products in the sport industry. Based on the concept presented in chapter 1 (that the sport industry is broad and includes industry segments, such as fitness management, recreation and professional sports), any product that fulfills the sport, fitness, or recreation- related needs or desires of a consumer is considered a sport product. This requires a broad concept definition of sport product. Drawing on the definition of sport and the sport industry in chapter 1 and the general definitions of product in this chapter, the definition of *sport product* is any good, service, person, place, or idea with tangible or intangible attributes that satisfy consumer sport, fitness, or recreation related needs or desires.

Return to chapter 1 and read again the section on what exists in the sport industry. Using our definition of sport product, those items are all sport products offered to fulfill consumer sport-related needs or desires. With so many sport products in the industry it is necessary for the sport marketer to identify differing consumer needs and desires in order to create and offer products that will fulfill those needs and desires. The most common method is product classification.

Sport Product Classifications

An initial step in planning products is the determination of what type(s) of product(s) to offer. This task involves studying a particular product category, also known as a product market or an industry segment. A product category may be defined as a group of products that are either exactly alike or with homogeneous characteristics. The reasons for studying product categories or segments are similar to the reasons for studying and segmenting consumers. A thorough understanding of your product, its benefits and functions, and its utilities, along with understanding the same about your competitor's product, is critical to product management. Constant study of your product and all products like it will guide decisions concerning product development or diversification, pricing strategies, distribution tactics, and promotional strategies.

This information provides the basis for the sport company to define its product(s), make decisions concerning opportunities or threats, develop appropriate marketing plans, develop a successful product mix, and determine the right time for product differentiation and deletion.

One method of classifying products is based on the consumer. In this method, products are traditionally classified in two very broad categories: consumer products and business products. *Consumer products* are those products offered to the final consumer for personal or household use (Evans & Berman, 1987). *Business products* are those products offered to organizations for use in the production of other goods and services, in the operation of a business, or for resale to other consumers (Stanton et al., 1991).

This is especially evident in the sport industry because of the sheer size of the industry and the extent and diversity of products. There are both consumer products and business products. *Consumer products* in the sport industry include tangible goods, such as a softball bat, team uniforms, golf clubs, and a ski boat. There are consumer service products in the sport industry that may be classified into one of three categories: rented-goods service, owned-goods service, and nongoods service (Evans & Berman, 1987).

A rented-goods service is the renting of a product for a period of time. Some examples in the sport industry include the following: A fitness center rents a fitness video to clients; a tennis center rents tennis rackets to members; a tennis center rents court time; a park near a lake rents a jet ski on an hourly basis; a snow ski resort rents skis for a day or a week; a marina rents a houseboat for a weekend or for a week.

Owned-goods services include those services to repair or alter something that the consumer owns. Some examples of owned-goods services in the sport industry are replacing broken strings on a tennis racket; getting golf clubs cleaned at the club; getting numbers, names, and logos put on a softball uniform; having a boat's engine repaired; getting a wheelchair repaired in order to play in a basketball game.

Nongoods services do not involve a good at all. This category includes personal services offered by the seller. In the sport industry some examples include: tennis lessons, golf lessons, summer basketball camp, or child-care services offered by a fitness center. This category also includes those services offered by sport management or sport marketing companies that specialize in managing and/or marketing a sporting event for consumers. For example, you hire a sport marketing company to market and manage every aspect of a large marathon in your city.

Business products in the sport industry are those products offered to sport businesses for use in the manufacture of sport products, in operation of a sport business, or for resale. Hillerich & Bradsby, manufacturers of the famous Louisville Slugger bats, purchases wood as a material used to make wood baseball bats (Pitts & Fielding, 1987). A golf club manufacturer purchases graphite and other materials to produce golf clubs. A running shoe company purchases a variety of rubber, leather, and other materials in order to make running shoes. A bicycle manufacturer purchases aluminum to use in the manufacture of light-weight bicycles. If the sport marketer understands these types of classifications, the marketer will understand consumer type and what the consumer is looking for.

Industry Segmentation

Industry segmentation is another method used by marketers to classify products and buyers. *Industry segmentation* is defined by Porter (1985) as the division of an industry into subunits (industry segments) for purposes of developing competitive strategy. An *industry segment* is a combination of a product variety and a group of consumers who purchase it (Porter, 1985).

Some industries contain just one product. More typically, an industry contains a variety of product items sold to many existing or potential consumers who vary in many ways. The sport industry contains a wide variety of products offered to a great variety of consumers—final and business. Trying to keep up with every product in the sport industry would be practically impossible! It becomes important and even necessary that the sport marketer focus on a section or segment of the total industry. This guides the sport marketer in the identification of marketing opportunities and threats within a specific product market and in the development of an appropriate marketing mix (Day, Shocker & Srivastava, 1979; McCarthy & Perreault, 1990; Porter, 1985).

The Pitts, Fielding, & Miller Sport Industry Segmentation Model (1994) (presented in Figure 8.1) presents a new and unique study of products in the sport industry. The authors used a portion of the Porter (1985) model for industry segmentation and used product function and buyer types in segmenting the sport industry. Three sport product industry segments were identified. These are the sport performance segment, sport production segment, and sport promotion segment.

The information is important to the sport marketer in developing an understanding of the product segment within the sport industry in which the company's product(s) fits, identifying and monitoring the competition, and

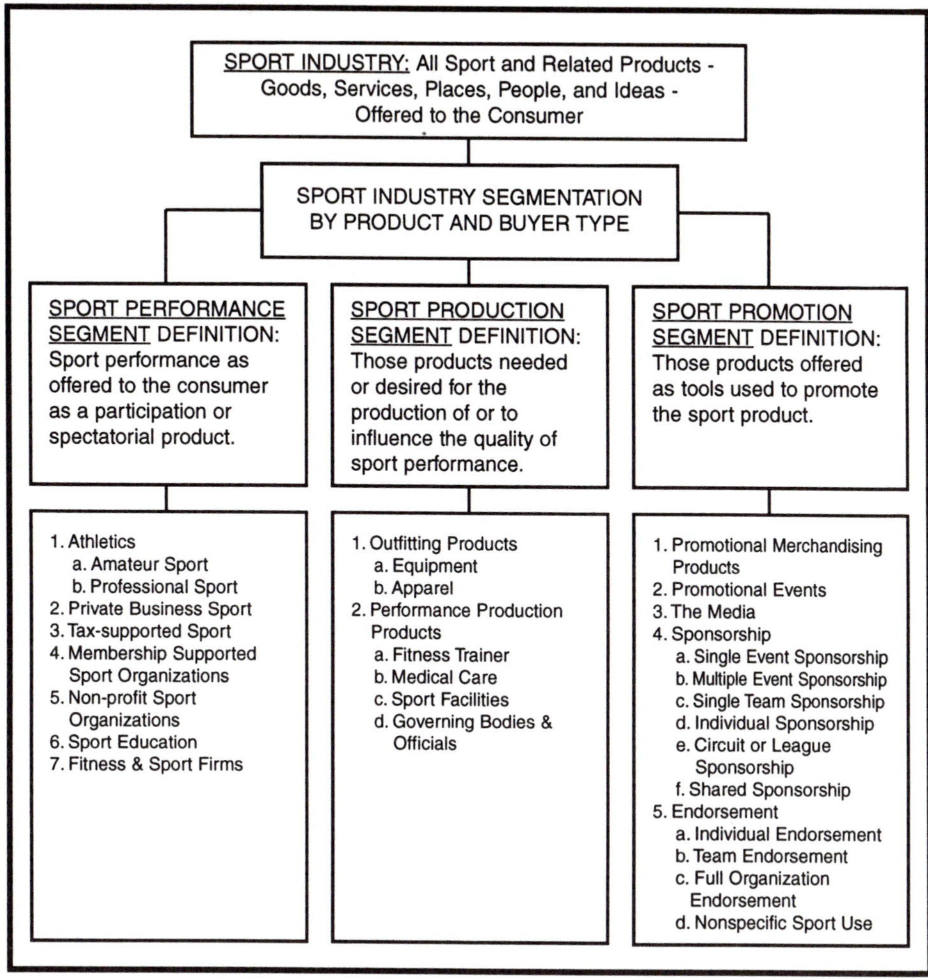

FIGURE 8.1 - The Sport Industry Segment Model
Source: Pitts, Fielding, & Miller, 1994

determining product management strategies (Figure 8.2).

The *sport performance industry segment* consists of sport performance as a product. Sport performance is offered to the consumer in two ways: as a participation product and as a spectatorial product. Each of these may even be considered separate segments as the marketing of participation and spectatatorial

THREE REASONS FOR UNDERSTANDING SPORT INDUSTRY SEGMENTS

1. TO UNDERSTAND THE COMPANY'S PRODUCT.
2. TO IDENTIFY AND MONITOR COMPETITORS.
3. TO DETERMINE PRODUCT MANAGEMENT STRATEGIES.

FIGURE 8.2 - Three Reasons for Understanding Sport Industry Segments

TABLE 8.3 - Examples of Products in the Sport Performance Industry Segment

SPORT PERFORMANCE INDUSTRY SEGMENT		
	PARTICIPATION	SPECTATORIAL
EXAMPLES OF:		
SETTING	Collegiate Athletics Pro Sports Recreation Leagues	Collegiate Athletics Pro Sports Recreation Leagues
FORMAT	League Event Tournament Lessons Clinic Rehabilitation Seminar Camp Lab Olympics Matches	Games/Matches/Meets Contest
MARKETS	By age groups By gender and mixed By race By disability By sexual orientation By religion By skill level	By age groups By gender By race By disability By sexual orientation By religion
FUNCTIONS & BENEFITS	Fun Fitness gain Skill development Knowledge gain Weight loss Competition Stress management Entertainment Rehabilitative	Entertainment Fun Stress management Activity Support

Source: Pitts, Fielding, & Miller, 1994

products is different. However, they were placed in one category due to their similarities in function and benefit (Pitts et al., 1994). Functions and benefits include working out, stress management, fun, activity, competition, and entertainment. Examples include basketball, hiking, boating, swimming, jogging, camping, Frisbee throwing, martial arts, and many, many more. These activities are offered in a variety of settings, to a variety of consumer markets, and in a variety of formats (a tournament, a league, a one-day event, a single event, a weekend event, lessons, clinics, seminars, and many more). Table 8.3 shows some examples of the variety of sport performance segment products.

As a spectatorial product, sport performance is offered primarily in two ways: attending a sport event and spectating via television or video. Sport spectating has changed dramatically over the last few decades. The spectator is offered plush skyboxes, restaurants, and even a hotel in the sport facility; entertainment before, during, and after the event; and even spectator participation events during the sport event. These have become an integral part of the sport event spectator's package (Pitts et al., 1994).

The *sport production industry segment* is defined as including those products necessary or desired for the production of or to influence the quality of sport performance (Pitts et al., 1994). Most sport participation requires specific equipment and apparel before it can be properly performed. The equipment and apparel afford the production of the sport performance. Further, in an effort to enhance performance, specific products or services may be desired. This creates a demand for a variety of products and product quality for the production of sport and to enhance the quality of performance (Pitts et al., 1994). For example, Martina Navratilova can probably play tennis with any tennis racket. However, she prefers custom-designed rackets in order to enhance performance. She also purchases a number of other products that influence her tennis performance, such as a personal fitness trainer, weight-training equipment, a sports medicine person, sports medicine equipment and supplies, and a professional tennis coach. Figure 8.4 presents examples of products in the sport production industry segment.

The *sport promotion industry segment* is defined as those products used in the promotion of sport industry products (Pitts et al., 1994). Refer to Figure 8.5 for examples of products in the sport promotion industry segment. For example, college basketball can exist without promotion. However, promotional tactics can increase attendance and result in partial funding of the program. The competitors in all segments of the industry use a variety of promotional products and

1. Sport-specific equipment
2. Safety & protective equipment
3. Apparel: clothing, shoes
4. Facility
5. Performance enhancing products:
   - personal fitness trainer
   - fitness equipment
   - sports medicine care, equipment, & supplies
   - coaches
   - other staff
6. Governing organizations:
   - rules committees
   - officials: referees, umpires
   - governing associations
   - statisticians
   - scorekeepers, announcers, & other officials

FIGURE 8.4 - The Sport Production Industry Segment Examples

Source: Pitts, Fielding, & Miller, 1994

1. Promotional Merchandise: Merchandise with a logo might include caps, cups, key chains, bumper stickers, decals, mugs, hats, T-shirts, dress shirts, ties, napkins, sweaters, jackets, clocks, shorts, sweatshirts & pants, blankets, stadium seats, pencil holders, stationery, pens & pencils, and checks.

2. Promotional Events: offering an event or activity along with a main sport event to bring attention to the product. Examples include holding a Beach Boys Concert after a major league baseball game; offering a golf tournament to promote pre-game, half-time, and post-game events that surround the Super Bowl.

3. The Media: the media provide vast exposure for some segments of the sport industry. Sport marketers negotiate with television, radio, and print media for coverage of sporting events. The coverage promotes the sport event.

4. Sponsorship: Sponsorship is a two-way promotional tool. The sponsorship company provides funding for a sport event which is a form of advertising for the company. Sport marketers use the funding to produce and manage the event. The company providing funding gains exposure & promotional benefits. Examples include almost all college football bowl games; many of the women's and men's professional golf tournaments; the auto racing industry; the Olympics, Special Olympics, the Gay Games, and the Maccabiah Games.

5. Endorsement: Similar to sponsorship, endorsement is also a two-way promotional tool in the sport industry. Some examples include, Mary Lou Retton's picture on Wheaties cereal boxes which suggests her endorsement of that product; Michael Jordan's endorsement of Nike products.

FIGURE 8.5 - The Sport Promotion Industry Segment Examples
Source: Pitts, Fielding, & Miller, 1994

techniques. This creates a demand for promotional products, events, methods and people who specialize in promotion, marketing, public relations, and other related areas.

With a thorough understanding of the sport company's product, the sport marketer increases chances for successful sport product management strategies. However, sport products come and go. Sometimes, the product can be labeled a fad. In other cases, the product was simply not a good idea. If the sport marketer can identify the success level of a product, decisions can be determined that may save the life of the product or, at a minimum, save the company. This product analysis is called the product life cycle.

The Sport Product Life Cycle

Just as people go through changes and stages throughout their lifetimes, so do products. A person is born and goes through childhood, adolescence, young adulthood, adulthood, middle age, the senior citizen stage, and eventually death. A product begins life as an idea. It is then introduced onto the market, experiences a period of growth, a time of maturity, and even will decline and be taken off the market. One major difference between the person's stages and the product's stages is this: The person's stages may be measured using years of age. Death is certain. Although a product's stages may be measured using several factors, two of which are sales and profits, the amount of time in each stage can vary markedly. For example, a human's life span is estimated at approximately 74 years, whereas a product's time on the market can range from just a few short days to hundreds of years (for example, religion).

The product life cycle is a concept popularized by Theodore Levitt in 1965 (Levitt, 1965). It is a way to define and understand a product's sales, profits, consumer markets, product markets, and marketing strategies from the inception of the product until it is removed from the market. Studying your company's products and understanding the product life cycle stage in which each product qualifies are imperative to planning marketing strategies. Studying, understanding, and managing products and their life cycle stages can have considerable influence on the success of a company.

Through research it is known that (a) product lives are shorter now than in the past; (b) higher investment is now required for new products; (c) the marketer may use the product life cycle to adjust marketing strategies; and (d) the marketer may strategically establish a more successful product mix in relation to the product life cycle concept—planning to establish products in each stage of the cycle so that, as one product declines, another product is introduced. As an example, let us look at fitness centers.

In the 1960s and early 1970s, fitness centers were known as health spas. The typical spa offered only a few products: a small weight room, a small pool, rolling machines, and locker rooms with a sauna and steam room. Typically, no exercise classes were offered as the "instructors" were hired only to look good and sell memberships. With the "fitness boom" of the late 1970s, a new crop of fitness centers sprang onto the market, and existing spas found themselves in the decline stage of the product life cycle. The new health-conscious consumer wanted more, and the new companies jumped into the fitness product market offering much more in their facilities. Some of the existing spas changed while some did not. Those that did not eventually lost out to the new multipurpose fitness centers.

Today's fitness centers offer a much greater product mix. In most you will find a very large weight room, large pool, indoor running track, and a variety of exercise classes, such as aerobics classes, swimming or pool exercise classes, fitness and nutrition classes. There usually will be a few sports, such as tennis, racquetball, wallyball, volleyball, or basketball. The locker rooms are large, clean, and airy with a full service of towels, shampoo, hair dryers, toothbrushes and toothpaste, and deodorants. One also finds plush carpeting, beautiful lockers, and big-screen television sets complete with a VCR for your convenience in viewing specific video tape recordings also supplied by the center. In addition, you will probably find nice, large jacuzzis, saunas, and steam rooms. There will often be a number of other services, such as a child-care service (sometimes a child-size fitness center itself), laundry service, full clothing services, sporting goods and apparel shops, restaurant and lounge, and a small business office area (complete with phone, computer, and facsimile and copy machines) so the member can conduct business functions while at the center.

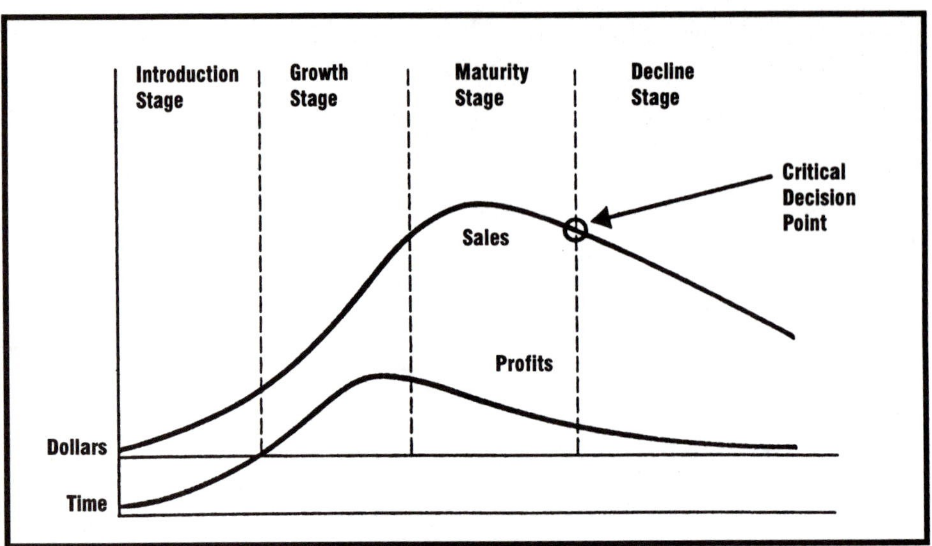

FIGURE 8.6 - The Product Life Cycle Stages

Stages Of The Product Life Cycle

The stages of the product life cycle are introduction, growth, maturity, and decline. The stages are shown in Figure 8.6. Sport management executives or marketers must be able to recognize in which stage of the product life cycle a product is at any given time. This determination will affect marketing strategy decisions.

The introduction stage is the period of time when a sport product is put on the market (offered to the consumer) for the first time. During this period of time, it is most likely that no one knows the product exists. The sport marketer must promote aggressively to make channelers, if existing, and the consumer aware of the product. Promotions stress information about the product, its features, and, perhaps most important, what the product does (or does for the consumer). Typically, sales are practically zero and profits are negative. The sport company has invested in manufacturing and promoting the product but has not begun to receive profits from sales. The product that is offered is one that probably went through many stages of refinement, such as idea generation, research and development, test marketing, and pilot trials. Investment during this period of time, for some products, may reach into the millions of dollars.

As Figure 8.6 indicates, sales are low and losses of profits are common. There is also a high percentage of product failure during this stage. The sport company may have the marketing research showing that there is a market for this product, but when the product finally hits the marketplace many things could have happened: The market may be no longer interested; needs or wants may have changed; or another company may have been first to the market and have established share. The sport company must promote aggressively during this stage to create demand for the product.

As demand for the sport product begins to develop and the product begins to sell, it enters into the next stage in the product life cycle, the growth stage. As Figure 8.6 indicates, it is during this stage that sales and profits rapidly and steadily increase. Although sales and profits may soar, the company may still be in danger. It is during this stage that competitors will enter the product market with identical or similar products. This competition will drive prices down and profits will decline. Aggressive pricing promotions, adjustments in costs, legal action against imitators, and other marketing strategies will help to stabilize profits.

After the bumpy road, the sport product may finally reach the maturity stage. It may have found a steady place in the market. However, during this stage, there still are many competitors and this keeps prices low, which keeps sales and profits down. It is also during this period of time that the product has been changed enough to finally meet the consumer's needs. Every company making the sport product has most likely discovered the successful product, price, and other marketing stategies that keep the product selling. Differences among competing products diminishes. It is at this point, however, that companies will begin to promote any difference in their product that they believe will gain some market advantage. Usually, pricing wars begin and continue until one or more companies are driven out of the particular product market. Critical marketing decisions must be made at this point.

During the decline stage, sales fall rapidly. There may be many reasons, some of which are new products on the market, a shift in trend, or new technology. Now the sport marketer is faced with the decision of terminating production of the sport product or making changes, sometimes drastic, to revive it. Of course, the sport marketer may also wait and see which companies drop out of the market. This can be a successful strategy because if a large number drop out, a company may become one of a few making the product and the cycle can be stopped. This tactic is risky as always when one plays a wait-and-see game.

It must be understood that each stage can be of varying lengths for any given product. The challenge to the sport marketer is to be able to recognize each product's life-cycle stage and make marketing decisions accordingly. For example, let us say that you are the manager/marketer for a multisport club. You are experiencing an unusually sharp decline in participants in the adult tennis leagues. Upon investigation, you find that most of those clients are now playing tennis at a different club because it is now offering child-care services any time it is open. You are faced with a decision: Make a change in what you offer or accept the loss of consumers to another company.

Table 8.7 shows a variety of examples of sport products in various product life-cycle stages.

The Product Mix And Product Management

Product management and product mix are critical elements of a sport company's business plan and marketing strategy. It is the sale of products and

TABLE 8.7 - Examples of some Sport Products in the Product Life-Cycle Stages

	PARTICIPANT SPORT ACTIVITY	SPORTING EQUIPMENT/CLOTHING	SPORT OFFERED AS ENTERTAINMENT (SPECTATOR PRODUCT)
INTRODUCTION STAGE	• snowboarding	• graphite composite softball bats	• men's professional soccer • women's professional boxing
GROWTH STAGE	• in-line skating	• in-line skates	• women's & men's professional beach volleyball • women's collegiate basketball • Women's professional golf
MATURITY STAGE	• softball • volleyball	• aluminum softball bats • spandex clothing	• men's professional baseball, basketball, football
DECLINE STAGE	• racquetball • boating • field hockey	• single-gear bicycle	

services that makes a company successful or may bring about failure.

Product mix is the complete set of all products that the sport company offers to the consumer. It consists of all of the company's product lines and all related services. A collegiate athletic program offers 12 women's and men's sports and promotional merchandise. A sporting goods manufacturer offers 10 different sport equipment products. The local fitness center offers a variety of fitness- and sport-related products, which include a full range of exercise classes, tennis classes and leagues, volleyball leagues, swimming classes and open swim time, a clothing and sporting goods shop, child-care services, equipment repair, laundry service, towel service, a restaurant and lounge, and many others.

The product mix may be measured by its product lines and items. A product line is a set of closely related products. For example, as Table 8.8 shows, a fitness center offers fitness, sport, clothing, and equipment as four of its product lines. Within each product line, there are product items. A product item is a specific product within a product line. Aerobics classes are a product item in the fitness center's fitness product line. Tennis, volleyball, and swimming are product lines. Each of these may consist of a variety of classes, leagues, and other items. In another example, a sporting goods manufacturer offers three product lines: softball equipment, baseball equipment, and tennis equipment. The softball equipment line consists of a variety of items: bats, gloves, batting gloves, softballs, and equipment bags. In a different example, a professional golf league offers two lines: watching golf and souvenir merchandise.

The product mix of a sport company may be described by its width, depth, and consistency. Width refers to the number of product lines offered. Depth refers to

TABLE 8.8 - Examples of Product Mix, Lines, and Items in the Sport Industry

SPORT COMPANY	PRODUCT ASSORTMENT (MIX)	PRODUCT LINE	PRODUCT ITEMS OFFERED IN THE PRODUCT LINE
FITNESS CENTER	Fitness Weight loss Restaurant and Lounge Aerobics Weight training Tanning Massage Testing-fitness; Cholesterol Sports leagues; Tennis, Volleyball, Swimming Pro shop	Aerobics classes	low-impact aerobics kid aerobics elderrobics advanced aerobics
		Weight training	body building free weight training sport-specific strength events
		Tennis	classes beginners' league intermediate leagues advanced leagues club tourney
COLLEGE ATHLETICS	Women's sports Men's sports	Women's individual sports	track field swimming cross-country tennis
		Women's team sports	basketball volleyball soccer
SPORTING GOODS MANUFACTURER	Golf equipment Tennis equipment	Golf	golf clubs golf balls golf umbrellas
		Tennis	tennis rackets tennis string tennis balls tennis ball retriever

Source: Pitts, Fielding, & Miller, 1994

the number of items within a line. Consistency refers to the similarity of product lines. The fitness center has a narrow width, for it offers product lines that are primarily of a fitness or sport nature. There is a wide variety of products offered

1. Classes Segmented By:	Age Groups Skill Levels
2. Instruction:	Individual Lessons Lessons for Doubles Play
3. Leagues Segmented By:	Skill Levels: beginners to advanced Gender: women's, men's, mixed
4. Clinics, Seminars:	For coaching, for individuals, for play strategy, for rules knowledge
5. Tournaments:	- Intramural - Extramural

FIGURE 8.9 - The Center's Tennis Line

within each, which means that the fitness center may be described as having depth. For example, the tennis line contains the following items: (a) classes: classes for age groups of 5 - 7 years old, 8 - 12, 13 - 15, 16 - 18, 19 -21, 22 - 25, 26 - 30, and in 5-year increments after; (b) classes for skill levels: beginner, intermediate, and advanced; (c) individual instruction; (d) leagues consisting of the following categories: skill groups ranging from beginner through advanced and within each are categories for women, men, and coed singles, and women, men, and coed doubles (see Figure 8.9). There may most likely be other items, such as special clinics or seminars, league tournaments, special tournaments, and competition with another center. The fitness center would be considered consistent as its product mix is focused on products of a similar nature.

Product management probably presents the major challenge facing the sport company. Products are what a company produces, if the company is a manufacturer, or what a company selects and buys, if the company is a wholesaler or retailer, in order to fulfill needs and desires of consumers. Effective management of the product is crucial to success. The remaining sections of this chapter are devoted to product management strategies.

Product management involves deciding which products to offer, what type of a product line to carry, when to keep or delete a product, when to add new products, and other product management strategies. In marketing terms, this includes managing the product life cycle, product positioning, new product development, product diversification, line extension, product identification, and product deletion. Decisions concerning these areas make up product mix strategies.

Product positioning involves trying to position a product appropriately in the market. A product's position is the image or perception that the consumer holds about the product's attributes, quality, uses, and other functions as these compare to other similar products. As was pointed out in the opening paragraphs of this chapter, a consumer does not simply purchase a product. The consumer wants to satisfy needs or desires. Products perform as the satisfaction agent.

Consumer perceptions are measured through marketing research. The research will show what the consumer thinks about a product and how it compares to another company's product. This information is important in making changes to the product or to the image of the product.

New product development as a strategy is the addition of a new product to a company's product line. There are many reasons a company might consider developing a new product including a need to stimulate sales, a desire to capture a new consumer need, a desire to improve the company's reputation, or a desire to expand.

There are consistently new products in the sport industry. In chapter 1 we discussed many factors that have positively influenced the growth and development of the sport industry. Some of those factors are the consistent offering of new sports, new activities, new leagues, new sport organizations for all populations, and new sport equipment. There are, perhaps, more sport equipment and clothing products than sports when considering that most sport activities require more than one piece of equipment, special clothing, and footwear per participant.

In the sport industry, it can be quite confusing when trying to determine which comes first: the sport or the equipment. In some cases, ideas for a new sport develop first. James Naismith developed some rules for a new sport and used a soccer ball. That sport today is basketball and requires very different equipment than was first used.

Every year the Sporting Goods Manufacturers Association (SGMA) convenes its "Super Show, a giant four-day sports gear bazaar" (Hiestand, 1992). There were approximately 85,000 sporting goods retailers, manufacturers, and buyers at the 1992 show in Atlanta, Georgia (Strauss, 1992). About 800 entrepreneurs were in the show's section for new products. That represents a fourfold increase over new products in the 1990 show (Hiestand, 1992). The new products varied in function and consumer market for whom the product was targeted. Some of the new products there included microwavable and freezable bandannas (for climate adjustment); an attachment for a hair dryer that dried ski boots and sneakers and cost around $15; and, for a mere $10,000 a "health environment capsule" that would provide "ionized air, brain wave stimulus and aroma therapy" (Hiestand, 1992, p. 3C).

Of course, not every new product introduced is successful. As a matter of fact, most new products fail. The failure rate is estimated to range between 33% and 90% (Peter & Donnelly, 1991). Companies spend tremendous amounts of money during the process to get a new product to the market. There are many elements involved in new product development. Some ideas require years of research that can involve scientists, technology, testing, manufacture of the new product, and promotion. However, with all the money and time invested in producing the new product, there is no guarantee that the product will sell.

There are some common reasons that new product offerings fail. The primary reason is failure to match the product to the consumer's needs (Peter & Donnelly, 1991). If the product will not do what the consumer wants, the consumer will not buy it. Further, this may be the result of poor consumer research, the company's failure to stick to what it does best, and failure to provide a better product at a better value than that of the competition (Peter & Donnelly, 1991).

Good product management and planning can increase the chances of new product success. As was pointed out in chapter 5, "Sport Marketing Research and Segmentation," and earlier in this chapter, information and research are primary keys in making decisions.

As pointed out earlier, there are many reasons a company offers a new product. Sometimes, a new product is not a brand-new product. It is a product that has been modified in some way as a means of offering a differentiated product or an improved product. For example, consider the variety of aerobics-type classes offered today. Some examples are hard aerobics, soft aerobics, waterobics, elderobics, jazzercise, and step-aerobics. All of these are not brand-new products.

1. A product that performs an entirely new function.
2. A product that offers improved performance of an existing function.
3. A product that offers a new application of an existing one.
4. A product that offers additional functions over an existing product.
5. An existing product that is offered to a new consumer market.
6. A product that is offered at a lower cost to attract new buyers.
7. A product offered as "upgraded" or an existing product integrated into another product.
8. A downgraded product or the use of less expensive parts or components in the manufacture of a product.
9. A restyled product.

FIGURE 8.10 - Nine Ways to offer a New Product
Source: Peter & Donnelly, 1991

Rather, they are a variation of the original aerobics product. In another example, arena football (football played in a small, indoor field with fewer players and a variety of rule modifications) might be considered a brand-new product because it is different from the original football sport. However, it is a variation of the original product. It is marketed as a different product—different from the regular 11-player game.

How many ways might one offer a new product? There are at least nine (Peter & Donnelly, 1991). Following are the nine ways with examples in the sport industry (also see Figure 8.10):

(1) A product that performs an entirely new function. When the snow mobile was introduced it performed a new function: motorized transportation across snow covered areas in a small personal-sized vehicle.

(2) A product that offers improved performance of an existing function. As an example, consider the introduction of new materials for wheelchairs. Aluminum and other composite materials offer the possiblity for wheelchairs to be light and durable. This provides wheelchair athletes the capability to enhance performance in athletic feats.

(3) A product that offers a new application of an existing one. Personal water crafts (more commonly known as the jet ski) were first introduced to be used as a recreational vehicle, a new toy for play on the water. Today, personal water crafts are used by police, emergency water rescue services, and coast guard operations for law enforcement, safety, and rescue functions.

(4) A product that offers additional functions over an existing product. In one example, a fitness center may offer more sports and services than another fitness center, thereby offering more functions to the consumer. In another example, weight-training equipment, one product is a single unit that allows the consumer to perform up to 12 exercises whereas another product is a single unit that offers only one exercise.

(5) An existing product that is offered to a new consumer market. This may be done either by repositioning the product or offering the product in new markets (market development). In an example of the latter, the National Football League (NFL) is trying to gain market development by offering its product—football games—in European and Asian countries.

(6) A product that attracts new buyers by offering a lower cost. When a new material is used for golf clubs, the existing clubs may be offered at a lower cost. Softball bats are offered in a wide range of prices. A fitness center may offer special priced memberships to first-time consumers for a limited period of time.

(7) A product offered as "upgraded" or an existing product integrated into another product. In one example, fitness centers offer a variety of possibilities for "upgrading" a consumer's membership. The consumer may purchase one level of membership with the possibility of "upgrading" it to another level. In another example, computers have been integrated into a variety of sport equipment as a method of "upgrading" the equipment. Playing a round of golf indoors in a small room is possible with the use of a computerized golf course system. Through the use of video, screens, displays, sensors, and other equipment, the consumer uses real golf clubs and golf balls to play a round of 9 or 18 holes of golf without stepping a foot outdoors.

(8) A downgraded product or the use of less expensive parts or components in the manufacture of a product. Many sporting goods and equipment manufacturers use plastics and other less expensive materials, parts, or

MARKETS	PRODUCTS	
	Present	New
Present	Market Penetration	Product Development
New	Market Development	Diversification

FIGURE 8.11 - Growth Vector Components
Source: Ansoff, 1965

components in their products. This changes the cost to produce the product and is sometimes promoted to the consumer as "new low price" or "we pass the savings on to the consumer" item.

(9) A restyled product. Examples include the almost annual changes in sport clothing, running shoes, and other sporting equipment.

In another approach to offering new products, Ansoff (1965) developed growth vectors, which are used by most businesses today (see Figure 8.11). These are product strategies involving present or new consumer markets and present or new products and include market penetration, market development, new product development, and product diversification. *Market penetration* is a strategy in which a company tries to sell more of its present products to its present consumer markets. *Market development* is a strategy in which a company tries to sell its present products to new consumer markets. *New product development* is the creation of new products. *Product diversification* is a strategy in which new products are added in an attempt to meet the needs of new consumer markets.

New Product Development Planning And Process

How does a sport company organize for new product development? The type of company and the products it offers will influence the eventual organization, planning, and process the company will use to develop new products. A fitness center that offers a variety of products must make a decision concerning the addition of new products, such as new sports, fitness activities, or even new tennis clothing in the pro shop. A tennis racket manufacturer will study the possibility and feasibility of manufacturing a new tennis racket. These are different types of companies: One is a manufacturer and the other a retailer. However, each must have and manage a new product development process. The process will involve hours and sometimes years of analyzing information concerning factors, such as consumer markets and product markets, cost of producing the product, cost to the consumer, the capability of the company to produce the product, distribution possibilities and cost, as well as promotion possibilities and cost.

Consider another and very different example: the National Basketball Association (NBA). For the NBA, a new product might be an additional team to the league or a modification of the rules of the game of basketball. The addition of a new team to the league requires analyzing consumer markets and product markets, production (start-up) costs, price (ticket prices) to the consumer, and many other decision factors. Modifying, adding, or deleting rules can change the game—the product—dramatically.

There have been many modifications to the game of basketball since it was invented. Some of those changes were instituted specifically to make the game more attractive to the consumer. For example, dunking was not allowed until the late 1970s primarily for safety reasons: Rims and backboards were not made for dunking and would break. Another reason was that the dunk was not considered to be a skill! A stiff penalty was levied against a player who dunked either during the warm-up period before a game or during a game: The player was ejected from the game. Dunking became a tactic. Coaches realized that a dunk motivated the team and excited the crowd. Specific players were instructed to dunk at key moments: during the warm-up period before the game or during the game. It was not long before coaches, athletic directors, and others involved in selling the game realized that the crowds loved to see someone dunk the ball. Soon the rules were changed, and rims and backboards were modified to be safe for dunking. The

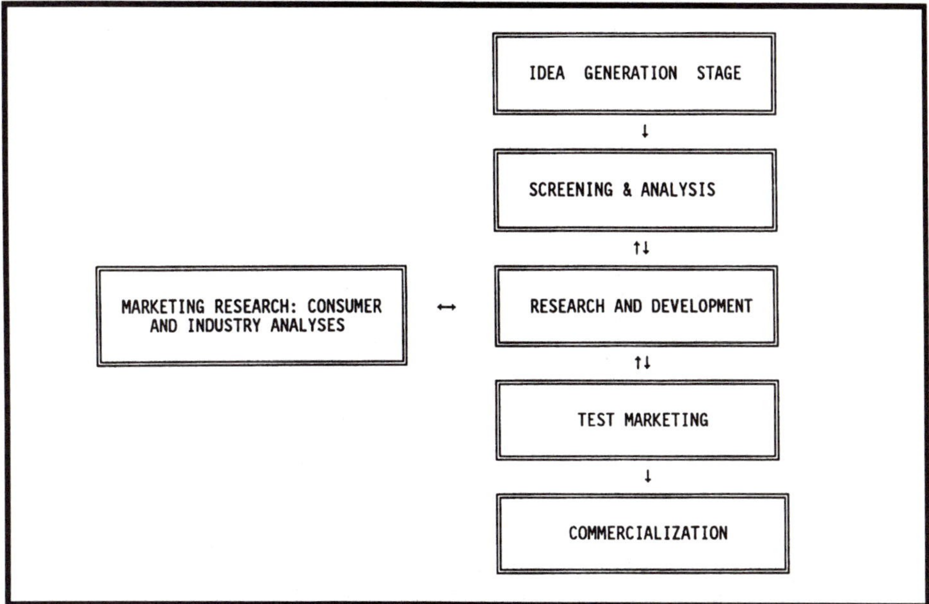

FIGURE 8.12 - Stages in New Product Development Process

dunk changed the game. Today there are even slam-dunking contests with large amounts of money, prizes, and titles involved.

Stages In The New Product Development Process

There are some common stages in the new product development process within most companies. These are idea generation, screening and analysis, product research and development, test marketing, and commercialization (Boone & Kurtz, 1989; Peter & Donnelly, 1991; Stanton et al., 1991). Figure 8.12 represents the stages within a new product development process a sport company might utilize.

The idea generation stage involves generating ideas for new products, product modification, or other types of product change ideas. This should involve information received through the company's marketing research concerning the consumer and product markets. Ideas may come from a multitude of sources. If the company has the resources, it may contain a product research and development department, commonly known around the company as the "R & D" department. It is the responsibility of the "R & D" people to generate product ideas, research them, and present feasible product ideas to company management. In other companies, product ideas must originate from various employees. In either situation, the company management must create an atmosphere that supports idea generation. In some companies incentives are offered for those employees whose ideas eventually result in a successful product. Eventually, a decision will be made to take the next step and study the feasibility of a product.

The next stage is product screening and analysis. This involves determining the feasibility of a product. This process includes determining if a product could be marketed profitably by the company, if the product fits with the company's mission, if the company has all the necessary resources or technology, or if it might be beneficial to form partnerships with other companies. Based on the conclusions drawn from the research, a decision will be made, and the product could move into the next stage.

In the product research and development stage, product ideas with potential are converted. The type of product and its conceived functions determine the type of testing. If the product is a tangible item, a model can be produced. The model will undergo a number of tests in an effort to develop the best possible product.

Type of product requires further discussion here because there are many different types of products in the sport industry. Remember our definition of product earlier in the chapter. Product is a concept that includes goods, services, people, places, and ideas. Also, remember that consumers are looking for a specific function—what the product will do. With this in mind, let us consider examples of each type of product and how it may be developed through testing.

Tangible Good. Softball bats provide a good example. The research and development department in a bat manufacturing company is considering the idea that aluminum might be a good material for bats. The purpose or function of a bat is to hit a softball. However, what the softball player wants is a bat that will hit a softball farther, consistently, and with control. The question, then, the company should consider is this: Will an aluminum bat meet those needs? Other questions are: Can aluminum bats be made?, What kind of aluminum can be used?, How much will it cost the company?, What kind of machinery and other equipment are needed to construct an aluminum bat?, Where might the company get the aluminum?, Will the aluminum bat function?, How can it be tested?, What will the consumer think about the idea of an aluminum bat?, Will the consumer accept—and purchase—a bat made of metal instead of wood?, Are any other companies considering making aluminum bats?, If not, can this company possibly be the first with this product?

If most of these questions can be answered positively, the company's next move is to produce some bats made of aluminum and test them in the company's laboratories. A variety of aluminum would be used in a variety of models. The bats would be put through a battery of tests. The company could also test the models by providing them to some softball players, teams, and leagues. The company would follow the players throughout the league and receive feedback from them. The information is used to make changes in the bat until reaching a point at which the players seem to be satisfied with the performance of one or more models. Further test marketing would include placing the bat on the market in a region and waiting for the results. If specific outcomes are reached the company would consider going into full-time production, getting the bats into more markets, and going into full promotion status.

Service product. The testing of a service product could follow this process. A fitness instructor at a fitness center overhears customers discussing why the center does not offer child-care services. The customers say that they would come to the center more often if they did not have to spend the extra amount of time, effort, and money finding a sitter. The instructor thinks providing a child-care service might be a good idea and takes it to the center's manager. The manager also thinks it might be a good idea and organizes a committee, headed by the instructor, to study the idea. The committee, after studying the idea and surveying their members, concludes that the center has the space needed, and could charge a small fee to cover the addition of an employee to manage the child-care center, and that the fitness center ought to offer the service for at least 6 months to test the idea.

Person. What might a company do if the company's products are people? As an example, consider a sport marketing and management company that specializes in managing and promoting professional athletes. The company's task is to try to find the best contracts and jobs for the athletes. The company uses the athletic and personal characteristics of the athlete as selling points. When the company considers the addition of a new product (adding another athlete) to its line of products (athletes already on contract) it will research many factors. Some of these factors are popularity of the individual, consumer markets (the variety and extent of demand for the athlete), cost to the company, and possible profitability. Further, the company might add the athlete for a one-year trial basis (test marketing).

Place. When the product is a place, research and development are contingent on factors such as the type of place (facility) and whether or not it exists. Let us look at an example of a facility that does not exist. The local state university has announced that it would like to have a new facility to house the women's and men's basketball and volleyball teams. The programs are very successful and have been nationally ranked in the top 25 for over 8 years. The existing facility was built in 1936. The process for determining the feasibility of this product can be very complicated. The university is a state-supported institution, which means that tax dollars are involved. The process might include the development of a committee to study the idea. The committee needs to gather information, such as facility needs, the cost of such a facility, current and potential resources, availability of space (land), ticket price structure, possible users of the facility, uses of the facility, expenses involved, and consumer surveys. This will involve working with contractors, architects, the state education department, state government, and many others. The committee could perform all the research or hire a marketing company to do the work. In this type of situation the university usually hires a marketing company to do the research. They should be careful to hire a marketing company with experience in the sport industry and with specific experience in sport facilities and sport facility research.

When the testing is complete and test results yield information, conclusions may be drawn about the product. The information from the research will guide decisions pertaining to moving to the next stage.

The test marketing stage is the next step in the new product development process. Test marketing involves selecting a specific market area in which to offer the product. It is usually offered with a specialized marketing campaign. The primary reason for test marketing is to determine how the product performs in a real market. In selecting the test market area, some factors to consider are size, control of selected promotional media, cost, the consumer markets, and the product markets.

A sports wheelchair manufacturing company has developed a wheelchair for basketball. The company offers the chairs in two large cities (test markets). The company's plan is to promote the wheelchairs in the two cities for a one-year period. If the wheelchair sells well in the two test markets, the company will expand to more large city areas.

You may decide to skip this stage as it can be very expensive. The decision to skip test marketing should be based on the conclusion that the new product has a very high possibility of selling and success.

The final stage is commercialization. Full marketing strategies are planned, and the entire company gets ready to make the necessary adjustments for the new product. Complete business and marketing plans are developed, implementation plans are identified, plans for production are developed, personnel considerations are established, and promotional efforts are determined. The product is finished and goes on the market.

Each sport company should organize its new product development process and attempt to manage the process for success. Management must remember, however, the high rate of unsuccessful new products and make a commitment to support the investment necessary for new product development.

Product Identification

Product identification involves establishing an identity for the product through the use of some identifying device. The primary purpose of product identification is to differentiate your product from other relatively homogeneous products. It also may be used as a strategy to increase the strength of the company or product image; to establish or to use an established reputation; and to facilitate market and product development strategies.

The most commonly used methods of product identification are branding and packaging. Branding is accomplished through the use of a brand, brand name, or trademark.

A *brand* is a name, symbol, term, or design intended for the identification the products of a seller (Bennett, 1988). It may consist of any combination of a name, word, letter, number, design, symbol, and color. A brand name is the word, letter, or number that can be vocalized (Stanton et al., 1991). The symbol, design or coloring is the brand mark. It can be recognized by sight and not expressed vocally. For example, the brand mark of Nike includes the word Nike and a mark that looks like a well-rounded checkmark. Nike calls it a "swoosh." One would never know that the symbol actually has an identifying name, however, until looking into Nike's legal papers that describe the Nike brand name and mark. It is at this point that the brand name and mark may become what is commonly called a trademark. The trademark is essentially a legal term. It is a brand that has legal protection; that is, it is protected from being used by other companies (see chapter 15). Why would a company want to use another company's trademark instead of developing its own identity? The reason is to confuse and trick the consumer. The consumer purchases the product thinking that the product is from a well-known company. What the consumer actually purchased is a copy—an imitation of another company's product. These products have become known as the "clones." For example, the consumer sees a mark that looks like the NIKE swoosh on a pair of sneakers. The consumer purchases the product because the price is very low (compared to the price for the real Nike product) and believes it is a deal too good to pass. In reality, the consumer has purchased an imitation product.

Success in branding lies in selecting a good brand name and mark. The company should select something that is short, easy to pronounce and spell, that suggests something about the product, and that is unique. Other factors to be considered are ethics, market segments, and current events. A company can do harm to its image and its product if its brand name or mark is insensitive to cultures, populations, or specific current events. For example, in 1993 Converse intended to release a basketball shoe called the "Run 'N Gun" until community groups in Boston, where Converse is located, protested the implications of the name. The name is derived from a basketball term used to describe a specific type of play. The protesting groups, however, pointed out that in today's society the word gun means a gun. Further, youths have actually been robbed and even murdered for their clothing and popular name brand shoes. Converse, recognizing its responsibility to young people, impending bad press, and a possible boycott, decided to change the name of the shoe. Its new name is "Run 'N Slam" (Moore, 1993).

There are three levels through which a consumer might progress in relation to branding. These are brand recognition, brand preference, and brand insistence. In the first level, brand recognition, a consumer is only aware of the existence of a particular brand. At the second level, brand preference, the consumer has developed a preference for a specific brand and will select it for purchase over other brands. At the third level, brand insistence, the consumer will purchase no brand over a specific selected one. It is, of course, the third level that is the goal of most companies. The third level, however, is difficult to achieve due to the speed at which competitors can enter the market.

Packaging is the activity of enclosing a product. It involves designing and enclosing the product in some type of package or container in an attempt to differentiate the product from others. In addition, the package should protect the product, should be a convenient size, easy to open, attractive so that it can be used as a promotional tool, and honest. While the sport marketer has many decisions to make concerning packaging, information guiding these decisions must also include consumer data. Because design and package costs are included in the final price of the product to the consumer, the marketer must know the price that a consumer is willing to pay for the product. Final decisions on packaging usually mean compromise when final cost becomes a major factor.

In the sport industry, there are products for which packaging takes on a slightly different meaning. Sport marketers have developed a way to "package" sporting activity events in an attempt to make the event more attractive to a greater diversity of consumer segments. "Packaging" a sport event involves enveloping the event with an array of activities, benefits, and products. In one example, sport marketers trying to sell season tickets to collegiate basketball games will create a variety of "ticket packages." The lowest cost season-ticket package might contain just the tickets and nothing else. The highest cost ticket package might include VIP valet parking, no parking fee, seats on or near the half-court line, admission to a pre-game and half-time reception, admission to a postgame party with the coach, and admission to the end-of-the-year banquet.

One of the shortest events in sports is surrounded by a month of activities. The event is a racing event over a distance of one mile and a quarter ("Derby winners 1875 to 1992," 1993). The race lasts just a few seconds over 2 minutes! The event is the Kentucky Derby—a horse race. The Derby's first race was in 1875, and since that time it has grown into a major money sport event with an attendance of over 120,000 (McMasters, 1993). In 1971, there were 12 events and activities surrounding the Derby (Harris, 1993). In 1993, there were 63 official Kentucky Derby Festival events and activities and countless unofficial events, parties, socials, and other activities. Of the 63 events, 12 were sports events. These included the following:

- the Derby Festival Budweiser $1 Million Dollar Hole-In-One Golf Contest
- the Derby Festival Thunderball University of Louisville Spring Scrimmage
- Derby Festival Miller Lite Volleyball Classic (sand volleyball)
- the McDonald's Derby Festival Basketball Classic Night of the Future Stars
- the Derby Festival Great Balloon Race
- the 20th Annual Derby Festival Mini-Marathon
- the 20th Derby Festival Bodybuilding Extravaganza
- the 20th McDonald's Derby Festival Basketball Classic

- the 13th Derby Festival American Life Soccer Tournament
- the Derby Festival Bass Classic
- the Derby Festival USAC Midget Auto Races
- the Derby Festival Fightmaster Golf Tournament for Exceptional Children
- the Derby Festival Miller Lite Pro Beach Volleyball Exhibition
- the Derby Festival Pro-Am Golf Tournament
- the Derby Festival Great Steamboat Race.

The Kentucky Derby race is held every year on the first Saturday in May. The official Kentucky Derby Festival events and activities in 1993 began April 7, and the last event was held on May 14. The events surround the Derby race providing a multitude of activities and entertainment events for the consumer. Hence, the Kentucky Derby is a "packaged sports event."

Sport event packaging goes beyond events and activities to include often-overlooked factors, such as facility cleanliness, friendliness of workers and staff, and prompt attention to a variety of consumer needs while attending the event. Everything included in the package is designed to create an atmosphere in which the consumer believes that she or he is getting plenty more than just spectating the event.

Product Deletion

For most products, the time will arrive when the product no longer is fulfilling a need or desire for a consumer. The sport marketer must be able to identify that time and make the decision to eliminate the product. The decision should be based on an analysis of the product's situation: sales and sales trends, profits trends, cost analysis, and product life-cycle stage. There are also indirect factors to be considered, such as the effect of eliminating a product on the company and employees, the effect of eliminating a product on other companies, and the effect of eliminating a product on the consumer.

If the sport company has decided to eliminate a product, there are some techniques that may be used in order to decrease the many effects that its elimination could have. For example, the product could be "phased out" over a period of time. This will allow everyone involved in the production of the product and the consumer to begin to make the transition toward the day that the product is no longer offered.

Chapter Summary

Products are the company. Products provide benefits and fulfill functions. The sport consumer looks for products that will satisfy specific needs or desires. In the sport industry there is a vast array of products. Product needs to be understood as a concept because a product involves tangible and intangible characteristics.

The wide variety of sport products available to the consumer in the sport industry requires some method of classification. Product classification typically involves an analysis of the consumer and, in particular, consumer needs and desires. It is the function of the product for the consumer that is the reason for its existence.

The product life cycle is a concept that must be understood by the sport marketer. Product management strategies are influenced by the stages in which the company's products might be categorized in the product life cycle. Product mix and product development strategies are also influenced.

New product development is important to the sport marketer because new products are a consistently offered in the sport industry. When the sport marketer understands the industry segment in which the company's products exist, informed decisions and strategies may guide the company to the successful addition of a new product.

The sport company must establish an identity for the product through product identification. This can include branding and packaging. Packaging is the activity of enclosing a product. There are some products in the sport industry that require a different kind of packaging—surrounding the product with an array of other products, activities, and events.

Product deletion is also a sport management and marketer's responsibility. A time will come when a product will no longer fulfill the needs or desires of the consumer. At this critical point, a decision must be made concerning the elimination of the product.

Questions For Study

1. What is a product? What is a sport product? List examples of sport products.
2. Why do people purchase sport products?
3. Define these terms: form utility, time utility, place utility, and possession utility. Give an example of each.
4. What is product classification?
5. What is the product life cycle? What are the stages in the product life cycle?
6. Give examples of sport products in each product life cycle.
7. Why is it important for the sport marketer to know in which stage of the product life cycle each of the sport company's products may be categorized?
8. What is the product mix? Why is it important?
9. How many ways might a sport company offer a new product?

10. What is the new product development planning process? What are the stages?
11. What is product identification? Why is it important? How is it used in the sport industry?

Learning Activities

1. Using the definition of sport product in this chapter, create a list of 10 sport products for each of the categories: goods, services, people, places, and ideas.
2. Using the Pitts, Fielding & Miller Sport Industry Segmentation Model, list products offered to consumers and business consumers in your city or community.
3. Determine in which stage of the product life cycle each of the products you listed in activity 2 falls.
4. Interview some of the sport businesses, organizations, or other enterprises in your city or community and ask about new product development and new product research and development.
5. Conduct a class study of product identification. On overhead transparencies, show company brand names or logos and ask students to try to identify each.
6. To study how today's sports events are packaged, attend a small sporting event and a large sporting event. Take a notebook. Make a list of everything that involved and surrounded the events: parking, pre-event events (such as pre-game shows), and other activities and services offered.

References

Ansoff, H. I. (1965). *Corporate strategy.* McGraw-Hill: New York.

Bennett, P. D. (Ed.). (1988). *Dictionary of marketing terms.* Chicago American Marketing Association.

Boone, L.E., & Kurtz, K.L. (1989). *Contemporary marketing.* Chicago: The Dryden Press.

Day, G.S., Shocker, A.D., & Srivastava, R.K. (1979). Customer-oriented approaches to identifying product-markets. *Journal of Marketing, 43*(4), 8-19.

Derby winners 1875 to 1992. (1993, March 29), *Call To The Post,* p. 54.

Evans, J.R., & Berman, B. (1987). *Marketing.* New York: Macmillan Publishing Company.

Feld, J. (1988, August). Different kind of money back guarantee boosts member retention for Arizona chain. *Club Industry,* pp. 16-17.

Harris, R. (1993, March 29). How eventful! Where did all those Derby Festival events come from, anyway? *Call To The Post,* pp. 14, 84.

Hiestand, M. (1992, February 3). Coming soon to sports stores near you. *USA Today,* p. 3C.

Levitt, T. (1965, November-December). Exploit the product life cycle. *Harvard Business Review,* pp. 81-94.

McCarthy, E.J., & Perreault, W.D. (1990). *Basic marketing: A managerial approach.* Homewood, IL: Richard D. Irwin, Inc.

McMasters, L. (1993, March 29). Then there was the time a thrown shoe held up the Derby. *Call To The Post,* p. 62.

Moore, M.T. (1993, February 17). Converse makes fast break to rename shoe. *USA Today,* p. 1B.

Peter, J.P., & Donnelly, J.H. (1991). *A preface to marketing management* (5th Ed.). Boston, MA: Irwin, Inc.

Pitts, B.G., & Fielding, L.W. (1987). Custom-made bats and baseball players: The relationship between form utility and promotion—J. A. Hillerich's contribution to sporting goods marketing. *Proceedings of the North American Society for Sport Management Conference, 2.*

Pitts, B.G., Fielding, L.W., & Miller, L.K. (1994). Industry segmentation theory and the sport industry: Developing a sport industry segment model. *Sport Marketing Quarterly,* 3(1), 15-24.

Porter, M.E. (1985). *Competitive advantage: Creating and sustaining superior performance.* New York: The Free Press.

Pride, W.M. & Ferrell, O.C. (1991). *Marketing: Concepts and strategies.* Boston: Houghton Mifflin Company.

Stanton, W.J., Etzel, M.J. & Walker, B.J. (1991). *Fundamentals of marketing.* New York: McGraw-Hill.

Strauss, G. (1992, February 3). Sporting-goods makers hang on to optimism. *USA Today,* p. 1B.

Tarpey, L.X., Donnelly, J.H., & Peter, J.P. (1979). *A preface to marketing management.* Dallas, TX: Business Publications, Inc.

CHAPTER 9

PRICING STRATEGIES FOR THE SPORT INDUSTRY

What do I get for my money? This is a question asked by consumers everywhere. What the consumer pays for something and what the consumer believes he or she gets for the money vary from one consumer to another. As an example, let us consider a conversation that took place between two individuals about two boats. Consumer A believes that Boat 1 is the best buy because the boat has more features and instruments than Boat 2. Consumer B believes that Boat 2 is a better buy because the engine has more horsepower. Consumer A points out that the price of Boat 1 is slightly lower than the price of Boat 2. Consumer B replies that the reason is that Boat 2 has a larger engine, and engines are expensive. Consumer A argues that Boat 1 has more safety features, such as a built-in automatic fire extinguisher in the engine compartment. Consumer B argues that Boat 2 has a good-looking color combination and that a more powerful engine is necessary to produce the speed and power needed when pulling waterskiers. Consumer A states that waterskiing isn't fun anymore and everyone's favorite toys are tubes and kneeboards.

The discussion will go on for hours, days, or even weeks. Which consumer is right? Both are right insofar as each is willing to pay a particular price for what each believes is the best buy. Which one is the best buy? The consumer defines best buy according to need and desire. In addition, the definition will change from situation to situation and from product to product.

Determining the price of a sport product is difficult. The sport marketer cannot fail to consider that price is perhaps the most sensitive element of a product for the consumer. The price, from the consumer's perspective, is the amount of money the consumer must sacrifice for something. In addition, money is relative. Every consumer has a unique amount of money to spend and only a specific amount to spend for sport products. Further, there are many other factors that affect the consumer's decision to buy. These and other factors that affect the determination of price, pricing objectives, pricing methods, and pricing strategies will be discussed in this chapter.

We first define price and consider it as a concept and look at the many ways it is presented to the consumer. Second, we present what we call the four Cs affecting price determination. Third, we present the concept of elasticity of demand. Last, pricing methods and strategies that can be used in the sport industry are presented.

What is Price?

Simply stated, *price* is something a consumer exchanges for products. Boone and Kurtz (1989) define price as "the exchange value of a good or service and the value of an item is what it can be exchanged for in the marketplace" (p. 339). There are two terms to understand in these definitions—exchange and value. *Exchange* is the trading of something for something else. The form of exchange may be money, services, or other forms for the exchange of products from the seller to the buyer. The original system of exchange was bartering, or trading. If you wanted to get corn, you might expect to trade wheat for it. If you wanted a boat, you might have to trade a couple of cows. Eventually, something called money became the trading means of choice. Today, currency is the most common means in the process of exchange used by the consumer to obtain wanted or needed products.

Value is not an easy term to define. One definition states that value is a "quantitative measure of the worth of a product" (Stanton, Etzel, & Walker, 1991, p. 240). Where do we begin to determine the quantitative worth of a product? In the example of trading, or bartering, a couple of cows for a boat, the individuals involved negotiate over the exchange. If the individual who wants the boat—the buyer—believes that two cows are too much to trade for the boat, that means that two cows are "worth" more than the boat. The individual with the boat—the seller—believes that the boat is "worth" two cows. The bartering, or negotiating, will continue until an agreement can be reached. If an agreement cannot be reached, we can conclude that the buyer believed that the value of the boat was not worth two cows. The buyer might decide to not make the trade. The seller has lost a deal.

This is exactly what takes place in today's marketplace. The buyers and sellers negotiate over price. Negotiation takes place in more than one form—verbal and nonverbal. For example, negotiation over some products might be realized through nonverbal communication when the consumer decides not to purchase a particular product because of the price. This can force the seller to set a different price—or face no sales! In the negotiation over some other products, such as cars or boats, verbal negotiation takes place. The buyer and seller negotiate until an agreement can be reached. As a matter of fact, negotiation over price is expected for some products in the United States. In some other countries, negotiation, sometimes called bargaining or haggling, over prices is expected and part of the culture. For example, anyone who has been to certain cities in Mexico will agree that negotiation is commonplace among the street vendors. If the buyer does not haggle over the price and pays the asking price, the buyer is considered foolish and an "easy target" by the seller. The seller will pass the word to other vendors. Some vendors consider the buyer rude if the buyer does not negotiate. Other vendors are insulted if the buyer does not negotiate.

There can be many factors involved in the determination of value and it can have several meanings. This is because each individual involved in determining the value of a product has a unique perspective. For example, let us revisit the opening discussion of this chapter concerning the two consumers discussing two boats. Each individual holds attitudes, preferences, values, and beliefs, a certain amount of expendable money, an amount of money each thinks should be spent on a boat, and other ideas that will affect what each believes ought to be the price, or value, of the boat. In other words, many factors besides price affect the establishment of the value of a product. Hence, we can suggest that price is a reflection of value.

Price is presented to the consumer in a number of ways, and this is also true in the sport industry. One reason for this is to give identification to the product through the price title. Another reason is to soften the blow—other words are easier on the ear than the word "price." Take a look at the following examples of words used in place of the word price that can be found in the sport industry.

- A *licensing fee* is the price a sports apparel company pays a university for the right to sell a t-shirt with the university's logo on it.
- The *ticket charge* is the price paid to enter a facility and watch a basketball game.
- *Membership fee* is the price to use a fitness center's facilities.
- *Admission* is the price paid to enter the water sports park.
- *Rental* is the price paid to use a water tube at the water sports park.
- A *league fee* is the price a softball team must pay to play in a softball league.
- A *sponsorship fee* is the price the local bank pays to be the sponsor of a Special Olympics event. (What the bank gets for its money is advertising and goodwill exposure.)
- *Registration fee* is the price paid for a daughter to attend the summer basketball camp.
- A *signing bonus* is part of the price a professional basketball team pays to assure the services of a player.
- A *salary* is the price a professional baseball team pays for the services of coaches and players.
- *Commission* is the extra bonus-oriented price a sports marketing company would pay its sales people for their services.

- *Shipping and handling* are the price a sporting goods company pays to get its products moved from one place to another.
- The *purse* is the price the Ladies' Professional Golf Association (LPGA) pays the golfers to participate in a tournament.
- A *bid* is the offered price for an item at a sport art collection auction.
- An *endorsement fee* is the price a sport shoe company pays to have a famous athlete like Florence Griffith-Joyner state that she endorses—believes in, favors, prefers, supports—the products of that company.
- *Broadcasting rights fee* is the price a television station company pays to televise a volleyball match.
- A *consulting fee* is the price the city government pays a sport marketing company to analyze the feasibility and marketing status for a possible new all-sports facility.
- A *franchise fee* is the price one pays to enter a team in a professional sports league.

These are some of the words used in various segments of the sport industry. The words give definition and identification to the product. This creative use of language is also part of the company's promotional efforts: Price is used as a promotional tool. This illustrates the interrelatedness of marketing mix elements.

Price Determination

Price can be a complex element of marketing for the sport marketer. The sport marketer must consider a multitude of factors. However, these factors can be organized in order to consider them in a managable manner. They fall primarily in four categories: the consumer, the competitor, the company, and the climate (environment). Each of the 4 Cs is presented next with a brief description.

The consumer. Although the price for something is a sensitive factor for the consumer, the consumer considers much more than the price in making a purchase decision. The consumer also considers factors, such as product quality, warranty, company service agreement, refund policy, the consumer's image and reputation, and product bargain. Each factor is weighed in the consumer's analysis according to what the consumer will get of each one for the price. For example, if the consumer is considering the purchase of a fitness center membership, services included in the membership package will be considered. Since this package costs more than another, how many services are included and will they be used by the consumer?

In addition to the factors mentioned, the consumer's buying decision is also affected by the decision-making pathway to reach conclusion. Along the path the consumer's decision process could be affected by the opinions of friends, family members, a significant other, and salespeople. The consumer could also be affected by age, income, education, geographic location, race, sexual orientation, and gender. Other factors include the consumer's personality, favorite activity, religion, and lifestyle. In addition, some consumers will research a product and its price to inform the decision to be made. There is information available through consumer product reports, product research labs, and government and private product testing organizations.

The study of the consumer's consideration of price is an element of a specialized field of study called consumer behavior. We recommend that the sport marketer read extensively in this area.

The competitor. There is another factor the sport marketer cannot ignore—the competitor. More specifically, the sport marketer cannot ignore the competitor's prices and pricing strategies. The price in the marketplace—prices being used by the competitors—should be given serious consideration when determining the price to place on a product. For example, let us say that you are in the process of planning to build and manage an indoor soccer facility. Presently, there are three indoor soccer facilities in the same city. You decide, without investigating the competitor's prices, that you will establish the price, or league fee, for two of your products as follows:

1. women's advanced league — $400
2. men's advanced league —— $400

When your facility opens you get no entries in either league. Upon investigation you discover that the consumers—soccer players—are buying the product—playing—at the other three facilities. You approach some of them to ask why and find that they believe your price is too high. You investigate the prices of the other facilities and find the following:

FACILITY A:	Women's advanced fee —- $300
	Men's advanced fee —— $300
FACILITY B:	Women's advanced fee —- $280
	Men's advanced fee —— $300
FACILITY C:	Women's advanced fee —- $295
	Men's advanced fee —— $295

The amount that the consumers of indoor soccer were willing to pay had been established. The consumers had been paying a specific amount for soccer for quite a few years and were not willing to pay more.

Aha! You decide that there is a simple solution! You will set the price very much below your competitors! You set the fee at $100 for each of the leagues. This time, a couple of teams register and pay the $100 but there are not enough teams to fill the eight slots needed. Therefore, you have to cancel them and return the money to those who had registered.

Once again, you investigate by talking to the consumers. This time you discover that the consumers thought that the price you set was some kind of a hoax with plenty of other hidden charges that would eventually add up to the $400 you originally wanted to charge. In addition, some of them told you that they were concerned with what they would get for only $100! In other words, they thought that $100 was a very low price to pay for soccer and that they would not get a quality product.

This situation reflects two factors in price consideration: first, the consumer's perception of the value for a product; second, careful analysis of the competitor's prices.

The company. Another important piece of the puzzle is your company. What are the factors in your sport company that will affect setting the price of a product? Some of these are materials, equipment, rent or mortgage payment, payroll costs, maintenance, renovation, promotion, and dividends to stockholders. If the company is a manufacturer, it cannot put a price on a product that does not, at a minimum, cover the cost of producing the product. If the company is a retailer or wholesaler, the price must at least cover the cost of the purchase of the product.

The type of sport company will also affect price determination. Generally, there are two types—nonprofit and for-profit. Nonprofit sport companies include those that are supported by government funding, such as community recreation facilities, and nonprofit sport companies supported by membership fees, such as a YMCA. Usually, these are tax exempt. For-profit sport companies are the opposite—companies owned by individuals, groups, or large conglomerates that do not receive government funding support and are not tax exempt.

There is a difference in the costs associated with producing similar products in nonprofit and for-profit enterprises. For example, a nonprofit community fitness center gets a variety of tax breaks. Therefore, the total cost of producing the sport product is less than the total cost for a for-profit fitness center. This allows the nonprofit sport company to set decidedly lower prices for the same products than the for-profit sport company offers. Hence, for-profit sport company owners complain that this is unfair competition (Berrett, Slack, & Whitson, 1993).

Nonprofit sport enterprises are giving special attention to raising prices, however, in the early 1990s. The reason is decreasing government and charitable funding. As state government's budgets are struggling during the early 1990s, the proportion of funding to recreation and sport facilities is decreasing. Nonprofit companies reported a decrease in charitable giving in the early 1990s due to the recession and the change in tax laws governing charitable giving—less of a given amount is deductible on a person's income tax calculations. As a result, some companies have implemented higher fees and other states are giving it serious consideration (Brademas & Readnore, 1989; McCarville & Crompton, 1988; Reiling, Cheng, & Trott, 1992).

The higher fees will have an impact on consumers and the companies. It will be up to the sport marketer to analyze carefully and estimate the effects of higher prices. Reiling, et al (1992) found that higher fees for camping in a state park would result in a decrease in the number of low-income campers but would not adversely affect high-income campers. In addition, as you will learn later in this chapter, the company might lose some consumers if prices are increased, but may make a greater profit.

The climate. The climate includes those factors that are primarily external and that the sport marketer cannot directly control. These include factors, such as laws pertaining to pricing, government regulations, the political climate, the economic situation, and local public attitude. For example, after a major hurricane devastated the south Florida area, many local businesses increased prices of some products significantly. Service station managers raised gas prices almost 100%. Building-supply stores raised prices on items like plywood, lumber, nails, hammers, and roofing materials. The people in the area complained loudly. The media heard their complaints and covered the stories. The business managers were treated to significant negative scrutiny and press. The issue became an ethical one—it was greedy to increase prices at a serious time of devastation and need. Many managers argued and tried to justify their price increases, but many gave in to the pressure and lowered their prices.

The economy can have perhaps the most direct effect on the sport company's pricing strategies. The early 1990s in the United States were labeled the "Age of Disinflation" (Farrell & Schiller, 1993). America was in the grips of recession involving high unemployment rates that slow economic growth. Even with interest rates their lowest since the late 1970s, consumer spending was very low. When consumers aren't buying, the consumer price rate—known as inflation—falls. Therefore, if a company can not raise prices to cover costs and company objectives, it is forced to change pricing strategies.

The sport marketer cannot afford to develop something referred to as tunnel vision. Tunnel vision means that the person has stopped paying attention to or studying all factors affecting a situation and has become lazy or egotistical, paying attention to only one or a few factors. The sport marketer must constantly study all factors involved in order to make educated decisions.

The Concept of the Elasticity of Demand

The sport marketer must understand a marketing concept called the elasticity of demand. Here is a simple definition: changes in the market (sales) when there is a change in price. Elasticity is a measure of how consumers react—consumer sensitivity—to changes in price (Boone & Kurtz, 1989; Howard & Crompton, 1980; Peter & Donnelly, 1991; Stotlar, 1993; Tarpey, Donnelly & Peter, 1979). The following questions can help you understand this concept:

1. What will happen if we raise the price of a sport product? If fewer consumers purchase the product, how many is "fewer"? How will that affect revenue, profit, and sales?

2. What will happen if we decrease prices? Will more consumers purchase the products? How will this affect revenue, profit, and sales?
3. Is there any guarantee that any change in price will result in a change in consumer purchase pattern?

The sport marketer can answer these questions only through estimation or experimentation. The sport marketer can attempt to estimate what will happen when a change is made to the price. The following example illustrates the concept of elasticity of demand estimation.

Wet'n'Wild Water Sports Park. The cost of admission to the Wet'n'Wild Water Sports Park is $8 for a full-day pass. If the price is increased to $10, our first analysis is that there will probably be an immediate drop in attendance. This drop may level off and the final effects will be minimal when this situation is considered over a long period of time and if the increase in revenues from sales equals or is greater than current revenue from sales.

If there is a decrease in the attendance number, we can conclude that the demand for this product is relatively inelastic. Refer to Figure 9.1 in which the graph illustrates the $2 increase and attendance figures. The graph shows that although the attendance number decreased from 320,000 to 300,000, total revenue increased from $2,560,000 to $3,000,000—an increase of $440,000 although there was a decrease of 20,000 buyers. This means that this situation is relatively inelastic because the change in price results in a parallel change in revenue (DeBrock, 1991; Stanton et al., 1991; Stotlar, 1993).

Figure 9.2 illustrates the estimate of what could happen if there is a drastic change in consumers. If the number of buyers drops from 320,000 to 240,000—a difference of 80,000 buyers—and this decrease results in a loss in revenue,

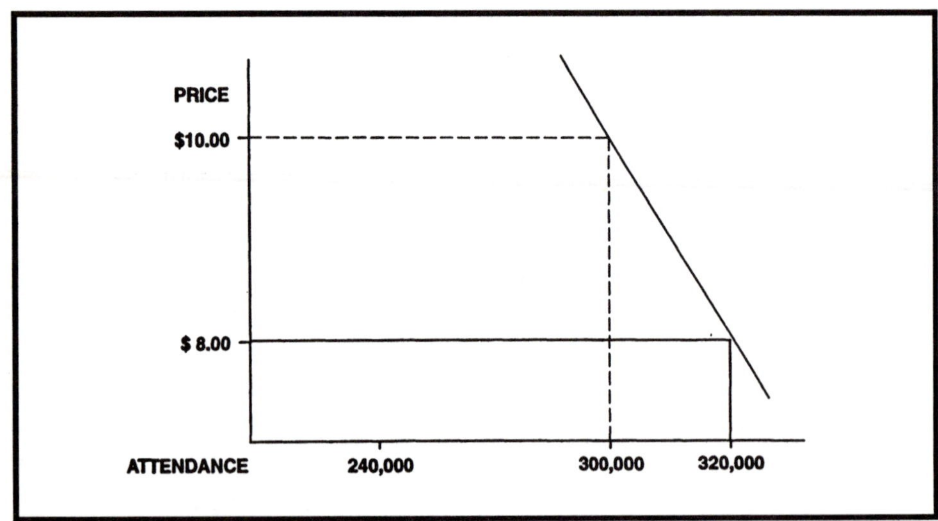

FIGURE 9.1 - Elasticity of Demand at the Wet'n'Wild Sports Park. This situation is considered to be relatively inelastic.

demand is relatively elastic—a change in price causes an opposite change in revenue (Stotlar, 1993; Walsh, 1986). The higher price and fewer buyers resulted in a $160,000 decrease in revenue.

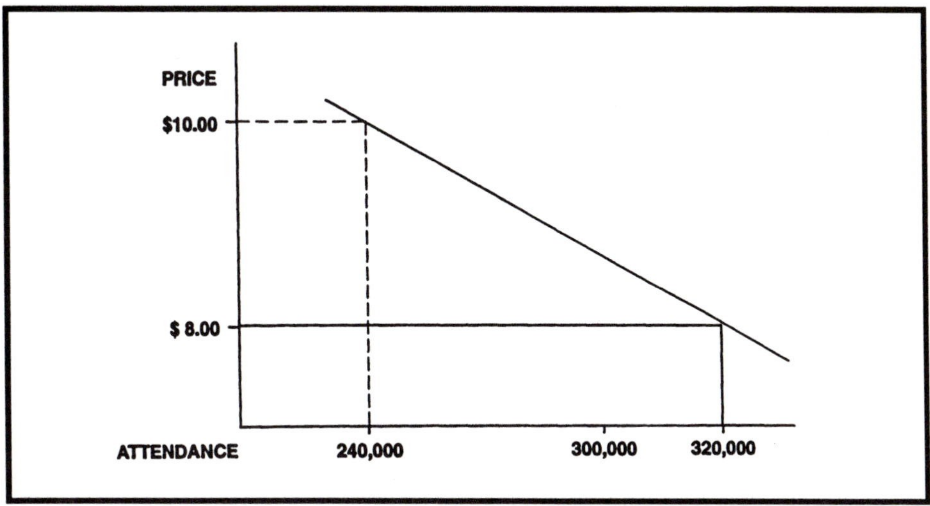

FIGURE 9.2 - Elasticity of Demand at the Wet'n'Wild Water Sports Park. This situation is considered to be relatively elastic.

Determinants of Elasticity

What causes elasticity and inelasticity of demand? First, consider the situation at the beginning of the chapter: the consumers comparing two boats. There are many factors affecting their decisions to buy. One factor is what they would "expect" to pay for a specific boat with a specific set of features. This "expected price" is what the consumer thinks the product is worth (McCarville, Crompton, & Sell, 1993). The expected price usually is one somewhere within a range of prices with relative minimum and maximum limits: a price most frequently charged, price for similar products, price of the brand usually purchased, or the price last paid (Winer, 1988). For example, the consumer might expect to pay between $100 and $300 for a one-year membership in a fitness center because that is the range of prices for that product in today's market. In another example, a consumer might believe that a fair price for a new pair of running shoes is "not over $80." If a consumer has "shopped around" this means that the consumer has compared prices of a product at two or more places. This is also precisely what the sport marketer should do! As one means of estimating setting a price, shop around—compare prices of the same or a comparable product. If the product seems to sell well within a specific range of prices, this is a fairly accurate estimate of "expected price," or what the consumer expects to pay and is paying.

Some of the other factors that affect elasticity include the following: product status as a necessity or luxury; product substitute availability; frequency of purchase; proportion of income available for a specific product; economy; brand loyalty; competition (quantity and quality); quality of the product; product specialization; and time frame of demand (Boone & Kurtz, 1989; Brunson & Shelby, 1993; Howard & Crompton, 1980; Pajak, 1990; Peter & Donnelly, 1991; Raju, Srinivasan, & Lal, 1990; Stotlar, 1993; Stotlar & Bronzan, 1987; Stotlar & Johnson, 1989; Tarpey et al., 1979). Each of these factors is presented next with a brief description.

Necessity or luxury product. Price can be relatively inelastic if the product is a necessity and elastic if it is a luxury. For example, football pads are a necessity, and there are no substitutes. Therefore, the buyers must pay the set prices. On the other hand, going on a sports adventure trip is a luxury, and there are plenty of substitutes. Therefore, prices must be set specific to consumer markets because the consumer does not have to spend money for a trip.

Product substitutabilty. Have you ever seen or heard these advertising words: "There is NO substitute!", "Accept no substitute!" or "No other product compares!" The availability of substitutes for products can have a strong effect on elasticity. Those sport products or other products that can meet the consumer's needs, wants, or desires are direct competition for the consumer dollar. In the recreation and leisure research, substitutability is defined as "an interchangeability among activities in satisfying participants' motives, needs and preferences" (Hendee & Burdge, 1974). More recently, Brunson & Shelby (1993) offered the following definition:

> The term *recreation substitutability* refers to the interchangeability of recreation experiences such that acceptably equivalent outcomes can be achieved by varying one or more of the following: the timing of the experience, the means of gaining access, the setting, and the activity. (p. 69)

Using this definition, the sport marketer must study two factors: what the consumer is looking for and the potential substitutes for the sport marketer's product. With this knowledge, the sport marketer can incorporate pricing and other marketing mix strategies to try to keep the consumer from selecting the substitute.

Frequency of purchase. The frequency with which the consumer must purchase a product affects elasticity of demand. Frequency can be linked to necessity. For example, if a consumer has a consistent need for athletic tape to stock the sports medicine clinic, pricing strategies can be set according to the frequency of purchase. In another example, if the sport product is such that there is a very low frequency of purchase, such as the need for a sport marketing study on building a new student recreation center for the university, price will likely be much higher.

Income. An individual's income limits the amount of money a consumer has available to spend on discretionary products after all the bills are paid. As income increases, the percent of income a consumer has to use for food and bills decreases. This means that the percent of income available for discretionary purposes increases. An individual with a lower income spends a larger percentage on food and bills and is therefore left with a smaller percentage for discretionary spending. For example, Consumer A's take-home income is $25,000 and Consumer B's take-home income is $50,000. Both use approximately 40% of their income for necessities, such as mortgage, food, vehicles, insurance, utilities, phone, and cable TV. Forty percent of each income is presented below:

$25,000 x 40% = $10,000
$50,000 x 40% = $20,000

Now calculate how much money each consumer has left for discretionary spending:

$25,000 - $10,000 = $15,000 or $1,250 per month
$50,000 - $20,000 = $30,000 or $2,500 per month

Consumer B has more discretionary income than Consumer A even though each uses the same percent of income for necessities.

The economy. The economy affects elasticity of demand. For example, how does recession impact consumer spending and setting prices? As stated earlier in this chapter, the early 1990s have been labeled the "Age of Disinflation" (Farrell & Schiller, 1993). Inflation is the rising price level measured in percentages over a period of time, usually annually. Inflation in the United States reached double-digit proportions in the late 1970s and early 1980s, eventually reaching 13.6% in 1980 (Boone & Kurtz, 1989). Since 1990 inflation has decreased from an annual 5.4% to a 1993 rate of 2.7% (Farrell & Schiller, 1993). Forcing this period of "disinflation" are recessionary factors, such as high unemployment, slow economic growth, increased fierce global competition, and worldwide overcapacity. What this means to the sport marketer is that when the consumer has less money to spend due to unemployment or is spending less money due to the fear of losing employment, the company will begin to feel the effects. The sport marketer must either redesign pricing strategies or implement significantly radical ones.

Brand loyalty. A consumer can become brand loyal. This means that the consumer will purchase only a certain brand product. As an example, Consumer A believes the running shoes of the Smith Company are the best and only shoes that fit everything the consumer is looking for in a running shoe and, more important, that the Smith Company is the only company that the consumer has come to believe in. The consumer will buy the shoes and probably other products from the Smith Company. Consumer B will buy running shoes from any company as long as they fit and the price is right. In this example, Consumer A is loyal to one brand.

Most companies strive to create brand loyalty within their consumers. They will even use this as part of their advertising. Have you ever seen or heard the advertising slogans presented here: "Our customers always come back." "Once a Smith customer, always a Smith customer"?

Brand loyalty applies to the sport industry in another unique way: something called the hard-core fan. A hard-core fan is someone who picks and supports a particular team, or sport, and will stick with it through good times and bad. For example, a hard-core fan of a university basketball team whose college colors are are gold and white may be heard to exclaim, "My blood runs gold!"

The competition. The prices of products of the competition will affect elasticity of demand. Sometimes "price wars" evolve between two or more companies or between companies within an entire industry. For example, the fitness-center industry experienced such phenomenal growth in the late 1970s and throughout the 1980s that the market was saturated with fitness centers. Almost all fitness centers offered the same set of products to the consumer. Therefore, the only difference between centers was the price. If the manager of a fitness center wanted to stay in business, prices had to be lowered; some prices were below the cost of the product.

The sport marketer must study the competition's prices and pricing strategies in order to be able to make educated decisions and to set marketing strategies that will compete best with the competition.

Product quality. A sport product's quality will affect consumer purchasing and, hence, elasticity of demand. If the consumer knows, or even suspects, that a sport product is of poor quality, demand will be relatively elastic. Thus, if prices are increased, the consumer simply will not buy, believing that the product is not worth the increase.

Product specialization. The specialization of a sport product will affect elasticity of demand. For example, a softball player must use a softball glove to participate in softball. A softball glove is a specialized sport product. There are 29,426,000 estimated softball participants over the age of 6 in the United States in 1991 (American Sports Data, Inc., 1991). All of them must have this specialized piece of sport equipment to participate in softball. Therefore, the consumer (the softball participant) will purchase this product because it is the only product to perform the function they need. However, there are many softball glove manufacturers and retailers. The consumer has a wide range of choice. This keeps the price down.

In another example, the manufacturer of Louisville Slugger bats, the Hillerich & Bradsby Company, produced a specialized product in the early development of the company: handmade, custom-made wooden bats (Fielding & Pitts, 1988; Miller, Fielding & Pitts, 1993; Pitts & Fielding, 1987; Pitts & Fielding, 1988). The company concentrated on selling their handmade custom-made bats to professional baseball players. Hillerich & Bradsby claimed that their bats were specialized and that they were the only bat manufacturers in the bat business who could make bats the way they did. Hence, many professional players were loyal customers.

Time frame of demand. Another factor affecting elasticity of demand is the time frame of demand: the amount of time a consumer has or is willing to take in the process of making a purchase. Following are three examples. If a soccer player needs athletic tape to wrap an ankle before a game and forgot to purchase the tape in plenty of time before the day and time of the game, the player will be under pressure and will pay almost any price for the tape. The player must stop at the closest store to purchase the tape and does not have time to "shop around" for the best price. In another example, consider the consumer who wants to buy a new softball bat. This individual currently owns a bat and is fairly satisfied with it. The new bat purchase is a consideration for the future. Therefore, this consumer is under no time pressure to purchase and can "shop around" for exactly what she or he wants and for the price she or he wants. In another example, a college athlete is pursued by several agents trying to persuade the athlete to retain their services if and when the athlete ever wants or needs an agent. The athlete can be under great time constraints as the senior year approaches.

Pricing Objectives for the Sport Marketer

One of the most fundamental management skills necessary for positively affecting success is setting objectives. Objectives give direction to determining the price and pricing strategies. Pricing objectives should derive from the established marketing objectives that were established in line with the sport company's objectives and mission. A question the sport marketer must always ask first is, "What results does the company expect to occur as a result of the price?" The objectives should be clear, forthright, quantitative, realistic, and achievable, and should establish vision for the future

The following are examples of pricing objectives from a variety of authors. Consider each one for its use and effectiveness in the sport industry.

Howard and Crompton (1980) outlined six pricing objectives commonly used in establishing prices in the park and recreation industry. These are

1. efficient use of all financial resources
2. fairness or equitableness
3. maximum opportunity for participation
4. rationing
5. positive user attitudes
6. commercial sector encouragement.

Peter & Donnelly (1991) listed the following as potential pricing objectives:

1. Target return on investment.
2. Target market share.

3. Obtain maximum long-run profits.
4. Obtain maximum short-run profits.
5. Promote growth.
6. Stabilize the market.
7. Desensitize customers to price.
8. Maintain price-leadership arrangement.
9. Discourage entrants to the market.
10. Speed exit.

Tarpey et al. (1979) listed those above and the following:

1. Avoid government investigation and control.
2. Maintain loyalty of middlemen [and women] and get their sales support.
3. Avoid demands for "more" from suppliers.
4. Enhance image of firm and its offerings.
5. Be regarded as "fair" by customers.
6. Be considered trustworthy and reliable by rivals.
7. Create interest and excitement about the item.
8. Help in the sale of weak items in the line.
9. Discourage others from cutting prices.
10. Make a product "visible."
11. "Spoil the market" to obtain high price for sale of business.
12. Build traffic.
13. Achieve maximum profits on product line.
14. Recover investment quickly.

Pride & Ferrell (1991) offer seven categories of pricing objectives:

1. survival
2. profit
3. return on investment
4. market share
5. cash flow
6. status quo
7. product quality.

Boone & Kurtz (1989) provide the following categories of pricing objectives:

(1) PROFITABILITY OBJECTIVES

- specified return on investment
- specified total profit level
- increased total profits above previous levels
- specified rate of return on sales

(2) VOLUME OBJECTIVES

- increased market share
- retention of existing market share
- service to select market segments
- specified market share

(3) MEETING COMPETITION OBJECTIVES

- meet competitive price levels

(4) PRESTIGE OBJECTIVES

- creation of a readily identifiable image for the company and/or its products

It is the responsibility of the sport marketer and management of the sport company to establish the pricing objectives. Each objective has potential positive and negative consequences for the company and its consumers. The sport marketer and all of management must analyze the consequences and make their decision based on this knowledge and on the direction they want the company to go. Once the objectives have been identified, the next step is to plan the methods and strategies that have the best potential in achieving the objectives.

Pricing Methods and Strategies for the Sport Marketer

After you have established pricing objectives, a next step in setting prices for your sport products is deciding on specific methods and strategies. A method is a way of doing something, especially in accordance with a definite plan of action. A strategy is a detailed plan of action by which an individual or company intends to reach objectives and goals. In this section we will present some common pricing methods and strategies that may be used in the sport industry with a brief description of each.

<u>Going-rate pricing</u>. This is a method applied when the company wants to keep prices at the going rate—the average price of your competitors for same or equivalent products (Howard & Crompton, 1980). For example, a check of all

membership prices charged at fitness centers will be used to determine the going rate.

Demand-oriented pricing. This is a pricing method whereby the sport marketer ascertains the price potential customers are willing to pay for a particular product (Howard & Crompton, 1980). Determination of the price potential customers are willing to pay can be done through consumer survey or studying the competition.

Price discrimination. This is a pricing method in which different prices are charged for the same sport products (Berrett et al., 1993; Walsh, 1986). This method utilizes consumer demographics and other factors. For example, sport companies use variables such as the following:

- age — senior citizen discounts; under-12 prices
- income — a sliding-scale pricing method according to income
- facility use — peak prices for peak-use times
- corporate rate — skyboxes sold to companies for luxury suites at the arena.

Peak-load pricing. This is the method of charging different prices for the same products demanded at different points in time (Walsh, 1986). It is very similar to demand-oriented pricing. This method involves charging higher prices during times when product sales will have a peak time. The primary selling time for softball bats is in March, April, and May just prior to softball season. Prices during this period will be a little higher than they will be for softball bats during December and January.

Seasonal pricing. This pricing strategy is used when a sport product is affected by the seasons and usually relies on specific seasons. Snow ski resorts charge higher prices during winter when there is plenty of snow and skiers want to go skiing. Lower prices are charged during summer months. During the summer, houseboat rental fees are almost twice the amount charged during winter.

Average cost pricing. This method uses the following formula (Howard & Crompton, 1980):

Average Cost Price = Average Fixed Cost + Average Variable Cost

where:

Average Fixed Cost = Total Fixed Costs / Number of Participants

and:

Average Variable Cost = Total variable Costs / Number of Participants

The first step in average cost pricing is to determine which fixed costs and variable costs you will use in the formula. Fixed costs are those expenses within the sport company that are constant, such as mortgage or rent, payroll, utilities, and phones. Variable costs are expenses, such as short-term loan payments, temporary staff, short-term facility rental, and equipment purchases or rental.

Once these have been determined the formula can be used. Howard & Crompton (1980) give the following example:

IF: Total Fixed Costs = $1,000

Total Variable Costs = $500

Projected Number of Participants = 100

THEN: the Average Cost Price (ACP) =

$1,000.00 / 100 + 500 / 100

THUS: ACP = $15.00

<u>Penetration pricing</u>. This pricing strategy is used when the sport company wants to penetrate a market using price as a primary marketing tactic (Boone & Kurtz, 1989). Prices are relatively lower than other prices for the same products on the market. This is typically used as a first-time offering of a product. For example, a sport marketing company will be opening for business. They decide their pricing strategy will be penetration pricing. They set prices for their services much lower than those of other companies to try to secure consumers. The company must use a promotion message that speaks to product quality. You'll remember we discussed the problem of setting price too low. Once the product achieves some market recognition, prices can be slowly increased over a period of time.

<u>Cost-plus pricing</u>. In this pricing method, the price of the sport product is based on the cost of the product plus a desired profit (Stanton et al., 1991). If the cost to produce one game of indoor soccer is $40, the price for a game will be $40 plus any amount of profit desired. Therefore, if the indoor soccer facility wants to make $60 of profit from each game, the price of one game will be $100. This will be multiplied by the number of games in a league round of play (usually 8-10 games). If there are 10 teams in the league and the schedule is a round-robin schedule, each team plays each other team once, giving each team 9 games. Apply the round robin formula for determining how many games will be played (Byl, 1990):

N X (N-1) / 2 = TOTAL NUMBER OF GAMES*
(*N is number of entries)

In this example, we find that 10 x 9 / 2 = 45 games.

Hence, there will be 45 games in the league. If the price per game is established at $100 the total price for all 45 games is $4,500

Your next step is to determine what to charge each team. The common method is to charge a league fee: Divide the $4,500 by the number of teams entering. Thus, $4,500 / 10 = $450. At this point in the formula, each team will pay a league fee of $450. Now add the "PLUS" amount to the $450.00. This amount can be any amount needed or desired provided, of course, that the "PLUS" amount won't put the price out of reach for the consumer. The "PLUS" amount can be added according to goals and objectives for the company. For example, the company wants to start saving for the purchase of some equipment and wants to be able to purchase the equipment at the end of 2 years. Use the cost of the equipment divided over 2 years and divided among all teams in all leagues in all sports to determine the "PLUS" amount to add to the cost.

Break-even analysis. This method for pricing is determined through an analysis of costs and revenue, more specifically, when the costs of producing the product equal the revenue taken from the sales of the product (Pride & Ferrell, 1991). If Central College sells $200,000 worth of tickets to its sports events and the events cost the college $200,000 to produce, the college broke even. In this example, however, Central College didn't make any profit. Break-even analysis will determine how many tickets need to be sold at what price to first break even, and every ticket sold after that point generates profit.

To use break-even pricing effectively, the sport marketer first determines the break-even point for a product using several different prices. This allows the sport marketer to determine total costs and revenue for each price being considered. Table 9.3 illustrates this method using different prices for tickets to Central College's events.

Short-term pricing methods. There are many short-term pricing methods. Some of these include the following:

- discounts: quantity — the more you buy, the lower the price per unit
- special sales

TABLE 9.3 - Calculating the Break Even Point Using Different Prices

TICKET PRICE	QUANTITY TO SELL	REVENUE	EVENT COST	BREAKEVEN-POINT (units that must be sold to break even)
$2.00	100,000	$200,000	$200,000	100,000
$5.00	40,000	$200,000	$200,000	40,000
$7.50	26,666	$200,000	$200,000	26,666
$10.00	20,000	$200,000	$200,000	20,000
$15.00	13,333	$200,000	$200,000	13,333

Calculating the break-even point using different prices. If Central College sports events average 200 paying attendees and there are 100 events, the total number of paying attendees to all events is 20,000. The break-even price is $10 and the break-even point is 20,000. Thus, if the ticket price is set at $10, Central must get 20,000 paying attendees to break-even. In this example, Central will not make any profit at $10 per ticket. Central will want to consider setting the price above $10 to make a profit. At $15 per ticket with 20,000 paying attendees, Central will profit $100,000.

- trade-in allowance
- rebates
- clearance sales
- promotional sales

Product line pricing. This method involves setting specific price minimums and maximums for each product line (Boone & Kurtz, 1989). Acme Tennis Racket Company can carry three lines of rackets differentiated by price: the $500 line, the $300 line and the $100 line.

Chapter Summary

In this chapter we outlined and discussed pricing for the sport marketer. We discussed the broad conceptual definition of price, exchange, and value. We looked at the 4 Cs of price determination and discussed each one in relation to its effect on price and the pricing strategy. We discussed the concept of elasticity of demand and its effect on price. The determinants of the elasticity of demand were presented. Last, we looked at several pricing objectives, methods, and strategies that can be used by the sport marketer.

The decision-making process for pricing for the sport marketer is not an easy one. There are many factors that must be considered, studied, and understood before establishing the price for a sport product. The sport marketer will be making educated decisions and decisions that will have increased positive potential when all factors have been analyzed and the pricing decisions are based on research.

Questions For Study

1. How does the consumer perceive "price?"
2. Discuss the concept of price.
3. List some examples of words used in place of the word price that can be found in the sport industry. Explain why these words are used.
4. What are the 4 Cs of price consideration? Discuss each and give examples.
5. Discuss the concept of the elasticity of demand.
6. List some examples of pricing objectives for sport.
7. List and describe some pricing strategies for the sport industry.

Learning Activities

1. Identify sport businesses, organizations, or other enterprises and their products in your city or community that use these pricing strategies: going-rate pricing, demand-oriented pricing, price discrimination, seasonal pricing, short-term pricing, and product line pricing.

2. Identify in your city or community some of the sport businesses, organizations, or other enterprises that use the price titles as presented in this chapter, such as licensing fee, admission, and purse.

References

American Sports Data, Inc. (1991). *American sports analysis: Summary report.* Hartsdale, NY: American Sports Analysis.

Berrett, T., Slack, T., & Whitson, D. (1993). Economics and the pricing of sport and leisure, *Journal of Sport Management, 7,* 199-215.

Boone, L.E., & Kurtz, D.L. (1989). *Contemporary marketing.* Orlando, FL: The Dryden Press.

Brademas, D., & Readnore, J. (1989). Status of fees and charges in public leisure service agencies. *Journal of Park and Recreation Administration, 7,* 42-55.

Brunson, M.W., & Shelby, B. (1993). Recreation substitutability: A research agenda. *Leisure Sciences, 15*(1), 67-74.

Byl, J. (1990). *Organizing successful tournaments.* Champaign, IL: Leisure Press.

DeBrock, L. (1991). Economics. In B. Parkhouse (Ed.), *The management of sport: Its foundation and application* (pp. 56-73). St. Louis: Mosby-Year Book, Inc.

Farrell, C., & Schiller, Z. (1993, November 15). Stuck! How companies cope when they can't raise prices. *BusinessWeek,* pp. 146-148, 150, 154-155.

Fielding, L.W., & Pitts, B.G. (1988, May). *From the Buster Brown bat to the Babe Ruth Autograph model: The progressive market penetration and market development of the Louisville Slugger 1907-1920.* Paper presented at the conference of the North American Society for Sport History, Tempe, AZ.

Hendee, J.C., & Burdge, R.W. (1974). The substitutability concept: Implications for recreation research and management. *Journal of Leisure Research,* 6, 157-162.

Howard, D.R., & Crompton, J.L. (1980). *Financing, managing and marketing recreation and park resources.* Dubuque, IA: Wm. C. Brown Company Publishers.

McCarville, R., & Crompton, J. (1988). Selected local park and recreation financial indicators in the first half of the 1980s: A challenge to conventional wisdom. *Journal of Park and Recreation Administration,* 6, 46-54.

McCarville, R.E., Crompton, J. L., & Sell, J.A. (1993). The influence of outcome messages on reference prices. *Leisure Sciences, 15,* 115-130.

Miller, L.K., Fielding, L.W., & Pitts, B.G. (1993). The rise of the Louisville Slugger in the mass market. *Sport Marketing Quarterly, 2*(3), 9-16.

Pajak, M. (1990). Every fly ball is an adventure. *Athletic Business, 14*(3), 26.

Peter, J.P., & Donnelly, J.H. (1991). *A preface to marketing management* (5th ed.). Boston, MA: Irwin, Inc.

Pitts, B.G., & Fielding, L.W. (1987, June). *Custom-made bats and baseball players: The relationship between form utility and promotion—J.A. Hillerichs contribution to sporting goods marketing.* Paper presented at the conference of the North American Society for Sport Management, Windsor, Ontario, Canada.

Pitts, B.G., & Fielding, L.W. (1988, June). *From product orientation to market orientation: The Frank Bradsby impact on the Louisville Slugger sales.* Paper presented at the North American Society for Sport Management, Champaign, IL.

Pride, W.M., & Ferrell, O.C. (1991). *Marketing concepts and strategies.* Boston: Houghton Mifflin Company.

Raju, J.S., Srinivasan, V., & Lal, R. (1990). The effects of brand loyalty on competitive price promotional strategies. *Management Science, 36*(3), 276-305.

Reiling, S.D., Cheng, H., & Trott, C. (1992). Measuring the discriminatory impact associated with higher recreational fees. *Leisure Sciences, 14*(2), 121-137.

Stanton, W.J., Etzel, M.J., & Walker, B.J. (1991). *Fundamentals of marketing.* New York: McGraw-Hill, Inc.

Stotlar, D.K. (1993). *Successful sport marketing.* Dubuque, IA: Brown and Benchmark.

Stotlar, D.K. & Bronzan, R.T. (1987). *Public relations and promotions in sport.* Daphne, AL: United States Sports Academy.

Stotlar, D.K., & Johnson, D.A. (1989). Assessing the impact and effectiveness of stadium advertising on sport spectators at Division I institutions. *Journal of Sport Management, 3*(1), 90-102.

Tarpey, L.X., Donnelly, J.H., & Peter, J.P. (1979). *A preface to marketing management.* Dallas, TX: Business Publications, Inc.

Walsh, R. G. (1986). *Recreation economic decisions.* State College, PA: Venture Publishing, Inc.

Winer, R. (1988). Behavioral perspective on pricing: Buyer's subjective perceptions of price revisited. In T.M. Devinney (Ed.), *Issues in pricing: Theory and research* (pp. 35-37). Lexington, MA: Lexington Books.

CHAPTER 10

DISTRIBUTION IN THE SPORT INDUSTRY

Overview

A sport business has to get its product to the consumer or the consumer to the product. There are many ways this can be done, and the selection of the method is contingent on the type of product.

There are tangible products that must be moved from the manufacturing site to a point for purchase, such as a retail store. A manufacturer of snow skis must determine how to get the skis from its manufacturing plant into the consumer's hands. The company can invite the consumer to the plant. However, a manufacturing plant can not readily serve as a retail store. Most plants are large buildings surrounded by parking lots for their employees and can be very dangerous for someone who is not an employee familiar with the safety regulations of the plant. The management of the company must decide how to move the skis to a place that will be a safe shopping place for the consumer. In addition, placing the skis in the right shopping place is a good promotion technique which enhances the chances of selling them. Therefore, moving products from the place of production to the place of selling is linked to promotion.

There are also intangible products in the sport industry. Basketball is an intangible product: It is not a physical object. Certainly, basketball players are physical objects. However, the game, as it is being played, is intangible. One can see it, but cannot touch it or take it home as one can take home a softball bat. Therefore, the intangible attributes of the game of basketball must become the selling focus of basketball as a product. If you have ever watched the NCAA Women's or Men's Final Four Championship games on television, you have been exposed to something that sport marketers call "hype." Hype is the "hyping" of a sporting event, talking about it in an extreme amount, comparing everything imaginable between the players and everyone else who will be involved, comparing every tiny, no matter how obscure, statistic between the two teams, discussing the conditions of the arena and the court, and every aspect possible. The hype is used to create and peak interest to the point that a consumer believes that she or he must watch the game and experience the event.

Although basketball is a sport product that cannot be moved in the same sense that a manufacturer moves softball bats from the plant to the retail store, many of the same principles apply. To distribute the basketball game, the arena becomes the retail store. The players will be the manufacturers of the product—the game. Further, although the basketball game will be the focus for the evening in this particular store, there will be many other items offered: food and drink; souvenirs, including shirts, caps, and shorts; and novelty items, including key chains, coffee mugs, and drinking cups. The hype and other offerings are an attempt to get the consumer to go to the arena and consume the product—the game.

In this example the consumer must go to a distribution point that is also the place of production. In other words, some sport products must be consumed at the same moment that they are produced. This is not unique to the sport industry. The arts and entertainment industries sell products that must be consumed at the same moment they are being produced. Some examples include concerts, ballet, and live theater.

The LPGA and the PGA sell a spectatorial product—watching professional golfers. They must decide the best way to get the product to the consumer. In this type of business, however, the product is not a material good that can be shipped to a retail store. The professional golfers will manufacture golf. The manufacturing plant is a golf course. The consumer is purchasing the opportunity to watch—spectate—professional golfers. The consumer must travel to the golf course to get the product—watching professional golfers. The LPGA and PGA may be called the manufacturer or producer. They could also be called a service provider because selling sports activities for spectators to enjoy is providing a service of entertainment.

Another possibility for distributing this type of product is to televise the event. In this way those consumers who cannot travel to the golf course can stay at home and watch the event.

In this chapter you will learn about distribution in the sport industry, the role of distribution in marketing strategy, the selection of a distribution network, and the types of distribution intermediaries available for moving sport industry products.

What is Distribution?

As we stated earlier, the sport business must determine how to get its products from the manufacturer to the consumer. *Distribution* is the process of getting the product to the consumer. It involves identifying distribution channels or intermediaries, determining the cost of distribution, determining the best distribution process for a specific product, and determining distribution intensity.

The distribution system selected is contingent on the type of product, what is best for the sport company, the consumers, and other factors.

As you learned in chapter 8, there are many different kinds of products in the sport industry. However, all products fit into one of two categories: tangible products or intangible products.

Distribution of Tangible and Intangible Products in the Sport Industry.

Tangible products are physical objects. Most are manufactured in mass quantities at a factory and must be moved—distributed—to a place of purchase—retailer or wholesaler. For example, running shoes are manufactured in a factory and must be moved to a retailer to be sold.

Intangible products are not physical objects and include products such as services, places, and ideas. Many intangible products are not produced until ordered by the consumer. In a fitness center in which laundry services are offered, the consumer must order the service, then simply leave dirty laundry in a bag in a certain spot. The center will perform the service and return the clean laundry to the locker area.

Products offered as entertainment are also intangible products. Sports events offered for entertainment purposes are scheduled for a specific date, time, and place; and the consumer must be available at that time and be able to go to the place where offered. A basketball game, for example, can be offered as an entertainment product.

A significant difference between the tangible running shoe product and the intangible laundry service or basketball game is something called "shelf life." *Shelf life* is the amount of time after a product is manufactured that a product can remain in a good and consumable condition. The running gear product has a shelf life—it is manufactured and can exist for quite a long period of time until sold. The laundry service has a shelf life. The service is produced and then awaits the consumer to take possession. The basketball game, however, does not have a shelf life. The game cannot be manufactured and put on the shelf until a consumer purchases it. As a matter of fact, the game is not manufactured until the players play the game. In other words, the game is simultaneously manufactured and consumed.

The game must be consumed at the same moment it is being produced. If not, it is not consumed and perishes. That game will never be manufactured again. There is, however, through the use of video and audio tape, a secondary product that the consumer may purchase and through which the consumer may watch the game: video tape recordings of the game sold to the consumer.

Because of the perishable shelf life of spectator sports events, today's spectator sports marketers are taking great pains to increase what consumers get for their money and for the amount of time spent at the event. Hence, most spectator sports events offer a variety of sideshows, concessions, services, souvenirs, and even rewards in the form of door prizes or fourth-quarter drawings.

In a different sport product—participation sports—some providers are offering the consumers more than participation for their money and time. To attract more runners, management and marketers of many marathons and 10K runs offer much more than just the running event. Many offer the consumer t-shirts, concessions, pasta dinners, door prizes, a reward for every entrant and every one who crosses the finish line, child-care services, changing and shower services, medical care services, insurance, souvenirs, and photographs of the runner crossing the finish line. Some of these are included in the price of entry, and some are sold separately.

For some types of products in the sport industry for the sport marketer, HOW and WHEN the product is packaged and offered to the consumer are an important part of distribution. Almost all running events are offered on Saturday morning. Professional football games are offered on Saturdays, Sundays, or Monday evenings. Softball leagues are offered during the summer months and on weekday evenings. The local college women's and men's basketball games are offered in evening slots. This is an important element of distribution called time, place, and possession utility.

Time, Place, and Possession Utility Through Distribution

Distribution offers time, place and possession utility to the consumer. *Time utility* is getting the product to the consumer when the consumer wants it (Boone & Kurtz, 1989). *Place utility* is getting the product to the consumer where the consumer wants it (Boone & Kurtz, 1989). *Possession utility* is creating possession of the product for the consumer (Boone & Kurtz, 1989). Therefore, distribution is the system through which the producer gets the product to the consumer when, where, and how the consumer wants it. More and more women's basketball fans want women's basketball games at prime times (weekday and weekend evenings, prime-time slots, such as 7 or 8 p.m.), in a great facility (in the same arena usually used only by the men's team), on a major broadcasting station (the major broadcasting networks, not the hard-to-find stations). They also want season tickets, giving them rights to specific seats for the entire season instead of "admission-at-the-door and no reserved seating." Spectator sports marketers are listening, and more women's basketball is being offered in prime time slots, on major broadcasting stations; and pre-sold tickets and season tickets are being offered. This offers the product to the consumer when, where, and how the consumer wants it.

Therefore, a primary objective of distribution in the sport industry is to offer the product to the consumer when, where, and how the consumer wants it. In another example, a manufacturer of sporting goods must distribute the goods to places where the consumer is most likely to purchase the goods. For example, Hillerich & Bradsby, manufacturer of the famous Louisville Slugger baseball and softball bats, has a manufacturing plant in Louisville, Kentucky. Their bats, however, are sold around the world. Therefore, H & B must decide on a method, or more than one method, to move the bats from the plant to places around the world where the consumer is most likely to purchase them. Those places are usually sporting goods retail stores and department stores with a sporting goods department. Some of the methods involved in moving the goods include moving them by truck, plane, ship, or train.

The Distribution System

The truck, plane, ship, and train mentioned above are examples of distribution intermediaries. Others include wholesalers, retailers, agents, brokers, distributors, sales agents, and shippers. *Distribution intermediaries* are those individuals or organizations through which products are moved from producer to consumer. They are the links through which products move on the route from manufacturer to consumer. The sport business management, as part of the overall marketing plan for a product, should have decided before a product is manufactured which intermediaries will be best for the company, the product, and the consumer. The determination of distribution intermediaries is a part of the development of a distribution plan (Evans & Berman, 1987).

Types of Distribution Intermediaries

There is a variety of distribution intermediaries available to the sport marketer. Some of these are listed and briefly described here.

Wholesaler. A company operating primarily to buy goods in large quantities and resell to retailers or final consumers (Peter & Donnelly, 1993).

Retailer. A company operating to buy goods to resell to consumers (Peter & Donnelly, 1993).

Agent. Someone, or a company, who acts as an intermediary that does not take title to the goods and performs a basic function of bringing together a buyer and a seller (Boone & Kurtz, 1992).

Mail order. A company that buys direct from the manufacturer and offers the products through a mail order system (Cravens & Woodruff, 1986).

Distributor. A wholesale intermediary (Peter & Donnelly, 1993).

The plan is called the distribution system (also sometimes called a distribution network or distribution channel). The *distribution system* is the system developed for moving products from producer to consumer (Peter & Donnelly, 1993).

How does one construct a distribution system? There are hundreds of systems because there are hundreds of companies in the business of moving products and because there is no one best system for any one business. The distribution system selected must be one that is effective and efficient for the manufacturer or producer, the intermediaries, the product, the company, and the consumers. In addition, the company must give serious consideration to the environment. The management must not think that the fastest or most economical method for moving products is automatically environmentally friendly. A question a sport marketer or sport management executive will always face is one of ethics: If something is good for the company, is it compatible with the environment, and is it ethical to proceed?

A distribution system can range from simple to complex. A *simple distribution system* is one in which only the manufacturer and the consumer are involved as depicted in Figure 10.1. In a simple system, the sport product moves from the manufacturer directly to the consumer. There is no intermediary involved. A few examples include the following:

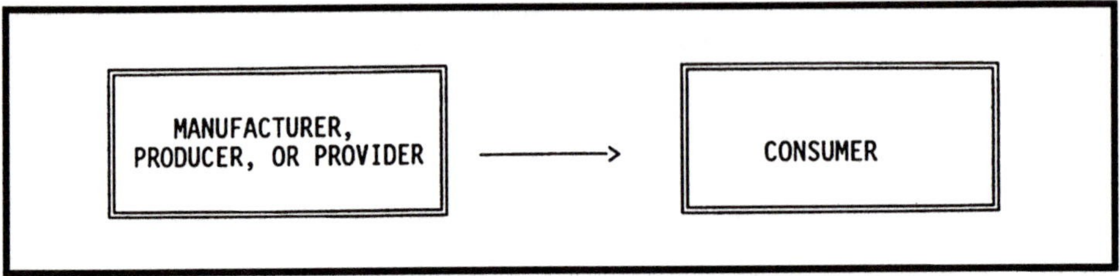

FIGURE 10.1 - A Simple Distribution System in the Sport Industry

- a golf club manufacturer that sells directly to a golf resort and country club;
- an aluminum manufacturer that sells to a softball bat manufacturer;
- a sport marketing company that sells directly to a client;
- a tennis pro who sells lessons directly to a student;
- a sport facility construction company that sells directly to a college athletic department;
- a city parks and recreation department that sells basketball leagues directly to teams;
- a promotional T-shirt company that sells directly to the college book store; and
- a professional football championship game that sells directly to the spectator.

A *complex distribution system* is one in which one or more intermediaries are involved in the movement of the sport product from the producer to the consumer. Examples of routes of a complex system are illustrated in Figure 10.2. In one network the product moves from the producer to an agent to a retailer and then to the consumer. In another network the product moves from the producer to a distributor to a retailer and then to the consumer. In another network the product moves to a wholesaler and then to the consumer.

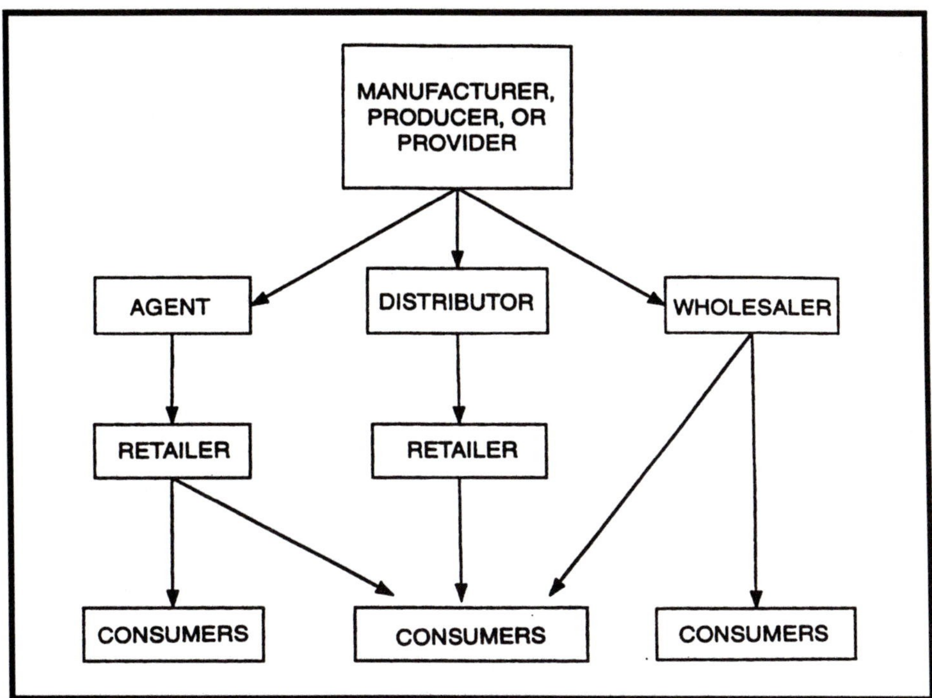

FIGURE 10.2 - A Complex Distribution System in the Sport Industry

In most instances in which intermediaries are involved, the final price of the product to the consumer is higher. Hence, the popularity of a phenomenon called the "outlet store" or "factory-direct" store. No intermediaries are involved, which keeps the cost of moving the sport product very low. This means a lower price to the final consumer and an increased profit margin for the manufacturer. When intermediaries are involved, the price of the product to the final consumer is driven up. For example, the manufacturer sells the sport product to a distributor, who sells it to a retailer who sells it to the final consumer. Each entity involved must make a profit. Therefore, an aluminum softball bat that costs $3.75 to manufacture will be sold to the consumer for $39.95. Figure 10.3 illustrates this process and what happens to the price of the product along the way to the consumer.

If the final price of Producer A's bat is much higher than the price of Producer B's bat, producer A must make a decision: (a) leave the higher price intact and develop a promotion that tells the consumer why the higher price is justified or (b) use a different distribution system that will possibly produce a lower price to the consumer. There is a catch: The sport marketer must be aware of something

Cost to Manufacture Bat	$3.75
Packaging	1.25
Shipping Charges to Distributor	.50
Other Expenses Such as Advertising	3.50
Manufacturer's Total Cost	9.00
Manufacturer's Profit Margin	+3.50
Manufacturer's Price to Distributor	12.50
Shipping Charges to Retailer	.50
Other Expenses	.50
Distributor's Cost	13.50
Distributor's Profit Margin	+5.00
Distributor's Price to Retailer	18.50
Retailer's Expenses	2.00
Retailer's Profit Margin	+19.45
Retailer's Price to Consumer	$39.95

FIGURE 10.3 - Example of a Sport Product's Increasing Cost as it moves through a Distribution System

called price fixing. It is illegal for the sport marketer to try to control the retailer's final price to the consumer if the retailer is not a store that belongs to the manufacturer. In other words, the sport marketer cannot control the final price. The sport marketer is free to suggest a retail price. However, if the marketer tries to force the retailer to offer the product at a specific price, the marketer is committing a form of price fixing.

Selection of a Distribution System

At first glance, the task of selecting a distribution system might seem overwhelming because there are so many options. However, if the sport marketer will first consider the factors that will affect the final selection, this will help guide the decision-making process.

An important element to remember is that the distribution system should be consumer driven. The considerations of the consumer should perhaps be the overriding factor. After all, it is the consumer who will purchase the product. Therefore, the product should be offered to the consumer when, where, and how the consumer wants it: time, place, and possession utility. One idea is to begin with the consumers of the product and trace the path from the consumer to the manufacturer.

Another important question to consider is, which distribution options are available to you? Some sport marketers spend hours creating and designing elaborate distribution systems only to discover that intermediaries do not exist or will not provide service in the way needed.

Factors affecting selection. The many factors that affect the final selection of a distribution system, or channel, are presented in Figure 10.4. It is important that the sport marketer analyze each factor, how they are interrelated, and how the distribution system considered fits with the overall marketing objectives.

THE CONSUMER
Characteristics: number, geographical location Needs: purchase behavior, when needed, how needed, where needed Psychographic Characteristics: promotion
THE SPORT COMPANY
Strengths and weaknesses: financial, location, availability of distribution options
THE SPORT PRODUCT
Type of Product: tangible, intangible, shelf life, packaging and shipping requirements
THE COMPETITION
Characteristics: number, geographic location, distribution methods
THE CLIMATE
Legal: laws, regulations, policy Political: who is in office; what is "politically correct & incorrect" Economic: cost, inflation, & other economic factors Ethical: rights issues and other ethical considerations
DISTRIBUTION CHANNELS/INTERMEDIARIES
Availability of Channels: What intermediaries exist and are available to you? Characteristics: types, location, cost, strengths and weaknesses, acceptance of product, ability to handle product

FIGURE 10.4 - Factors to Consider in the selection of a Distribution System

Adapted from Evans & Berman (1987), Boone & Kurtz (1992), Cravens & Woodruff (1986), and Peter & Donnelly (1993).

Determining Distribution Intensity

One of the elements of distribution that the sport marketer must decide is the intensity of the distribution of the product. The degree of distribution intensity will affect sales of the product. *Distribution intensity* is the amount of distribution selected for a particular sport product. Distribution intensity ranges from intensive to exclusive and is contingent upon most of the same factors that affect the sport marketer's decision on distribution channels. Table 10.5 illustrates the range of intensity.

TABLE 10.5 - Continuum of Distribution Intensity and some Sport Product Examples

	INTENSIVE	SELECTIVE	EXCLUSIVE
WHERE DISTRIBUTED:	everywhere possible	a few places	a few select places
EXAMPLES: Basketball Game	.TV & cable channels .radio taped for later broadcast .taped for sale in-person	.in-person .only one TV channel .two radio stations	.in-person .only one TV channel
Softball Bats	.every sporting goods outlet possible: stores and department stores	.only half of all sporting goods stores	.only one select sporting goods stores

Intensive distribution. If the sport marketer chooses an *intensive distribution strategy*, then the product will be offered in as many places as possible. In the examples given in Table 10.5, softball bats would be offered everywhere possible: all sporting goods stores, pro shops, department stores with sporting goods departments, and other outlets. A basketball game would be offered through as many outlets as possible: many television channels, many radio stations, in-person viewing, taped for later broadcast, and videotaped for later sale.

The type of distribution intensity selected becomes part of the advertising message to the consumer primarily to let the consumer know where the product is available and to establish status quo for the product or company. An advertising message used to let the consumer know might be "widely available" or "available at all local sporting goods stores."

Selective distribution. If the sport marketer selects a *selective distribution strategy* the product will be offered in a limited number of places. The softball bats will be offered only in sporting goods stores. The basketball game will be offered through one local television station, one local radio station, and in-person viewing.

Exclusive distribution. With *exclusive distribution* as a strategy, the sport marketer will offer the product in one or a small number of outlets. The softball bats will be offered in only one sporting goods store. The basketball game will be offered only through one television station or in-person viewing.

Another factor affecting the decision on distribution intensity is advertising dollars. In intensive distribution, much of the advertising effort falls with the place of distribution. In exclusive distribution, much of the advertising effort lies with the producer, although the outlet selected can claim to be the "exclusive outlet" for the product.

Another factor is image. Exclusive distribution creates an image of exclusivity and prestige. The advertising message will sometimes include the words "available only at Smith's Sporting Goods."

Chapter Summary

The sport marketer must decide how to get the product to the consumer through the selection of a distribution system. The selection process is affected by many factors, including the consumer, the company, the product, product positioning, the climate, and distribution systems available to the sport company. Distribution intensity will determine how extensively the product will be made available to the consumers.

Questions For Study

1. What is distribution?
2. Describe the different kinds of distribution in the sport industry.
3. What are distribution intermediaries? Give some examples.
4. What is a distribution system? Give some examples of systems in the sport industry.
5. What are the factors that affect the selection of a distribution system?
6. What is distribution intensity? Give some examples of each type.

Learning Activities

1. List some tangible and some intangible sport products offered in your city or community. Create a distribution system for each.

References

Boone, L.E., & Kurtz, D.L. (1989). *Contemporary marketing.* Fort Worth, TX: The Dryden Press.

Boone, L.E., & Kurtz, D.L. (1992). *Contemporary marketing.* Fort Worth, TX: The Dryden Press.

Cravens, D.W., & Woodruff, R.B. (1986). *Marketing.* Reading, MA: Addison-Wesley Publishing Company.

Evans, J.R., & Berman, B. (1987). *Marketing.* New York: Macmillan Publishing Company.

Peter, J.P., & Donnelly, J.H. (1993). *A preface to marketing management* (6th ed.). Boston, MA: Irwin, Inc.

Chapter 11

Promotion in the Sport Industry

People will not buy a product if they do not know it exists. The first purpose of promotion is to tell people about a product. Therefore, promotion is a very important part of the marketing mix for a sport company. It is such an important variable that there are companies that sell promotion as promotional products and services to companies who want them. And there are so many of this kind of company that promotion is considered an industry. There are marketing firms and sport marketing firms, advertising firms, agents who specialize in promoting sports people or teams, and companies that specialize in producing promotional products, such as logo t-shirts, bags, cups, mugs, hats, towels, key-chains, watches, jackets, flags, banners, trinkets, and drink coolers. Further, within the promotion industry there is specialization. For example, there are companies that specialize in manufacturing products that will be sold to companies that specialize in printing on the products the logos, trademarks, brand names, or other images a company might want. There are companies that specialize in creating and managing the logos, licensing, and merchandising for a sport company (Pitts, Fielding, & Miller, 1994).

All Pro Championships, Inc. is one such company. This company, located in Louisville, Kentucky, manages the promotional merchandising and licensing for the Super Bowl and for the Kentucky Derby. These events are annual events and are quite large events when one considers the number of people involved, consumers, media attention, and audience. All Pro creates the logos and images that will be the official logos and images each year for the Super Bowl and the Kentucky Derby. All Pro manages obtaining the legal status for the logos and images. This gives All Pro, the Super Bowl, and the Kentucky Derby full legal rights to and control of the logos and images. If a company such as a local convenience store wants to sell Super Bowl or Kentucky Derby shirts and mugs, it must be licensed to do so. This means that it must pay a licensing fee to All Pro for the right to sell the merchandise. All Pro also controls the merchandise sales. Therefore, the store must purchase the merchandise through All Pro. There are many stores and individuals who want to sell the official merchandise of the Super Bowl and the Kentucky Derby because there are hundreds of thousands of people who want to purchase the merchandise for a variety of reasons.

Promotion is a very important element in the sport industry as in other industries because it is the communication tool of the industry. Again, people will not buy a product if they do not know it exists. In the sport industry communication is used to inform, educate, remind, or persuade people. The people to whom the sport company will communicate are existing and potential consumers. In addition, the sport company communicates to the general community, the business community, and the media. Therefore, it is correct to state that promotion is a form of communication.

In this chapter you will learn about promotion as a marketing mix variable. We will define it, outline the process of promotion planning, define promotion objectives, present the variety of promotion types, present the concept of promotion mix, and discuss the decision-making process for forming promotion strategies. In chapters 12, 13, 14, and 15 you will learn about specific promotional methods used in the sport industry.

Defining Promotion and Sport Promotion

The best place to begin understanding promotion is in defining it. Let us start with a dictionary definition. *Promotion* is a form of the word "promote." *To promote* means to persuade, to build up, to encourage, to advance, to exalt, to elevate, and to build a good image. *Promotion* is the act of promoting (Websters, 1989). Promoting can include activities designed to inform, to gain attention, to encourage action such as participation or purchasing, and to disseminate information. From a sport marketing perspective, activities of promotion to inform or educate might include advertising, direct mailing, or circulating informational flyers. Activities to persuade someone to buy a product might include scheduling a Madonna concert in conjunction with a sports event to encourage people to go to the event, bringing Shaquille O'Neal to your sporting goods store to sign autographs to encourage people to go to your store, or giving away 1,000 Bud Light can huggies to the first 1,000 people who go through the gates at your college basketball game to encourage people to go to the game.

From a general marketing perspective, Boone & Kurtz (1992) define promotion as "the function of informing, persuading, and influencing the consumer's purchase decision" (p. 526). Another definition is that promotion is "any form of communication used to inform, persuade, or remind people about an organization's goods, services, image, ideas, community involvement, or impact on society" (Evans & Berman, 1987, p. A43).

In a sport marketing perspective, promotion is applied to the sport industry and is defined as:

Sport Promotion: the function of informing or influencing people about the sport company's products, community involvement, or image.

In this definition the many segments of people to whom the sport company promotes are a significant factor when developing promotion strategies. The sport company promotes to the end consumer, the business consumer, the general community, the business community, and the media. To inform means that the sport company wants to tell them something. To influence means that the sport company wants a specific action from the person. Usually the final action wanted is a purchase action.

Each promotion action selected is based on the objectives of the promotion. The sport company will select a specific type of promotion, or form of communication, based on the objectives.

The Process of Communication

Communication is a process of transmitting or interchanging information, thoughts, or ideas through speech, writing, images, or signs (Webster's, 1989). There is an objective for the communication, a sender, a receiver, and a message (Stotlar, 1993; Stotlar & Bronzan, 1987). The sender has an objective for the communication and develops the message based on the objective and the receiver. The message is customized to the audience to whom it will be sent. An appropriate method for communicating is selected based on which method the sender believes will be most effective for the message and for the receiver.

In the process described above, the sport company is the sender, the promotional method is the channel for the message, and the receiver can be existing or potential consumers, the general community, the business community, or the media. For example, if the sport company wants the general community to know that it is a company that cares about the community and one way it does this is by financially supporting the local children's recreation leagues, it may select a billboard in the community to disseminate the message. It may choose to have a message emblazoned on the billboard, such as "We care. We are the proud supporter of the Central Children's Sports Leagues. — Southland Sporting Goods—where your family shops for all your sporting needs." The company may use more than one method to reach the audience. It may choose to post signs around the children's ball park, send a flyer through direct mail to everyone in the community, and do a special sale in recognition of its involvement in the children's leagues. The company must decide which methods will be most effective in gaining the attention of its audience and imparting the message.

Let us look at an example of how the entire process might work. Management of the Ship Shape Fitness Center has decided to target senior citizens. Their objective is to sell memberships to those senior citizens defined as 60-plus. Some products designed for and to be offered to this group are customized aerobics classes, one-on-one weight training, partner walking, water shaping, and a 60-plus tennis league. T-shirts will be specially designed to give as awards for milestones and league winners. The company develops the following message to be used as its primary promotion slogan: "Fitness is good for you no matter how young you are!" Management believes that this message is positive and keys on the 60-plus person thinking of her or himself as young, not old. Promotional activities will include a one-week open house. The open house will include activities designed to educate the 60-plus person about fitness. There will be exhibitions to show how fitness can be a fun and attainable goal. Management decides that the center will get 50-, 60-, or 70-year-olds to perform the exhibitions. The objective for this is that the 60-plus person can see someone of his or her age exercising. The target group can relate to this much better than watching a very young and fit person exercising. The methods for communicating the message are selected based on the best method for reaching the audience. From their marketing research, management learns that this market most likely does not work outside the home, they are busy people and are not at home very much, and they do not watch a lot of television or listen to radio. Therefore, management conludes that the best way to reach the audience is through direct mail advertising. The piece will be informative, simple, and will include information about the open house and the center. Other promotional methods will include coupons for 2 free days at the center, a special half-price membership fee for the first year, and special membership fee discounts for every year after that.

The sport marketer in this example has identified a target market, selected a positive message, and developed promotional methods specifically for the market. The products added were designed for the market, and the prices were identified based on the market's income. Communication is the tool used in getting the message to the consumer.

Reasons for Promotion

One of the primary reasons for promotion is to let people know about your product. As stated at the beginning of this chapter, if no one knows about your product, no one will buy it. There are other reasons for promotion because there are many different messages a sport company wants to communicate to the people about its product or company. Let us look at some of those reasons for promotion.

<u>Promotion establishes an image</u>. The sport marketer has a reason for being in business and a mission for the company. The company was designed based on a specific market segment. Therefore, the sport marketer wants to communicate a specific image to the consumer and the community. The image may be luxury, prestige, convenience, cost-saving, one-stop shopping, or creativity. The message of the promotion will communicate the company's image. For example, if the company is a marina and the objective of the marina is primarily to service and house large, expensive yachts, the promotional mix and message should communicate luxury and prestige. The marina's name might be "Class One Yacht Club." The communication through promotional methods such as advertising might be a slogan, such as "Our home is your home at Class One Yacht Club" or

"Yachting is your luxury and your luxury is our business." Through the name of the company and the communication message in the slogan, the consumer is told that this marina is for the upper-class consumer who owns a yacht and that this company will take care of this consumer in the fashion to which she or he is accustomed.

Promotion can reposition the image of a faltering product. If a product is gaining a poor reputation, the sport marketer can turn around the image of the product. For example, personal watercrafts (PWCs), more commonly known as jet skis, have begun to get a poor reputation because of the loud noise level of the engine, the recklessness of the drivers, the increase in accidents, and the increase in numbers invading previously quiet water areas. The Personal Watercraft Industries Association (PWIA) and several PWC manufacturers have rallied and created a variety of promotional methods they hope will facilitate control of the reputation and turn it around. Their activities are directed at the end consumer, manufacturers, PWC rental businesses, and state and local water-governance organizations. Some of their activities include educational programs on safety (posters, videocassettes, bochures), research to decrease the noise produced by the PWC, rescue and education loan programs in which manufacturers loan PWCs to area coast guard offices or rescue units for their use, and loans to lake and beach lifeguard stations for rescue operations (Holland, Pybas, & Sanders, 1992). The cooperative promotional effort is to change the reputation of the PWC in order to positively affect sales.

Promotion creates awareness for new products. As stated earlier, if people do not know your product exists, they will not buy it. If the sport company is planning to release a new product, no one will know unless the company communicates this.

Promotion alerts the consumer to sales. The consumer will not know that the company will be having a sale unless you tell them. The sport marketer must identify promotional methods and the communication message that will tell the consumer about the sale: dates, times, type of sale, purpose of sale, and any other information the consumer might need. If your company is a sporting goods retail store and you are planning a Thanksgiving sale, you must create the promotion to tell the consumer. Another important factor is your decision on when and where to promote. For example, your Thanksgiving sale will be the Friday, Saturday and Sunday after Thanksgiving day. Perhaps the best promotion is an advertisement in the local newspaper, and the best time to run the ad is in the Sunday paper before Thanksgiving.

Promotion tells the consumer where your business is located. Although this sounds like a simple message, and it is, the consumer needs to know where the business is located. If the information is provided, the consumer does not have to spend extra time trying to find the business. This communication is usually handled within the promotion as a map depicting the location or as instructions on how to get there. Sometimes a business will use a well-known landmark as a locater. For example, a well-known landmark in the city of Louisville, Kentucky, is the Water Tower—an historic city waterworks facility situated on the Ohio River. Businesses in the area use the Water Tower as a locater. A boat retailer's advertisements include the words "next to the Water Tower." A restaurant uses the same words. An indoor soccer facility uses the wording "located close to the Water Tower." The purpose of the message in the promotion is to establish the location of the business.

Promotion Planning

Figure 11.1 illustrates the steps to be taken in promotion planning. *Promotion planning* is the process of developing all aspects of the company's communication effort. There are many factors that should be considered which will affect decisions concerning the promotion element of the company's marketing mix.

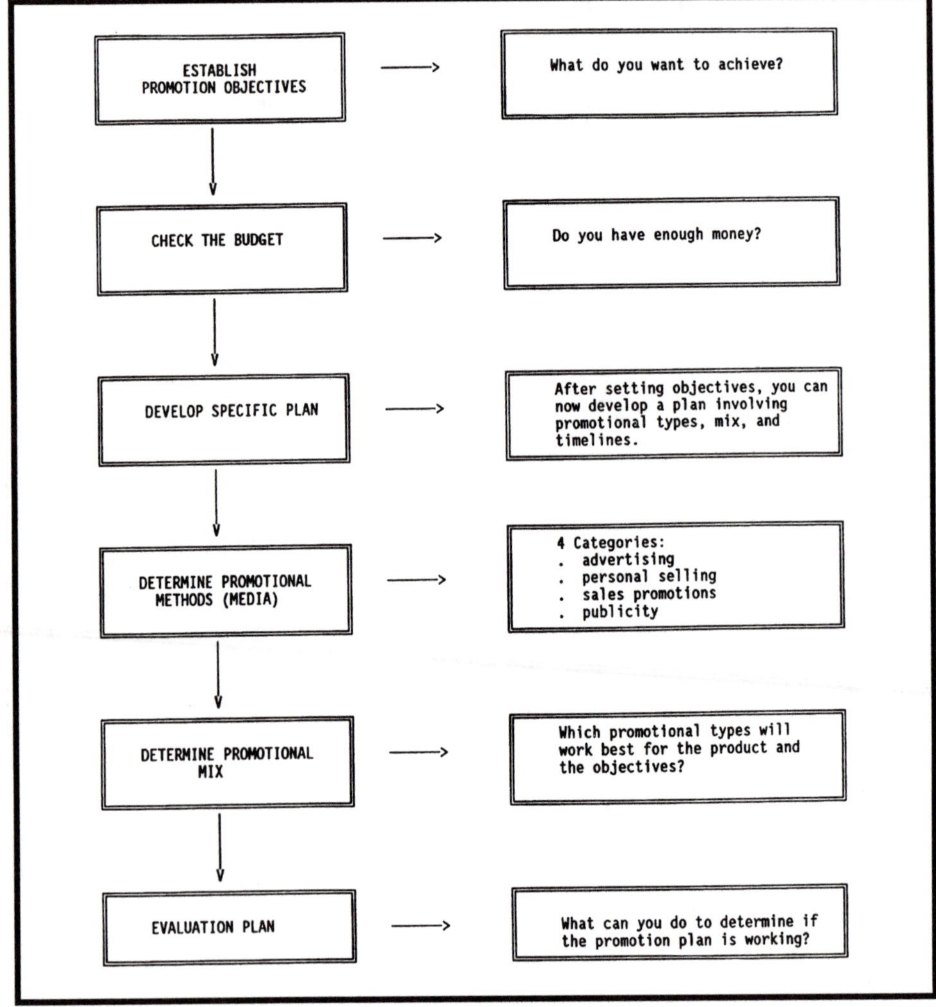

FIGURE 11.1 - Promotional Planning Model

Some of these are the consumer, the competitor, money and other resources, product life cycle, and mission and objectives of the sport company. The following sections discuss the steps in the promotion planning process.

Promotion Objectives

In the promotion planning process, the first step is to establish promotion objectives. The establishment of promotion objectives is based on this question: What does your company want to achieve in promotion? Some factors to consider include stage of product life cycle, reasons for considering a promotion plan, and resources available. The promotion objectives should derive from the marketing objectives, which should derive from the company objectives.

Promotion objectives are statements that specify exact actions desired by the company. They are based on what the company wants. Usually the objectives are demand oriented, education oriented, or image oriented. The overall objective is to affect behavior, knowledge, or attitude. Table 11.2 illustrates these objective types, purpose, outcome desired, message, and an example of each.

If the sport company wants to affect behavior, demand oriented objectives will

TABLE 11.2 - Sport Promotion Objective Types

TYPES OF OBJECTIVES:	DEMAND	EDUCATION	IMAGE
PURPOSE	To affect behavior	To affect knowledge	To affect attitude or perception
OUTCOME DESIRED	Consumer purchases the company's product	To educate or inform the consumer about the company or its products	Consumer thinks of company in specific terms: good, positive, brilliant, creative, fun, serious, etc.
MESSAGE	• persuasive • demand oriented	• informative • reminder	• informative • persuasive
EXAMPLE	A sport shoe manufacturer uses a famous male basketball player to persuade the consumer to buy its shoes.	A new sport marketing firm is opening. It places an ad in local business paper that tells story of company, what it does, its products and services, where it is located, and its hours of business.	A women's professional golf association uses TV and billboard ads to tell about its disadvantaged-youth golf-with-the-pros day held once a year. The association and the players pay for the youth to spend a day with the players golfing and participating in other events.

be established. The behavior that the company wants to affect is purchase behavior. The company wants the consumer to purchase its products and wants to persuade the consumer to do so. With this as an objective, the company must design a promotional method and message that persuade the consumer to buy.

If the company wants to educate or inform the consumer about something, education oriented objectives are developed. Usually, the company wants to educate the consumer about the company, its products, services, or other information. Typical information includes the location of the company, information on sales taking place, the company's offerings, or something about the company's products.

If the sport company wants to affect attitude or perception, it will develop image oriented objectives. The company wants the consumer or other to think in a specific way toward the company. Usually, the company wants the consumer to think positively about it.

Check the Budget and Other Resources

During the process of developing the objectives it would be very wise for the sport marketer to know how much money is available for promotion and if the company has other necessary resources available. This information will certainly have an impact on decisions made for promotional planning. Some promotional methods are expensive whereas others are inexpensive and still others are free. Television advertising can be very expensive. On the other hand, staging an open house is relatively inexpensive.

Idealistically, the sport marketer must determine what promotional methods are available that are most effective for the objectives. However, realistically, when this is determined, an inquiry should be conducted to determine if there are enough money and other resources to pay for and follow through with the promotional methods selected.

After checking the budget and other resources needed for the promotional methods selected, you will now develop a detailed plan of action involving selecting the most appropriate and effective promotional types, determine a promotional mix, and develop an evaluation plan.

The plan will include details concerning the objectives, budget, who will perform which tasks, the promotional mix and evaluation plan, and a detailed schedule with deadlines and timelines for each task.

Promotional Methods

There are four general categories of promotional methods: advertising, personal selling, sales promotions, and publicity. Most of these are discussed in detail in chapters 12, 13, 14, and 15. Table 11.3 illustrates the four categories and specific promotional methods available for the sport marketer in each category.

Advertising is any nonpersonal form of paid communications and is usually presented in newspapers, magazines, television, radio, signs, direct mail, sponsorship methods, and endorsement methods (Branvold & Bowers, 1992; Evans & Berman, 1987; National Park Service, 1991; Stotlar, 1993).

Personal selling is direct face-to-face promotion between the seller and a potential consumer (Peter & Donnelly, 1991). It also may include selling via the telephone, videoconferences, and interactive computer links (Boone & Kurtz, 1992). In addition, today there is selling through television. Consider those

TABLE 11.3 - Four Categories of Promotion Methods and Some Examples

ADVERTISING	PERSONAL SELLING	SALES PROMOTIONS	PUBLICITY
• newspaper ad • magazine ad • television • radio ad • direct mail • billboard ad • ads on buses, grocery carts, walls, etc. • sponsorship • merchandising • the logo	• sales force • public speaking	• telemarketing • price • point of purchase display • newsletter • giveaways • target market specials • sponsorship • special events • open house day • dinner, parties, etc. • exhibitions • merchandising	• press conference • press release • articles in local or other newspaper • coverage on TV or radio

television channels dedicated to bringing into your home hundreds of thousands of products. These are hosted by professional salespeople and a simple phone call to the company will complete the purchase of any product offered on the show. Personal selling is a major element in the sport industry. There are salespeople in the sporting goods stores, salespeople for sports apparel manufacturing companies to sell their products to retailers, promoters whose job is to sell a sporting event to television and sponsors, telemarketers whose job is to sell tickets for the team, and salespeople whose job is to sell advertising space in the Super Bowl Program. In addition, in the sport industry, individuals who are not trained salespeople become salespeople. For example, in college men's basketball, the players and coaches become salespeople for the program. They are scheduled to speak at local banquets and other activities. The coach usually has a local show aired once a week, and the coach usually is hired by local businesses as a "pitch person" in advertisements for their products.

Sales promotions consist of those promotional activities other than advertising, personal selling, or publicity activities that are designed to affect consumer attitude or behavior. Some sales promotions include telemarketing, price promotions, point-of-purchase display, newsletter, giveaways, sponsorship, merchandising, and special events.

Sales promotions are used extensively in the sport industry, especially for sporting events. One of the reasons is that there are many sales promotions that are relatively inexpensive and many that do not cost the sport company at all. For example, the Louisville Redbirds, a minor league men's baseball team, planned a Beach Boys concert immediately following one of the games. The promotional event drew three times as many spectators (almost 20,000) as other games (Branvold & Bowers, 1992). Other examples include the following:

- hosting a fun-run
- holding a barbeque for members of the fitness club
- giving away a car at the half-time of the football game as a door prize to someone in attendance
- hosting a celebrity tennis tournament
- holding a wellness fair
- holding an authentic Hawaiian luau
- holding an open house
- holding a live band aerobics evening
- getting a famous athlete to make an appearance in your store to sign autographs
- encouraging tailgating for the local college football game
- giving out free pass coupons
- hosting a holiday tournament

Publicity is any form of unpaid promotion. This includes the promotion or communication that comes in the form of being mentioned in a magazine or being the subject of an article in the local newspaper. Although it is usually free or at a minimal cost to the sport company, the disadvantage of publicity is that the company usually has no control over the content. This means that if the local paper wants to write an article about the company, the reporter can write almost anything wanted about your company.

Some sport companies try to influence the kind of publicity they believe will be developed and offered to the public. For example, most large college women's and men's athletic departments will stage a "press day." Reporters, journalists, and sports broadcasters are invited to come to "press day." They are encouraged to interview and photograph the athletes and coaches. Packets of material are offered to each individual. The packets contain information about the athletes and coaches, such as their records in high school, past season's records, highlights, hometown information, human interest information, and expectations for the upcoming season. There will also be plenty to eat and drink. The purpose for press day is to treat the press positively in the hopes that the press will return the positiveness through their stories, reports, articles, and broadcasts. The treatment doesn't stop here! At every sport event during the season there is a special room for the press. The "press room" will again contain packets of information, pictures, and current statistics about the season. Of course, there will be plenty of food and drink!

Most college athletics departments employ a full-time person, typically called a sports information director, to coordinate and manage the press and public relations activities for the college. The sports information director, called the SID, will have a staff ranging from one work-study student to a corps of employees, including an assistant SID, graduate assistants, secretaries, and several work-study students. It is the job of the sports information office to manage all of the public relations, media relations, and publicity activities for the athletic office. The office will develop the media guides, manage press day and the press room, develop the press packets, and make available up-to-the-minute statistics and general information. Although these activities are sales promotion activities, the target market includes the media, and the activities are designed to influence attitude and perception.

The Promotional Mix

After establishing the promotion objectives, developing the budget, and considering promotional methods that will work best for the company, product, and consumer, the sport marketer must determine its promotional mix. The *promotional mix* is the combination of promotional methods that will help the sport company meet its objectives in the most effective way. It is rare that a sport company will use only one method—for example, a college athletic program use only direct mail, a sport marketing company use only billboards, a sporting goods retailer use only newspaper advertising, or the Special Olympics use only merchandising. It is more typical and much more effective for the company to use a mixture of the methods.

The decisions about which methods to use are contingent on many factors. Figure 11.4 illustrates many of the factors that affect the decision on promotional mix. Each of these is discussed briefly here.

Each promotional method serves a different function (Evans & Berman, 1987). Advertising on television can reach a large number of consumers. Publicity can reach a large number of consumers but cannot be controlled by the company. Personal selling is effective if the salesperson is knowledgeable and influential, but it serves a very small number of consumers. Sales promotions are effective in different ways depending on the type of sales promotion. Each sales promotion attracts a different consumer and a different number of consumers.

The company will affect the promotional mix (Evans & Berman, 1987). Some promotional methods fit some companies better than others. Giveaways and Girl Scout night (sales promotions) are more effective for a minor league professional league baseball team than for a sport marketing company. Direct mail (advertising) is more effective for the New York Marathon than for the Super Bowl.

1. **A different function for each method**
2. **The company**
3. **Stage of product life cycle**
4. **Access to promotional methods**
5. **Channels of distribution**
6. **Target markets**
7. **The competition**
8. **Geographic dispersement of the consumer market**
9. **The product**
10. **Push or pull strategy**
11. **Laws**
12. **Sport company resources**

FIGURE 11.4 - Factors Affecting Decision on Promotional Mix

The stage of product life cycle will affect decisions concerning the promotional mix (Bradbury, 1990; Stanton, Etzel, & Walker, 1991). During the introductory stage the company should aggressively promote the product. This means that the promotion budget will need to be extensive. During the growth stage sales will increase. This means that revenue will increase. Promotional methods and aggressiveness will change and money put into promotion will decrease. In the maturity stage, the pace of sales may slow and will plateau eventually. During this stage, however, the product is established, and promotional objectives and methods will change. If a product is approaching the decline stage, promotional objectives and methods must change to avoid disaster. If the product is allowed to continue in this direction, eventually all sales will cease. Typically, promotion objectives and methods are aggressive. Sometimes, the product is repositioned and treated like a new product.

Access to promotional methods will affect which methods the sport company is able to use (Evans & Berman, 1987). Some methods may not be accessible to the sport company. Some of the factors that affect accessibility include the following:

1. Budget: Sometimes there is no money or not enough money for what the sport company wants to do. Advertising on television is more expensive

than advertising in the local newspaper.

2. Location of the promotional method: The promotional method may not be within the geographical location the sport company wants, or the method may not reach a particular geographical that the sport company needs to reach with a promotional method.
3. Requirements: The promotional method may have requirements that the sport company cannot meet.

<u>Channels of distribution will impact decisions on the promotional methods used</u> (Evans & Berman, 1987). Managers of specific channels may have requirements that the sport company cannot or will not agree with.

<u>Target markets of the sport company will influence promotional methods</u>. The promotional methods will need to be effective for each target market identified by the sport company. Target market factors to consider include geographic location, size, and all demographics and psychographics. Some promotional method factors to consider are listed below in the form of questions:

1. Which method will catch the attention of the market? Only sport marketing consumer research can answer this question. A true understanding of the consumer will guide the sport marketer to the decision concerning the method to which the consumer will positively react.
2. What kind of message will attract the consumer, and will the consumer be able to understand it? Again, consumer research will guide the sport marketer to the answer to this question. The sport marketer should develop the promotional message so that the consumer can relate to it and understand it. In other words, the sport marketer should consider writing the advertising message in the consumer's language.
3. Can the promotional method reach the intended target market? If a sport magazine is being considered as an advertising medium, does the target market subscribe to the magazine? For example, the Gay Games uses promotional methods that reach its specific target market: the lesbian and gay population around the world. Some of these are direct mail using mailing lists of prior Games participants and from lesbian and gay magazine publishers, merchandising advertisements in mail order catalogues, such as *Shocking Gray*, and advertising in lesbian and gay targeted magazines, such as *The Advocate*, *Deneuve*, and *Out*.

Signage — a form of advertising in a stadium or arena — is an effective promotional method for many companies (Stotlar & Johnson, 1989). Although most of the companies using signage are not sport companies, some sport companies do use signage. Signage has its roots in outdoor billboards. However, whereas a billboard has space and location limitations and captures the attention of the consumer for a few seconds as the consumer drives by, a sign in a stadium is in front of the consumer as long as the event lasts. Length of events can range from one hour to five hours. That amounts to a lot of impression time! *Impression time* is the length of time an ad or message is displayed within the consumer's line of vision. During an event such as the Indy 500, which lasts approximately 5 hours, signage can make a significant impact on impression time. The Indy 500 event is televised and attracts a large viewership. The signage will be everywhere, including on the cars and the drivers' suits and helmets (Ruff, 1992a, 1992b). The spectator attending the event is surrounded by the signage and the consumer watching the event on television will be impacted with the advertising. As the camera captures and focuses on a specific car, the television viewer will see the advertising on the car. As the camera follows the cars around the track, various signs come in and out of view. As the research shows, nearly 70% of the spectatorship can identify advertising they saw during an event (Stotlar & Johnson, 1989).

<u>The competitor will affect the promotional method selected for the sport company</u>. Although the promotional methods must be selected and designed for the consumer, equal attention must be given to the competitor (Schnaars, 1991). Promotional methods selected can impact sport marketing strategies, such as gaining market share, outmaneuvering a competitor in a specific area, such as price, market penetration, and advertising message. The sport company must spend time gaining an understanding of the consumer and what the consumer wants and, at the same time, must spend the same amount of time studying its competitors.

<u>Geographic dispersement of the consumer market will affect the promotional methods selected</u>. Personal selling is best for localized markets. However, as the location of the sport company's consumers spreads geographically, the company will have to consider promotional methods that will reach the consumers.

<u>The product and its elements will affect the promotional methods selected</u>. The type of product and the characteristics and elements of the product will impact the method and message of promotion. Some of the characteristics include product type (good, service, person, place, idea), customized versus standardized, differentiation, quality, features, performance, design, and product life cycle stage. Sport product characteristics should help guide the sport marketer in selecting a promotional method best for the product.

<u>Decision to use a push or a pull promotion strategy will affect the promotional method used</u> (Cravens & Woodruff, 1986; Peter & Donnelly, 1991). The objective of both strategies is to get the product into the consumer's hands. A *push* strategy involves trying to move the product into the channels of distribution and encouraging sellers to increase sales volumes. The strategy usually involves offering a variety of awards and enticements to the channellers. Many sporting goods manufacturers use this strategy. A company will offer

incentives or price breaks to a wholesaler or retailer increasing sales volume. A *pull* strategy involves strong promotion directed toward the end consumer in order to affect the consumer's demand for the product. The consumer's demand for the product acts to "pull" the product through the channels. The sport company's promotional methods are designed to target the consumer and create demand. The consumer in turn asks for the product. For example, if a sporting goods retailer does not carry a specific product, the consumer can ask the retailer to carry the product.

Laws governing promotion will affect selection of promotional methods. Local, state, and federal government agencies and consumer protection agencies have enacted laws, guidelines, and restrictions that affect a sport company's promotional efforts. Some of these include the Federal Trade Commission, the Food and Drug Administration, the Securities and Exchange Commission, the United States Patent Office, the Library of Congress, and the Department of Justice. Other organizations and groups also work to control promotions. Two of these are the National Association of Broadcasters and the Better Business Bureau. Further, individual companies exercise ethical decision making in selecting and developing promotional methods.

Sport company resources will impact the promotional methods decision. There are two types of resources within a sport company: material and nonmaterial. Material resources include money, supplies, equipment, and the like. Nonmaterial resources include human resources. Does the sport company have the resources necessary to accomplish the promotional methods it is considering? The critical bottom line may be the ultimate factor affecting the company's decision concerning promotional methods.

As you can see, there are many factors the sport marketer must consider and analyze in the process of selecting the promotional methods for the company.

Evaluation

What can the sport marketer do to determine if the promotion plan is effective? How can the sport marketer determine if one part of the plan is effective and another part is ineffective? The sport marketer must establish a method to determine if the plan or parts of the plan are accomplishing what the company wants. This is the best place to start—what the company wants. The promotion objectives outline what the company wants to achieve with the promotional plan. Is the plan accomplishing these objectives? In order to answer the question, the sport marketer must assess the outcomes of the plan. Typically, this is done through marketing research. Although chapter 5 details marketing research, the following is a brief look at how it can be used for determining promotional effectiveness.

Some types of marketing research are good for determining if the promotional plan is working. If the sport company wants to determine if certain forms of advertising are effective, it can conduct a consumer survey. The survey will provide answers for the sport marketer to analyze. In the analysis, the sport marketer must assess whether or not the advertising is accomplishing its goals. For example, the Blue Ridge Ski Resort wants to determine the effectiveness of the direct mail advertising its special two-for-one ski week. The sport marketer prepares a special skier check-in form that will be used for that week only. There will be questions on the form that ask the skiers to identify where and how they found out about the special. If 50% of the respondents state that they found out about the special in the direct mail they received, the sport marketer can make a subjective judgment about whether the promotional method was successful. If there were 12 people who came for the special, 50% is 6. If 6 skiers found out about the special through the direct mail they received, does that mean that it was an effective method? Before we can answer that question, we must ask, "How many direct mail pieces were sent to potential buyers?" If the answer is 1,000 pieces, 6 out of 1,000 could be determined unsuccessful. If the answer is 20 pieces, perhaps 6 out of 20, or 30%, may be considered to be a successful method.

Promotion and Legal Issues

There are laws, guidelines, regulations, policy, and perception that affect promotion. The primary reason for regulation is consumer protection. The sport marketer must study and understand all of the regulations in order to produce a legal and ethical promotional plan. These areas are discussed in the following sections.

Laws. The sport marketer must know, understand, and apply the laws to the promotional plan. Federal regulation involves two primary laws: the Federal Trade Commission (FTC) Act and the Robinson-Patman Act. The FTC Act prohibits unfair methods of competition. One area of unfair competition is false, misleading, or deceptive advertising. The Robinson-Patman Act outlaws price discrimination and has two sections on promotional allowances. These sections state that promotional allowances must be fair and equal.

Regulation by other organizations. There are many organizations that affect promotional activities. For example, the Better Business Bureau is a nationwide company that works as a consumer advocate and works to control promotion practices.

Industry control. Many industries and individual companies work to affect promotional activities of their counterparts. These controlling mechanisms, although they are not law, are very effective in regulating ethical and tasteful promotional practices of companies.

Promotion and Ethical Issues

Every aspect and function of the sport business must follow ethical guidelines usually determined partially by the company and partially by the public. Ethical considerations should be given serious attention in areas including sociocultural issues and environmental issues. The sport marketer cannot afford to assume that the population of the United States or even other countries is of a similar culture and similar lifestyle. Serious attention to socioeconomic factors, cultural factors, and other such factors will result in a responsible and leadership role for the business. In other words, it is critical that the sport marketer always work to "do the right thing" ethically and in socially responsible ways to position the company as people friendly and earth friendly.

Chapter Summary

People will not buy your product if they do not know it exists. Promotion is the tool of the sport marketer that communicates to the people about the company and its products. Sport promotion is the function of informing people about the sport company's products, community involvement, or image. Promotion can establish a company image, reposition a product, create awareness for a new product, alert the consumer to sales, tell the consumer where the sport company is located, and inform the consumer on where a product can be purchased. The steps of promotion planning involve establishing objectives, determining promotional methods deemed best for achieving those objectives, and developing a promotional mix. The sport marketer must know and understand the many factors that impact the development of the promotional mix. Finally, the sport marketer must know the laws and the legal and ethical issues surrounding promotion in today's society.

Questions for Study

1. What is promotion?
2. What is sport promotion?
3. Why is promotion important to the sport marketer?
4. What is the process of communication?
5. What are promotional methods? Give some examples in the sport industry.
6. What is the promotional mix?
7. What are the factors that affect decisions about the promotional mix?
8. What are legal issues affecting promotion?
9. What are ethics and what are some ethical issues the sport marketer should use in determining promotion strategies?

Learning Activities

1. Conduct a study of three different sport businesses, organizations, or other enterprises in your city or community. Determine the promotional methods used by each.
2. Collect print advertising of a variety of sport products from a variety of resources. Conduct a study of the ads and determine the target market(s) and the promotional message.
3. What are some populations recently objecting to the use of certain promotional messages and logos? In discussion groups, discuss the reasons and the ethical responsibility of the sport marketer.

References

Boone, L.E., & Kurtz, D.L. (1992). *Contemporary marketing.* Orlando, FL: The Dryden Press.

Bradbury, M. (1990). How club life cycles affect strategy. *Club Business International, 11*(7), 16, 35, 37.

Branvold, S.E., & Bowers, R. (1992). The use of promotions in college baseball. *Sport Marketing Quarterly, 1*(1), 19-24.

Cravens, D.W., & Woodruff, R.B. (1986). *Marketing.* Reading, MA: Addison-Wesley Publishing Company.

Evans, J.R., & Berman, B. (1987). *Marketing.* New York: Macmillan Publishing Company.

Holland, S., Pybas, D., & Sanders, A. (1992). Personal watercrafts: Fun, speed—and conflict? *Parks and Recreation, 27*(11), 52-56.

National Park Service. (1991). *Marketing parks and recreation.* State College, PA: Venture Publishing, Inc.

Peter, J.P., & Donnelly, J.H. (1991). *A preface to marketing management* (5th Ed.). Boston, MA: Irwin, Inc.

Pitts, B.G., Fielding, L.W., & Miller, L.K. (1994). Industry segmentation theory and the sport industry: Developing a sport industry segment model. *Sport Marketing Quarterly,* 3(1), 15-24.

Ruff, M. (Ed.). (1992a). The driving force. *AutoWeek,* 42(22), 37.

Ruff, M. (Ed.). (1992b). What's in a name? *AutoWeek,* 42(22), 37.

Schnaars, S.P. (1991). *Marketing strategy: A consumer-driven approach.* New York: The Free Press.

Stanton, W.J., Etzel, M.J. & Walker, B.J. (1991). *Fundamentals of marketing.* New York: McGraw-Hill, Inc.

Stotlar, D.K. (1993). *Successful sport marketing.* Dubuque, IA: Brown and Benchmark.

Stotlar, D.K., & Bronzan, R.T. (1987). *Public relations and promotions in sport.* Daphne, AL: United Stated Sports Academy.

Stotlar, D.K., & Johnson, D. A. (1989). Assessing the impact and effectiveness of stadium advertising on sport spectators at division I institutions. *Journal of Sport Management,* 3(1), 90-102.

Webster's encyclopedic unabridged dictionary of the English language. (1989). New York: Portland House.

CHAPTER 12

PROMOTIONAL METHODS IN SPORT

When you say the word promotion, many concepts come to mind, some good, some bad. Promotions can be defined as all corporate activities aimed at influencing consumer-purchasing attitudes and behaviors. However, to some people, promotions have come to mean some shady practice where misrepresentation and inaccuracy are used to sway the public into unwanted or unnecessary purchases. According to Ries and Trout (1986), consumers screen and reject a considerable amount of the product and marketing information delivered via traditional communication sources. As such, consumers may not be conscious of wants until their wants are stimulated by the sport marketer through an array of well-selected and designed promotional activities. Creating new concepts and ideas about wants and products or services to fulfill them is difficult; therefore, sport marketers must be proficient in their promotional strategy to move the consumer to purchase.

Promotions are an integral part of all communication efforts. Promotion has as its main objective the acquisition and retention of public acceptance of an idea, product, or service. This can be accomplished through effective communication with consumers. It is incumbent on the marketer to develop communications that are socially responsible and ethically sound. According to Bronzan and Stotlar (1987), there are four essential ingredients in promotional communication: the sender, the message, the medium, and the receiver. For messages to convey clear and succinct meanings, the sender must accurately create the message and put it in an appropriate media form. When the receiver encounters a message, it must be decoded and interpreted. Interpretation of the message is influenced by the receiver's emotional status, perceptions of the sender, and cultural disposition, among other factors. As a result, sport marketers use promotional communications to influence or change the attitudes, opinions, and behavior of consumers in the sport industry.

The primary components of promotion in the sport industry include advertising, publicity and public relations, personal selling, and sales promotion. These components exist in conjunction with each other and can be used by the marketer in harmony or separately to accomplish marketing and sales objectives. Experts refer to this as the promotional mix. An effective manager must be able to integrate the promotional mix into the total marketing function of the organization.

Competition between specialists in each area can defeat the purpose of the promotional mix. For example, the advertising department may claim that it can do more to produce results than can the sales force. On the other hand, the public relations department may assert that its activities are more effective than advertising. Therefore, a marketing manager must clearly understand the role of each component and be able to integrate their functions into the organization's overall business and marketing plan.

Advertising

The United States has only 6% of the world's population, yet it consumes more that 57% of the advertising (Ries & Trout, 1986). Hiebing and Cooper (1990) define advertising as a message which informs and persuades consumers through paid media. We are all aware of effective and ineffective advertising. Think for a minute about ads you have seen and enjoyed, but where you cannot remember the product; whereas other ads immediately bring a specific product to mind. All advertising firms plan for success, but it is not always achieved. Consider the short-lived Reebok campaign of "U.B.U." and Nike's long-running "Just Do It" advertising.

Advertising is a controlled medium. That is, the message delivered to the consumer is carefully crafted and controlled by the organization so that its content consists of only information that the organization wishes the consumer to receive. However, because advertising is controlled by the company, the credibility with consumers may be low. Recent studies have shown that 78% of consumers feel that advertisers exploit children, 70% believe that they make unfair brand comparisons, and 67% say that businesses make misleading or exaggerated claims for their products.

In sport, advertising can take many forms. There is advertising <u>of</u> sport products and services and advertising <u>through</u> sports events. The advertising of sport products and services is a multimillion-dollar industry. As an example, in 1992, Reebok spent over $95 million in advertising while the athletic shoe industry leader, Nike, spent over $115 million.

Advertising through sport is also a sizable segment of the industry. According to Stotlar (1993), sport advertising approaches $5 billion per year. Much of that total is spent by companies that use sport events and publications for advertising nonsport products. A primary motive for this activity is that sports present a wholesome image and a wide demographic profile from which specific segments can be targeted.

Advertising through sports events can also take the form of a sponsorship, as will be detailed in chapter 14. The research that has been done on sponsorship through stadium advertising (Branvold, 1992; Stotlar and Johnson, 1989) has shown that it is an effective media purchase.

A popular advertising-related promotional activity conducted by many sport organizations is the trade-out, the process by which a sport organization gives something of value (complimentary seats, stadium advertising space, program ads) to the media in exchange for advertising space or air-time for use in promotional activities.

Promotional trade-out programs within the university segment seek to do two things: increase the attendance at athletic events and increase overall support of the school's programs. Radio seems to be a popular choice as one of the media selected for trade-out campaigns. Many universities trade-out radio time for tickets at a cash-value ratio of about 3-1 favoring the university (Savod, 1987). Some universities have negotiated deals with major TV markets using coveted football or basketball tickets as barter. Newspaper and billboard space can also be included in this strategy (Savod, 1987).

One university in particular used a 50-station radio network to blanket their state plus critical consumer areas in adjoining states. During the summer and early fall, radio tapes were made by varsity football players discussing their football program and the upcoming season. In this setting, you need to make sure that all of your activities are in compliance with collegiate rules. These plans were particularly successful in encouraging advertisers who had rejected traditional appeals for direct advertising (Savod, 1987). Additional coverage of this topic is in chapter 14 in dealing with leveraged media sponsorships.

Publicity

Publicity is one of the most important terms in designing a promotional mix. Hiebing and Cooper (1990) indicate that publicity differs from advertising in that, although it informs and affects consumer attitudes, it is free. As with advertising, the primary objective of publicity is to draw attention to a product, an organization, or an event. However, because publicity comes from a third, presumed neutral party, its credibility is greater than that of advertising (Stotlar, 1993). Also, publicity, because it is free, is an uncontrolled media tool with the content and delivery regulated by the media outlet.

All sport marketers should realize that publicity alone will not sell tickets, raise funds, win supporters, retain members, or sell merchandise, but publicity can be helpful in conveying ideas to people so that these ends can be more easily attained.

Publicity should be planned with these guidelines in mind:

1. Too much publicity can be poor public relations, because often at a given point people tend to react negatively to excessive publicity.

2. The amount of publicity absorbed is important, not the amount printed.
3. The amount of publicity disseminated does not necessarily equal the amount used.
4. The nature of the publicity eventually tends to reveal the character of the institution or department it seeks to promote, for better or worse.
5. Some publicity an institution or department receives originates from outside sources.
6. All promotional activities do not result in publicity.

A successful publicity program depends on the development of an effective plan. This plan should incorporate the following elements:

1. identification of publicity needs
2. recognition of appropriate media sources
3. development of goals for each source
4. creation of a specific methodology for targeted sources
5. implementation through selected promotional materials
6. assessment of publicity outcomes.

The primary objective of publicity is to draw attention to a person, an organization, or an event. Sometimes attention is directed to the sport organization in negative situations: Accusations, accidents, and indiscretions can occur in any sports organization, and unfavorable publicity often results. One of the worst mistakes that a public relations practitioner can make is to give additional publicity to bad news by attempting to deny or explain the problem (Helitzer, 1992). In one-to-one communication, a dialogue can exist and a general conclusion as to the truth can be reached. However, mass media do not operate on a one-to-one basis. Since the readers, listeners, or viewers of stories are not always encountered on the same days, only part of the audience that saw or heard the original story will hear or see the rebuttal. Thus, the part of the audience who receive only the rebuttal begin to seek additional information and impetus to the "crisis" and those who only received the original story remain unaffected by the rebuttal.

Personal Selling

Personal selling is defined as an oral presentation with potential customers for the express purpose of making a sale. Commitment to personal selling as opportunity is one of the keys to effectiveness. There is an understanding among those in sales that communicating how a product or service can benefit the consumer is paramount. Within this approach is the belief that without the salesperson, consumers would not be capable of realizing the benefits of consumption and that personal selling, therefore, is the most important aspect in the promotional mix.

You may not personally adhere to that philosophy, but there are many sellers who do. They see their role as providing the link between the organization and consumers, so that consumers' lives may be enhanced by the product or service to which they were introduced.

Success in personal selling depends heavily on locating potential consumers. Connor (1981) said that "if you can master one skill in selling, become a master prospector. It will guarantee your future success" (p. 14). What exactly is prospecting? It is building a viable portfolio of potential clients and customers which positions the salesperson for work. Just as many executives go to the office, the person in sales consults the prospects data base. The question arises, just how do you go about creating a client base with potential customers? For the sport marketer, this often leads to the marketing information system discussed in chapter 6. You should also remember the traditional 80-20 business adage where 80% of your sales usually result from 20% of your customers.

Sales Promotion

The term sales promotion has been characterized as "a catch-all for all communication instruments that do not fit into advertising, personal selling or publicity categories" (van Waterschoot & Van den Bulte, 1992, p. 87). In their review of contemporary definitions, van Waterschoot and Van den Bulte (1992) indicate that sales promotions are activities of short duration that are intended to move consumers to an immediate exchange.

In the sport industry, several examples exist that can be categorized as sales promotions. Point-of-purchase displays are particularly effective. In retail sporting goods stores, displays of products are often used to tie the product with previous advertising. The phrase "as seen on TV" should be familiar to most sports consumers. Point-of-purchase displays can also initiate recall of sponsorship. A cardboard cut-out of Steffi Graf in front of the tennis racket section could stimulate the consumer's memory of her recent victory and move the consumer to purchase the racket that sponsors her tournament play.

Trade shows have also been effective sales promotions for sporting goods companies. The Sporting Goods Manufacturers Association has conducted nationwide trade shows for many years with the express intent of motivating large-scale retail chains to order merchandise "hot off the line." The International Health, Racquet and Sportsclub Association (IHRSA) (formerly the International Racquet and Sportsclub Association—IRSA) has organized and run trade shows in the fitness industry for many years with great success. Many club managers place orders directly at this show because they have been able to compare equipment from different companies first-hand, and based upon what they see, initiate the purchase. As you can see, this type of activity is crucial to marketing success.

Sport organizations can also serve nonsport businesses' sales promotions through incentives. Concepts where purchasers receive free tickets to a sporting event with the purchase of a particular item may move that person to purchase. Store appearances of a sport celebrity at point of purchase can also stimulate immediate sales.

Although sales promotions have been referred to as a "catch-all" category, they strike at the heart of marketing, finalizing the exchange. Sales promotions must be incorporated with other elements in the promotional mix.

Promotional Activities

Most business enterprises find it necessary to create special activities to promote their programs, products, or purposes. Hiebing and Cooper (1990) define promotions as a marketing tool that provides extra value or incentive directly to consumers. Intercollegiate athletics and interscholastic sports must likewise engage in promotional activities. From a philosophical viewpoint, some people engaged in athletic programs may prefer to be exempted from promotional activities so that they might devote more of their creativity, time, and energy to the actual conduct of athletic events. Unfortunately, those days have passed, and promotional activities are necessary for survival.

Traditional promotions, such as the "hat day," "bat day," and "poster day" events continue to be quite popular with both fans and sports organizations. The results of research studies into the effectiveness of these activities are varied. In some cases, they have produced large increases in overall attendance, whereas at other times they have produced increases only for those specific events where people have attended primarily to obtain the free novelty. Sport marketers should not jump to the hasty conclusion that it is negative if a person attends an event for the express purpose of getting a free product. Sport can serve an effective (and profitable) role in linking consumers with products from sponsors.

Promotional activities that involve high school, collegiate, or amateur players require the exercise of considerable caution. Many sport governing bodies have restrictive guidelines regulating the appearances of athletes in commercial activities. In some instances, if an athlete is associated with a specific product or company, he or she may be declared ineligible for amateur competition. For these and other reasons, you must make sure that your marketing practices conform to all standards of professional ethics.

Some promotional activities seek to draw attention to the team, event, or product by awarding prizes to attendees. Several sports teams have sponsored contests where spectators ticket stubs were drawn at random for chances to win prizes by scoring goals (soccer, hockey), kicking field goals, or shooting baskets. These events usually are scheduled prior to the contest or between periods of play. The cost to the sport organization is minimal because the prizes often can be secured from sponsors as a trade-out for name recognition during the event.

Some of the possible promotional activities associated with athletic events that have proven profitability are presented below.

1. Banquets to honor the participants of various sport teams through tributes to coaches, players, and support staff. These can be effective as award ceremonies where special acknowledgment and honors are accorded either employees or prominent citizens. To obtain the maximum promotional value, you should prepare personal stories, pictures, and awards in advance.
2. Exhibitions of new products, protective sports gear, or the latest in sport fashion. These have also proven to produce positive media coverage.
3. Team reunions in conjunction with a reception, dinner, and game.
4. Events, including guest days or nights for senior citizens, persons with disabilities, disadvantaged youth, Boy Scouts, Girl Scouts, and other groups who attend games. Often these programs are enhanced by coordinating the event with a civic or service club where the members of the club provide transportation and supervision.
5. Sports clinics for various age groups in popular sports. These can expose and profile your staff for the media. Clinics also can be conducted on prevention and care of injuries, new fitness programs, or a myriad of other sport-related subjects.

A unique aspect of many sport programs is the desire of the public to associate with players, coaches, or employees. Successful organizations often make these people available through a Speakers Bureau. This can take many different forms: colleges and universities could offer their coaches, fitness centers could provide their instructors, and corporations could offer their leading salespeople for inspirational and informative talks. Many sport organizations circulate the list of speakers available to various organizations that may have the desire for guest speakers, whereas more aggressive organizations actively seek speaking engagements for their employees.

Publications

Every sports organization will produce some type of promotional publication at one time or another. The purpose of organizational publications is usually to transmit knowledge or information to the public. A publication also communicates various aspects about the sport organization, style, approach, attitude, and image. For this to be effective, it must also be consistent. Herein lies the dilemma for managing promotional publications in many sport organizations. Do you create one single office that is responsible for all publications, or do you allow each department to produce its own publications to fit its individual needs?

Because publications are so crucial in the promotion and marketing of a company's goods and services, most sport organizations have one central unit that is responsible for the organization's publishing. Centralization of this promotional function reduces several problems that have been encountered with sport organizations.

A major problem for many sport organizations is the dreaded desk-top publisher. With the popularity of computer-based publishing programs for personal computers, everyone thinks she or he can be in the publishing business, and he or she can. According to Herman (1992) the "freedom of the press belongs to the person who has one" (p. 25). For your organization, this means that you might have untrained people creating and disseminating material to the public about your products and services. The pitfalls here are tremendous. Poorly written, poorly designed, and inaccurate information may be presented to consumers without your knowledge or control.

Three different methods of addressing this problem have been presented. Herman (1992) suggests that you can have a centralized system, a franchise process, or an "official" publications policy. In the centralized system, one office handles all of the printing and publishing for the entire organization. This system affords the greatest amount of control and consistency and is very effective in protecting the organization from unprofessional or inaccurate publications. The limitations with this system are that it requires a relatively large staff and the demands on one unit often fluctuate during different times of the year, which creates ineffective staffing patterns.

The franchising of publication operations can be effective because individual units are allowed to produce their own promotional materials. Not only do the units often have a better idea of exactly what they need, but they also often have a better idea of the unique benefits of the product or service in which the consumer may be interested. The franchise allows a representative from each unit to approve any publications from that unit. To qualify as a unit representative, a person has to undertake special training from a publication specialist. This option retains some of the advantages of the centralized system in control, yet it decentralizes responsibility and workload.

The "official" publication method provides the least control of the three options. This policy limits the central publishing unit to the "official" publications of the organization (catalogs, brochures, advertising copy, etc.). All other units are free to produce their own newsletters or internal releases. This does remove the concept of a "publications police" from the two previous systems; however, it also allows for the uncontrolled production of promotional literature. There is also a high probability that "unofficial" publications find their way into the public eye, creating confusion and occasionally crises.

Regardless of the administrative structure, special brochures about your sports organization are effective in increasing exposure and publicity. Most commercial sports organizations utilize an annual report for communicating with both internal and external publics. As a controlled medium, this document can be effective in creating favorable impressions about the organization in the minds of employees, clients, and prospective investors. In sport these have been used by sporting goods companies, professional and collegiate teams, fitness centers, and commercial recreation enterprises.

Sports teams have, for many years, prepared and distributed game programs as promotional publications. Boeh (1989) indicates that although sports teams have many advertising and promotional opportunities, game programs are still the most popular and reliable. Irwin and Fleger (1992) have found that the game program can be effective as a promotional tool through providing team history and contest information and also as a source of revenue. Data from their research indicate that although attendance figures over the past few years at collegiate events declined, program sales increased significantly. The average sales data showed that currently 1 in 10 football fans and 1 in 13 basketball spectators purchased a program.

The philosophy surrounding the game program is of significant importance. If you are going to be competitive with other advertising media, then you are in the advertising business. If you cannot, you are really asking for philanthropy and contributions. This position/philosophy needs to be established early.

If you decide you are in the philanthropy business, you must recover enough advertising revenue to offset printing costs. These "advertisers" must know that they will not receive the same exposure for their dollar as they would with other media. This does not, however, automatically mean that they will not purchase an ad. In many small towns, the advertisers are willing to support your organization through the purchase of an ad, irrespective of a cost-benefit ratio. Boeh (1989) advises that the sponsor should not be led to believe that he or she will receive the same advertising impact that other media offer. Rather, advertising in your game program should be explained as a way for the sponsor to support the athletic program with a donation and receive recognition in the form of an ad.

The way to determine if you are truly in the advertising segment is to calculate a CPM (cost per thousand impacts). In doing so you present the cost of advertising in your program on the same basis as other media sources, such as the local newspaper. Although your ad costs are typically higher, few people keep newspapers as souvenirs.

Irwin and Fleger (1992) present several ways for sport marketers to manage game programs. The options they cite for producing profits and exposure provide valuable information in the area.

Chapter Summary

Promotional systems are central to effective sport marketing since they relate directly to the consumer's decision to purchase. As the various promotional activities described in this chapter indicate, there is no single approach that suits every situation. Promotions are limited only to one's imagination. Sport marketers must carefully analyze a particular setting, become knowledgeable about ideas tried by others, and create a promotional mix that best fits their specific organization.

What must be done is to insure that all promotional activities are successful. Obviously, there is no single, simple answer. Yet, this chapter has provided some basic principles, guidelines, and practices that will improve your chances of success.

Fundamental to the success of all promotional activities is the confidence of the manager. Oftentimes, those who succeed are the ones who believe they will. Although it is highly unlikely that any sports organization can implement all the promotional methods outlined in the chapter, a complete study should be made of available opportunities. A master plan for all promotional activities should be developed and executed on the basis of cost, time, and appropriateness.

Questions for Study

1. What is the relationship between promotion in sport to promotion in other entertainment industries?
2. Investigate the contribution of Mr. Bill Veeck to promotions in sports.

Learning Activities

1. Visit a local media outlet (radio, television station, or newspaper) and producer or editor to talk about their relationships with sports organizations. Prepare a contact sheet for that outlet complete with the names, position titles, and phone numbers of important people.
2. Investigate an advertising purchase for an athletic program or stadium scoreboard sign and determine if it is an equitable media buy compared to other advertising outlets.

Professional Associations and Organizations

Booster Clubs of America
200 Castlewood Drive
North Palm Beach, FL

Suggested Readings

Helitzer, M. (1992) *The dream job: Sports publicity, promotion, and public relations*. Athens, OH: University Press.

Irwin, D. L., & Fleger, B. (1992). Reading between the lines. *Athletic Management*, 4(3), 15-18.

References

Boeh, T. (1989, October). A program for selling. *Collegiate Athletic Management, 2*, 53-55.

Branvold, S. E. (1992). Utilization of fence signage in college baseball. *Sport Marketing Quarterly, 1*(2), 29-32.

Bronzan, R. T., & Stotlar, D. K. (1987). *Public relations and promotions in sport.* Daphne, AL: United States Sports Academy.

Connor, T. (1981). *The soft sell.* Crofton, MD: TR Training Associates International.

Helitzer, M. (1992). *The dream job: Sports publicity, promotion, and public relations.* Athens, OH: University Press.

Herman, J. T. (1992, April). From chaos to control. *Case Currents*, pp. 24-28.

Hiebing, R. C., & Cooper, S. W. (1990). *How to write a successful marketing plan.* Lincolnwood, IL: NTC Business Books.

Irwin, D. L., & Fleger, B. (1992). Reading between the lines. *Athletic Management, 4*(3), 15-18.

Ries, A., & Trout, J. (1986). *Positioning: The battle for your mind.* New York: McGraw-Hill.

Savod, B. (1987). Multimedia promotion program. NCAA *promotion manual.* Mission, KS: NCAA.

Stotlar, D. K. (1993). *Successful sport marketing.* Dubuque, IA: Brown and Benchmark.

Stotlar, D. K., & Johnson, D. A. (1989). Assessing the impact and effectiveness of stadium advertising on sport spectators at Division I institutions. *Journal of Sport Management, 3*(2), 90-102.

van Waterschoot, W., & Van den Bulte, C. (1992, October). The 4P classification of the marketing mix revisited. *Journal of Marketing,* 56(10), 82-93.

Chapter 13

Media Relations in Sport

The two most important aspects of media relations for the sport marketer include developing media relationships and developing media competencies. Media relationships will be a base from which all marketing and promotional strategies are launched. From the competency standpoint, the sport marketer must be knowledgeable about the specific formats, terminology, and media employed by the media.

Media is a broad term when used as a noun. It generally includes two categories, print and electronic. Within these categories, print media refers to newspaper and magazine publications whereas electronic media typically includes television and radio. Although the classification system has worked well for many years, technology is rapidly blurring the lines of distinction. Many television stations are owned by publishers, publishers are producing vignettes for television, and with electronic computer bulletin boards, some newspapers are never printed. Regardless of the labels placed on media professionals, sport marketers must develop sophisticated skills and nurture productive relationships.

Building Media Relationships

The media must be considered as clients. Effective relations with media outlets will provide significant opportunities for communicating marketing concepts and product information with other clients and customers. Radio, television, and newspapers are the traditional media sources with which the sport marketer must become familiar. By providing a high-quality service to the media, all marketing functions can be enhanced.

Principles of Good Media Relations

Sport marketers can develop confidence and respect by adhering to some basic principles or guidelines. According to Bronzan and Stotlar (1987) and Sports Media Challenge (1991) these include the following:

1. Be Yourself. Don't stiffen up, but rather relax and share your enjoyment in the sport.
2. Don't try to block the use of news through censorship, pressure, or trickery.
3. Be cooperative at all times; be accessible by telephone or in person.
4. Don't use jargon. Instead use words with which the public is familiar.
5. Don't pad a weak story; this practice tends to weaken credibility.
6. Use facts, not rumors, and be precise. Although initially facts may be more detrimental than the rumor, specific examples limit the story whereas rumors tend to remove all boundaries.
7. Don't stress or depend upon off-the-record accounts. If you can see a camera, microphone, or reporter's notebook, assume your words are recorded. Remember, the job of the media is to get facts and report the story. Asking a reporter to abide with off-the-record requests is unfair.
8. Give as much service to the media as possible. When news occurs, get the story out expeditiously. "Hot" news is desired by all reporters, so you must be willing and able to supply stories, pictures, statistics they wish, in the form they need and on time.
9. If a reporter uncovers a story, do not give the same story to another reporter. Treat it as an exclusive right.
10. Since news is a highly perishable commodity, remember that the media need news, not publicity.

Press Conferences

One essential aspect in providing service to your media clients is identical to the basic concept of marketing: Provide what your client needs. Press conferences can provide that service, but should occur only when circumstances warrant their use. Too often, a media relations director will call press conferences to disseminate the information that should have been in a news release. This causes the press to be wary of conferences. A press conference takes up a great deal of a reporter's day; therefore, if the press conference is to be a success, the information must warrant its occurrence.

Helitzer (1992, p. 222) provides several considerations for planning a successful press conference. He recommends that you assess the value of the press conference format. Simply put, "Is there a better way to release the information?" The timing of the press conference also is important. You must make sure that the key media people are available at the scheduled time. Although it is not always possible to check everyone's schedule, the media do have some times that are better than others based on the media source (morning paper vs. afternoon, radio vs. television).

If the decision has been made to conduct a press conference, the affected media must receive invitations. The invitation can be delivered to the media sources through the mail or in person. The former is the most efficient with the latter being more effective. The key decision factors often revolve around the number of media invited and the time it takes the organization to issue the invitations. If the decision was made to send the invitation through the mail, it is also advisable to place a reminder call a few hours before the conference.

The preparation and selection of the site are also important considerations. Here, Helitzer (1992) has some specific criteria. Ample space must be assured for the anticipated number of attendees. Parking, seating, telephones, refreshments, and the amount of materials available also will be designed around this factor. Attention also should be given to the electrical facilities present at the press conference site. All communication media, including the public address system, the podium height and lighting, projectors, and multimedia equipment, must be checked in advance of the conference.

First impressions are critical with the press conference. Therefore, you should have a registration table and press kits available for all attendees. The agenda or program for the meeting should be distributed along with any particular rules about the process of addressing the speakers.

Too often sport organizations attempt to use media for free advertising. If you want to serve the media, provide them with what they need: news. Your task as the sport marketer is to make what you have look like news. This could be a new product being introduced, announcements of new sales records, or even promotions and awards for company personnel.

Press Releases

Traditionally, sport marketers provide much of their information to the media in the form of press releases. The press release has been used by commercial, amateur, and collegiate sport organizations for many years and has become a familiar tool for dealing with the media. It has become the most common form of communication in the sport industry. Several authors (Bronzan & Stotlar, 1987; Helitzer, 1992) have presented criteria regarding successful press releases.

The press release must be written in a style that conforms to the needs of the media even though releases are generally not used exactly as received. The journalist must present the information in a way that attracts audience attention. For the electronic media, it is crafted into a usable form by the media, and for newspapers it is redesigned to fit the specific space allotted. In both situations, the release should be written in a style commonly referred to as the "inverted pyramid."

In scanning a newspaper, people want to see if a story is important to them prior to spending the time to read it. A headline is the first thing the reader will notice. There is some disagreement about whether a press release should have a headline attached. A recommendation would be to supply the headline and allow the reporter to make an editorial decision.

In the electronic media, the people listen to the lead-in and make decisions about the relevance of the topic. The piece must include the essentials of who, what, when, why, where, and how. This should be accomplished in the first paragraph. The media can then decide if the story is worth attention. The first paragraph also may account for all the room the story is allotted in the paper. Thus, the news release must include the details of the story or event in descending order of importance. A good news release, therefore, has three parts: the significance (headline), the essence (lead), the details (tail). Writing in this style (inverted pyramid) will more closely match the style of the reporter and will make it more likely that the information will appear in the media.

It is clear that simply grinding out releases is a costly waste of time and money. A University of Wisconsin study showed that of 300 press releases received in a 5-day period by a typical morning paper, 242 were rejected; of 339 releases in a 5-day period by a typical evening paper, 218 were discarded, 32 used as received, 42 rewritten and used; out of 113 publicity releases received in one week by a typical weekly newspaper, only 3 were used. Helitzer (1992) reports that only 10% of the information received by daily publications is ever used. These data clearly indicate that most press releases never appear in print and many are never even read as the news media sort through daily stacks of releases in order to select those stories they believe to be of most interest or benefit to their readers (Bronzan & Stotlar, 1987).

The quality of presentation has a bearing upon whether or not a release is used, and competition is intense. One method of improving the chances that a release will be used is to meet the standards expected in preparing and delivering the story. Some of the most critical areas in meeting these standards are the following (Bronzan & Stotlar, 1987; Helitzer, 1992):

1. All news releases should be double-spaced on white paper; use 8 1/2 by 11 inch paper; use only one side of each sheet of paper (Bronzan & Stotlar, 1987; Helitzer, 1992). If the information is sent via electronic transfer, spacing is unimportant as the information will be reformatted upon receipt.

2. Minimum margins of one inch on the sides and two inches at the top and bottom should be provided on each page (Helitzer, 1992).

3. The organization's name, address, and telephone number should appear on the release. Pre-printed stationery is acceptable, but the information can also be included in the upper left-hand corner of plain paper (Bronzan & Stotlar, 1987; Helitzer, 1992).

4. It is essential that the release contain a "contact" person in the sport organization. This should include full name, position title, address, and

phone number. News is a 24-hour business, and timely follow-up is an important feature for reporters and editors (Helitzer, 1992).

5. The words, "For Immediate Release" should appear on the upper right-hand corner of the first page on almost all releases, the exception being stories on future events or quotes from a yet-to-be-presented speech (Bronzan & Stotlar, 1987; Helitzer, 1992).
6. There is considerable debate over whether or not you should write a headline for the story, Helitzer (1992) indicates that a good headline assists the news organization with routing the information and can catch the attention of an editor, spurring more reading. Bronzan & Stotlar (1987), on the other hand, indicate that headlines supplied by the sports organization are rarely used; therefore, they are better left to the media.
7. Arrange paragraphs in their descending order of importance. This is known in the trade as the "inverted pyramid." Each succeeding paragraph should contain information that is less crucial than the preceding one. This style facilitates editorial decisions and enables the newspaper to cut the story to meet its space needs (Bronzan & Stotlar, 1987; Helitzer, 1992).
8. The essential facts and story line must be included in the first paragraph (Bronzan & Stotlar, 1987). According to Helitzer (1992) the editor will only read the first two paragraphs in making preliminary decisions about running or rejecting your release. Therefore, the first paragraph must include the five Ws: who, what, when, where, and why. This is part of the lead for the story and is used to bring the editor (and readers) into the remaining part of the story.
9. Short sentences should be used because they are more readable and understandable than longer ones. Depending upon the classification of words used, the length of the sentence should seldom exceed 17 words. Sentences that incorporate technical terms, figures, unusual names, or places must be short to ensure clarity and understanding. Paragraphs should be "purposely" short for easier reading (Bronzan & Stotlar, 1987; Helitzer, 1992).
10. All pages should be numbered at the top, and at the bottom of every page except the last one, use the word "More." You should also mark the end of the story by the word "End" or a series of circled ### marks (Bronzan & Stotlar, 1987; Helitzer, 1992).

Other useful tips for getting press releases into the media have been provided by both authors. When mailing press releases to the "Sports Editor," the individual's name should also be included so that it will be opened by the person performing those functions. Distribution times are very important because the print/broadcast deadline of the receiver can affect whether the release is available for use. If you personally deliver a news release, try to present it directly to the person who will make the decision on its use, avoiding the front desk if possible. Professional ethics indicate that, after delivering the release, you should depart without attempting to influence the use of the story.

Sport marketers must become familiar with the specific needs of different media outlets. What follows is an examination of the needs of the various media sources that may be utilized in the sport marketing field.

Newspapers and Magazines

Although newspapers have continued to be a mainstay of American culture, magazines in sport, health, and fitness and other publications that carry featured sports stories experienced phenomenal growth in the 1980s and 1990s. Newspapers and magazines are not imposed upon readers; the reader purchases one, or reads one that someone else has purchased. Thus, at the outset, there is some assurance of readiness to accept or expose oneself to the content. Generally, readers are interested in the content, and most influential citizens make it a practice of reading current newspapers and sport magazines. Since they often are read at leisure, there is time to digest the content of the items read and to formulate at least tentative opinions.

Sport marketing directors should become acquainted with the publishers, the highest ranking officer (the executive editor), the editor, the editorial page editor, and, finally, the managing editor, who is the working head of staff engaged in handling publication. A file of contacts should be formulated and kept in the media relations office so that essential information can be sent to an appropriate publication at any time. You also will want to determine which day or days are best for particular stories. Most authorities suggest that you chart the calendar for appropriate and inappropriate days based on the daily content of a publication and plan accordingly. Newspapers usually devote more space to stories than do magazines as a rule. However magazines often provide more specific material for the reader, so the impact of any story may be enhanced.

A common complaint from newspaper and magazine editors is that the purpose of some sport organizations is to seek free advertising. Experienced media personnel are quick to recognize this ploy, which severely strains relationships. Another familiar complaint is that sport marketers often attempt to color or censor the material, and the editorial personnel rightly believe that it is their duty to the readers to remove any bias that may have been included. Finally, the sport marketer must never attempt to use influence or pressure tactics to get an item in or out of the paper. Although this has been attempted where event sponsors have threatened to withdraw advertising from publication that did not give substantial media coverage to a sponsored event, the practice is considered unethical.

The style of material must also follow rules of the trade. The most accepted style manuals are those of the Associated Press and the New York Times. These books will guide you through proper abbreviations, formatting for statistics, and capitalization in product and team names (Helitzer, 1992). You should provide photographs whenever possible. Sports are action-packed activities, and high-quality photographs can catch the attention of editors and readers alike. A glossy-finish still-picture is preferred, with no more than two or three persons in the picture. You should identify photographs by typing the information about the event and all people in the picture on the lower half of a standard sheet of paper; then paste the upper half of the paper to the back of the photograph so that the caption material will drop down below the picture when it is withdrawn from the envelope.

Bronzan & Stotlar (1987) state that the major causes of rejection can be traced to common errors or omissions. Many stories are cited as having limited reader interest or being poorly written. Often the material cannot be distinguished from advertising, the use of which conflicts with traditional editorial policies. On occasion, some materials are obviously exaggerated or contain apparent inaccuracies. If stories or press releases are continually rejected, arrange to have a conference with the editor, reporter, or others involved to determine any problems that may exist. The stated purpose of this meeting should be to improve your service to the media and it is hoped that the results will yield more positive relationships between your organization and the print media.

Of course, newspapers and magazines also are valuable in calling attention to other forms of communication, such as forthcoming speeches, event, radio, or television programs. It is through this avenue that many sport marketers encounter the electronic media. Because radio and television are instantaneous communication media, they present special needs to which the sport marketer must attend.

Television

From the Olympic Games to a local coach's show, sport marketers will encounter television in many aspects of their work. Competition in the television industry increased markedly in the 1980s. Over 150 new cable networks were established, and 400 new stations came into existence ("ESPN Radio," 1993). Cross-ownership of cable and networks has produced some interesting programming choices. Viewers could see the first two rounds of US Golf Open on ESPN and the final two on ABC; it was the same with US Tennis Open on USA Network and CBS because the cable outlets are partially owned by the networks.

Regular network distribution is also changing. Pay-per-view has become available for regional broadcast of sports events. All of the major networks produce and telecast a variety of games on any given day. However, the local affiliates of the network select the contest that they feel will have the broadest appeal in the area. Yet because the other games are also available, the viewer can, for a fee, view the other game via cable with a few flips of a switch. There is no additional cost to the producer, a limited hassle for the distribution, and the consumer gets the desired product at a reasonable price.

Sports programming has increased 500% over the past 15 years primarily due to the increase in the available program sources. The types of programming that are traditionally available include regularly scheduled contests (MLB, NBA, college games, motor sports, and horse racing), made-for-TV events (*Superstars*, celebrity sport events, Goodwill Games), and sport anthology or talk shows (NFL films, ESPN). One of the early examples of made-for-TV sport was ABC television's *Superstars*. This program was the catalyst for other similar programs in the television industry. In the 1990s programs developed that were jointly owned by the network and the sponsor (pro beach volleyball—NBC and Miller Brewing Company).

This has created an interesting situation whereby some experts predict that if television ever stopped its sport coverage, the U.S. sport system would collapse. This brings to the forefront an intriguing point: TV and radio sports rights fees rose considerably in the 1970s and 1980s, but it seems the trend is over for the 1990s. In 1972 the National Basketball League got $9 million in TV rights, whereas their 1992 contract was worth $219 million. On the other hand, CBS paid $1.1 billion to Major League Baseball (MLB) for 1990-93 and lost over $150 million on the contract. In 1993, as a result of facing a 55% reduction in rights fees, MLB entered a partnership with ABC and NBC to form The Baseball Network. The joint venture guaranteed a minimum of $165 million in revenues each year over the first 2 years of the 6-year contract. Specifically, MLB owners will receive 87.5% of the first $160 million, with the networks splitting the balance. The next $30 million will be divided equally, and any revenues beyond $190 million will be shared on an 80-20 basis in favor of the owners.

The 1994-98 National Football League contracts did increase slightly over previous agreements. ABC paid $950 million (up from $925 million for 1990-1993) for Monday night games, the Pro Bowl, and the 1995 Super Bowl. NBC raised its previous commitment from $752 million to $880 million for 1994-98. NBC will continue to carry American Football Conference games. The change came in Fox Network's bid for the National Football Conference games (previously on CBS) at $1.58 billion including the 1997 Super Bowl ("Its Official," 1993).

If you want to have your event covered on television, the process is quite complicated. To obtain coverage you have to make what you have look like what the networks need. Television stations must pay for all programming, even reruns of *The Brady Bunch*. You can demonstrate that yours may be better and cheaper. Remember, it is your task to prove this to the decision-makers at the TV station.

The first step is to contact the programming director, not the sports person. When the contact is made, you will need to present a proposal for the coverage of your event. In general you will need lead time of about 2-3 months, 6 months if you are trying to obtain coverage on a network affiliate. As with most sport marketing areas, the sport marketer must be prepared. Some of the information that you will need to know includes data about television programming. For instance, you must know the difference between ratings and share.

The Nielsen ratings have long been the benchmark for measuring television viewing patterns across the United States. The system is based on a selection of

4,000 households equipped with a "people meter." This device records the viewing patterns of the household. The resulting data are transformed into ratings and shares. Ratings represent "the percentage of the total television households (approximately 93 million in the United States) that are tuned to a particular program" ("ESPN Radio," 1993, p. 13). Share, on the other hand, is "the percentage of those sets in use [at that specific time] which are tuned in to a given program" ("ESPN Radio," 1993, p. 13). To be successful, your event must be able to deliver competitive ratings and share for the station.

The outline of your proposal should include the following points:

- Explanation of the event
- Benefits to the station—previous rating/share
- Level of involvement—production, wild footage, telecast only
- Your facilities—hookups, staff
- Who has control—time/date, during event timing and running.

Although the number of programming and outlet sources has increased, so has the competition across sport. However, with a lot of hard work, it is possible to present your event on television.

Radio

Sport marketers can use radio in a variety of ways. Probably the most common is for a team to broadcast its games over an official radio network. These distribution outlets are important in providing the game to fans who cannot attend the game in person or to those who enjoy the casual atmosphere of listening to sports events without visual cues or traveling to the event site.

As an example, ESPN Radio Network provides 16 hours of sport programming per week, 7 hours each on Saturday and Sunday evening and 2 hours on Sunday morning. Agreements with affiliates require them to air the Sunday morning segment and 2 hours each on Saturday and Sunday night. The affiliates pay nothing for the program but receive no revenue from commercials. All commercial time is pre-sold by ESPN Radio ("ESPN Radio," 1993). In this situation, the station attracts listeners, but has a reduced capacity to earn revenues during all hours of operation. However, the station hopes that the listeners will stay tuned for additional programming and develop loyalty to the outlet.

The Continental Basketball Association also looked to radio to increase its power with sponsors. In 1991 it negotiated a deal with Star Communications for a CBA Game of the Week. The CBA arranged for call-in interviews with players and coaches, and in lieu of a rights fee, it accepted ten 30-second commercials. With these commercials, the CBA could offer them to sponsors in more attractive packages without incurring additional costs ("CBA," 1991).

Radio programming has also ventured into new territory. In 1991 radio introduced its own version of pay-per-view. TEAMLINE was created to allow people to listen to their favorite sports contest, even though they were out of the broadcast area. In its first year over 50 colleges and the majority of professional teams were available. In this interesting and unique way, TRZ Sports Services, owner of TEAMLINE, became a distributor of play-by-play sports. They were not a competitor of the radio stations (why would someone pay for the broadcast if they could tune in for free?), and they did not sell advertising, but rather used the original broadcast intact. This created significant win-win relationships. The contests could attract even larger audiences, this could give the broadcaster greater power to sell advertising, TRZ could make a reasonable profit (without production costs) and the customer, equipped with only a telephone (or preferably a speaker phone), could access desired products (Cohen, 1993).

Chapter Summary

The media relations should have as a goal the provision of accurate information for all media sources. This information should be be disseminated in a professional manner. Sport marketers must develop sophisticated skills and productive media relationships. These can most often be attained by working with the media and providing a high level of service. Quality press conferences and written material are essential in establishing the relationships. Radio and television programming are evolving in new directions, and top sport marketers will need to be current with technology and trends. As programming and outlet sources change, so will the competition across sport. Yet, with a lot of hard work, your marketing functions can be enhanced through effective media relations.

Questions for Study

1. What are the essential steps in obtaining electronic (television or radio) coverage of your sport event?
2. What are some of the differences between the impact of newspaper and magazine articles that would affect sport marketing?

Learning Activities

1. Contact a sport organization and obtain permission to attend a press conference. Take notes and compare them with material in the text.
2. Working with a local high school and city newspaper, attend a sport event and write a press release after the event. Make contact with the local newspaper and deliver your release. Go over the content with the editor and discuss the quality of the release.

Professional Associations and Organizations

College Sports Information Directors of America/ COSIDA
Campus Box 114
Kingsville, TX 78363

Suggested Reading

Helitzer, M. (1992). *The dream job: Sports publicity, promotion, and public relations.* Athens, OH: University Press

References

Bronzan, R. T. & Stotlar, D. K. (1987). *Public relations and promotions in sport.* Daphne, AL: United States Sports Academy.

CBA to get national exposure with new network radio deal, (1991, December). *Team Marketing Report,* pp. 2-3.

Cohen, Andrew (1993, April). For a good time call Teamline. *Athletic Business, 17,* 18-19.

ESPN radio network: One year later. (1993, Winter). *Between the Lines: Ernst and Young's Financial Newsletter for the Sports World,* 9, 10-11, 13.

Helitzer, M. (1992). *The dream job: Sports publicity, promotion, and public relations.* Athens, OH: University Press.

It's official: NFL dumps CBS (1993, December 21). *Greeley (CO) Tribune,* p. B1.

Sports Media Challenge (1991). *Pocket guide to media success.* Charlotte, NC: Author.

CHAPTER 14

MARKETING THROUGH ENDORSEMENTS AND SPONSORSHIPS

Introduction

The purpose of this chapter is to describe how sport organizations can enhance their marketing efforts through athlete endorsements and sport sponsorships. Although sport personalities and sports events have long been used by nonsport companies to sell products, the contents of this chapter will be confined to the use of endorsements and sponsorships by sport organizations.

As explained in the sections of the text on marketing and promotional mix, the sport marketer must incorporate all available resources to satisfy the sport consumer. That process can be expedited through opinion leaders. These are individuals who have specialized knowledge of your sport product or service and who can influence others in the purchasing process.

Individual athletes also have been used to provide sport product endorsements with the hope that their endorsement will result in increased sales. This can be an effective component of sport marketing when matched to target markets and applied appropriately with consumers. The scope of all marketing strategies and tactics must include attention to the organization's social responsibility and ethical business practices.

Just such a tactic was employed by sport shoemaker Reebok when their marketing research indicated that basketball player Shaquille O'Neal was the best known sports personality among 12 to 18-year-old boys. The ensuing relationship between Reebok shoes and O'Neal demonstrates the enormous power in the market place. Even before finalizing his initial NBA contract, O'Neal signed a $15-million deal with Reebok for a complete line (Shaq Attaq) of shoes and sportswear. This action furthered previous developments in athlete endorsement, which included the creation of product lines in consort with individual players (i.e., Nike's Air Jordan). In addition, basketball equipment manufacturers (Spalding, O'Neal; Wilson, Jordan) often tie specific products to players following the traditions established by baseball from the early part of the century (Zbar, 1992).

Opinion Leaders and Endorsements

Many sport companies use opinion leaders because of their knowledge and power within certain groups. They are usually considered by consumers to be "experts in the field." One college basketball coach said, "We're pretty good experts on basketball shoes. I've been around basketball shoes for 35 years probably .... I definitely talk to shoe companies about the style of shoes" (quoted in Brubaker, 1991, p. A1).

All of the major shoe companies use coaches as opinion leaders. Numerous college coaches have been paid as much as $200,000 per year to outfit their team in specific shoes. The considerable economic value generated from the national television coverage of these college games provides the incentive. Nike's budget for their college basketball coaches runs about $4 million and includes $600,000 in complimentary merchandise as well (Brubaker, 1991).. The exposure achieved through this endeavor comes not only in the arena but also through a company's support of the coach's summer sports camps where clothing for the coaching staffs, T-shirts, posters, and related merchandise can influence the impressionable youth market.

Youth programs represent the "grass roots" of the sport shoe market. If you want to move shoes, the youth market is the place to be. Establishing the purchasing patterns of customers early in their lives is a powerful tool in marketing. L.A. Gear selected this tactic in 1991 when it entered into agreements with several youth basketball leagues. According to a company spokesperson, "the reason we're involved in programs like this is obvious. You want to get kids used to wearing L.A. Gear" (quoted in Brubaker, 1991, p. A1).

It is not just the coaches of organized team sports that can be incorporated into endorsement as part of sport marketing plans. In the cheerleading and performance-dance industry, specialty companies often provide free shoes and apparel to the leading groups in the nation in an effort to influence the style selection and purchasing of other participants.

L.A. Gear seems to receive substantial value from their endorsees. A typical contract with a coach, for example, calls for the following (Brubaker, 1991):

1. Give L.A. Gear the use of the coach's name, nickname, initials, autograph, voice, video or film portrayals, facsimile signature, photograph, likeness and image.
2. Make L.A. Gear shoes available to the players and assistant coaches as well as cheerleaders, game personnel, ball boys and girls, and the team mascot.
3. Film a TV commercial and participate in two photo sessions the results of which may be exploited by L.A. Gear throughout the world

in any manner whatsoever.

4. Make eight promotional appearances in the United States and one abroad, designated by L.A. Gear.
5. Attend a company party, an annual retreat, or both.
6. Assist in the production of a promotional video on topics such as basketball fundamentals, physical conditioning, nutrition, academics, drug and alcohol education and preparation for the real world.
7. Comment favorably upon the the use of L.A. Gear products whenever possible.
8. Wear a sport jacket, sweater, or shirt bearing the L.A. Gear logo prominently displayed during all college basketball games and at other appropriate public activities.
9. Deduct $5,000 from the contract if team members do not achieve a 2.25 mean grade-point average each year.
10. Give L.A. Gear four complimentary tickets to each game. (p. A1)

Other ways of using opinion leaders in sport have included product sampling and prototype testing to receive input. Product sampling always generates a great deal of interest in the product and can be tracked to indicate the overall effect on sales. Often a product new to the market, or even pre-release prototypes, are distributed to key opinion leaders within an industry. This develops loyalty, and it can provide the company with reliable feedback on its products with only minimal costs.

Individual Athlete Endorsements

The use of individual athletes to endorse products has been a marketing practice in sport for decades. As early as the the 1936 Berlin Olympics, Adidas provided track star Jesse Owens with free shoes. Historically, the line between professional and amateur athletes was finely drawn. If an athlete were paid or received money from sport, he or she was a professional; if the athlete received nothing, she or he was an amateur. All of this has changed in Olympic sports, and although the Olympic Games offer no prize money, the athletes certainly collect from their endorsement deals. In 1981, the Olympic rules were modified. The International Olympic Committee (IOC) changed its regulations allowing each international federation to establish its own standards on the receipt of monies and the effect on eligibility. Currently, the IOC no longer even refers to athletes as "amateurs," but only as "eligible athletes."

Under this system athletes establish a trust fund that allows for the accumulation of monies to cover living and training expenses when the athlete cannot undertake professional responsibilities because of training and competition obligations. Theoretically, this keeps the athlete from being penalized for choosing to be an athlete rather than simply a company employee. However, Olympic-level athletes typically have to train year round. Monthly expenses are taken out of their trust fund to cover all living expenses. In late 1993, the International Amateur Athletic Association (the international federation for track and field) began to allow individuals to receive direct payments from event managers. Each individual was required to register with the association, and event organizers were allowed to pay only those participants whose names appeared on the registered list.

Probably one of the best lessons about individual athlete endorsements for a sports company is the 1992 Dan and Dave campaign initiated by Reebok prior to the Barcelona Olympic Games. Potential U.S. Olympic decathletes were used by shoe manufacturer Reebok to promote new models of their "Pump" training shoe. The ads ("To be settled in Barcelona") attempted to predict who would win the Gold Medal. However, Dan (O'Brien) failed to make the U.S. team. With over $30 million in the ad campaign, Reebok parlayed the "tragedy" into a bonanza of publicity worth several times the advertising costs. Incidentally, a Reebok-sponsored athlete did win the 1992 decathlon Gold Medal, Robert Zmelik from the Czech Republic. Prior to the Dan and Dave fiasco, the trend was in abundance at the 1984 and 1988 Olympic Games. Gymnasts Mary Lou Retton and Bart Connor came out of the games with endorsements that would make them financially secure for life.

Although many athletes cannot command large sums of endorsement money, a supply of free equipment is easy to obtain. Tennis player Gabriela Sabatini has secured numerous sponsorship deals, including Pepsi, Fuji, Rayban, Longines, Tacchini, to name a few; plus more in personal appearances. Jeansonne (1986) referred to the "evolving business-runner, so motivated by the monetary reward that he is losing sight of the sporting challenge" (p. 18). World-class track athlete Carl Lewis has been one of the more outspoken advocates for professionalism. His rationale has been that everyone benefits from the athlete's performance except the athlete. The event managers, the shoe companies, the television networks all profit from the exhibition of athletic talent. In Lewis' opinion, athletes who keep their bodies in perfect condition and provide the show should be assured a financially sound future.

Another phenomenon that has proven to be successful in the sport marketing industry is cross-promotion. If your sport enterprise sponsors and individual athlete and that athlete obtains other, nonsport endorsements, your company gets increased exposure. Take for example, Nike's sponsorship of Michael Jordan. When Michael Jordan appeared on a Wheaties box he was wearing Nike shoes and holding a Wilson basketball.

Endorsements with individual athletes do not exist without danger and controversy. Who controls the rights? Do team players have the right to select their own shoes, or do coaches have the power to demand that specific shoes be worn? Currently, the rights battle has been going to the player, but it will remain an issue for some time to come.

Another issue relates to organizational control. This has been particularly evident in the Olympic Games. During the 1992 Barcelona games, the U.S. men's basketball team had uniforms sponsored by Champion, and individual players each had his own shoe contract. However, the United States Olympic Committee had an agreement with Reebok for the medal presentation uniform. Because the players had not signed the USOC agreement (requiring participants to wear the USOC-designated presentation apparel) and because wearing a Reebok logo conflicted with their shoe contracts, a serious problem occurred. In the end, the players agreed to wear the Reebok uniforms, but unfolded the collar which covered the manufacturer's logo.

Similarly with Championship Auto Racing Teams (CART), the car owner has the rights to signage on the car and driver's suit, yet the drivers own the rights to the helmet. Top drivers on the circuit typically earn $200,000 from their helmet sponsorship alone. There are also a variety of personal appearance opportunities arranged with different sponsors that add to the revenues earned by the drivers.

Almost all sports organizations (NCAA, the NFL, the NBA, Major League Baseball, and the IOC) have so-called "billboard rules" (Woodward, 1988). These rules limit the size and number of logos that can appear on uniforms and equipment. Even with the tight rules many sport marketers find loopholes. At the Tour de France, the rules control the riders, but not their equipment—their cars; as a result, sponsors have literally covered the cars with logos and advertising.

Trends

Although sport marketers can still benefit from individual athlete endorsements, the risk is high (e.g., Ben Johnson, Mike Tyson, Dan O'Brien). Schlossberg (1990) indicated that the power of athletes in endorsing products has faltered. As a safeguard, many endorsement contracts have special clauses to cover instances where a player or coach is involved in a scandal. L.A. Gear's contract has a special termination clause that indicates that L.A. Gear can terminate the agreement at any time "if the coach wears another manufacturer's product, commits any act that 'tends to shock, insult or offend' his community, violates an NCAA rule, loses his job or becomes disabled/incapacitated and unable to perform" (Brubaker, 1991, p. A1).

There also seems to be a credibility problem with individual endorsements. In a 1990 survey, it was shown that a majority of consumers believed that sports celebrities were only endorsing products for the money (Schlossberg, 1990). According to Comte (1989) "it's too expensive to just have an athlete under contract. Within 10 years you'll see the syndication of athletes and companies" (p. 5). Much to Comte's credit, the prospect became reality when in 1993 Nike began operating its own sport marketing agency. As a result of the problems and risks with individual athlete endorsements, many sport organizations are considering sponsoring more events. Team and event sponsorships seem to be more in vogue than individual-athlete deals, signaling a trend for the 1990s.

Sponsorships

The initial question that must be addressed is whether a sport organization should use sponsorship in lieu of traditional advertising. According to the International Events Group (1992c) "sponsorship offers a number of distinct advantages over more conventional advertising techniques" (p. 7). Specifically, advertising delivers a straightforward commercial message, whereas sponsorships "get to people through a different source."

Sponsorship involves the company being prepared to make a commitment and support an activity; it says the company is going to be more people oriented than advertising suggests. In several ways, sponsorship is longer lasting in the terms of its commitment. (International Events Group, 1992c, p. 7)

The sponsorship of sports activities ranges from local beach volleyball tournaments and fun runs to the Olympic Games. In 1994 the deals ranged in scope from Nestlé Chocolate's $6-million agreement with the National Basketball Association (NBA) to Miller Brewing Company's $250,000-dollar sponsorship of Gay Games IV. Collectively, these events can provide sport marketers with an array of opportunities to market their products and services. As outlined at the beginning of this chapter, the discussion of sponsorships will be limited to their use as marketing tools for sport organizations. Although they have been extremely successful and widely used by nonsport companies, that treatment will not be included in this text.

Worldwide, corporate spending on sport sponsorship increased dramatically during the 1980s and 1990s. Data for 1994 set spending at $10.9 billion, with $4.25 billion dollars spent in North American alone. Europe contributed $3.4 billion, Pacific Rim businesses added $2.2 billion, and $1.1 billion was generated by other nations. The estimates for 1995 calculated by International Events Group projected an 11% increase over 1994 spending with an additional $10 billion spent on related promotions and merchandising activities. The rate of increase slowed somewhat in the early 1990s over the double-and triple-digit increases in the late 1980s. Growth in the industry has been recorded as 17% from 1992-1994 and 11% during 1991 (International Events Group, 1994b). This is in contrast to 30% increases in 1989 and a 500% change covering the 5 years from 1983 to 1988 (Stotlar, 1993).

In 1993, over 4,200 companies engaged in sport marketing activities, and almost every sport organization from local fitness centers and high school to the Olympics and professional sport leagues was looking for sponsors. As the number of sports organizations desiring an affiliation with sponsors grew, the leverage in the industry changed. This created a situation where the sponsor could weigh the offers from competing organizations seeking sponsors and keep prices down. As a result, during the early part of the decade, the momentum shifted from the organizations to the sponsoring corporations. In the environment of the 1990s it is increasingly important for sport managers to be skilled in the methodologies and techniques of sponsorship as a management component. A successful sponsorship arrangement can serve as a positive marketing vehicle for any sport organization.

Rationale for Pursuing Event Sponsorships

Sport organizations can buy into event sponsorship for a variety of marketing reasons. Probably the major reason for sport marketers to employ sport event sponsorship is to generate funds for conducting the event. Few events will generate enough capital from ticket and concession sales to cover event costs. In their 1988 proposal to Apple Computer, the AAU Junior Olympics asked for $1.5 million in sponsorship while contributing only $50,000 to the funds needed to operate the event (Gallup, 1988).

The 1994 World Cup in soccer was successful in building an alliance of television networks and sponsors so that the goals of each group could be accomplished. The event organizers, FIFA and World Cup USA, wanted to involve sponsors, obtain revenues, and present soccer in the traditional manner. To accomplish this, all three entities had to work together. When the broadcast rights were awarded to ABC and ESPN for $11 million, it was understood that there would be limited opportunities for the sale of commercials. Unlike many professional sports in the United States, soccer has not altered the rules of play to allow for "TV timeouts." Together, the organizers, the networks, and the primary sponsors (Coca-Cola, McDonald's, Snickers, and Mastercard) agreed to combine the sponsor's logo with the game clock, which would be inset in the screen during play. The sponsors also received commercial air time during the pregame, halftime, and postgame shows. All three groups achieved their goals as a result of this agreement the first of its kind in sports television. The networks obtained a prestigious event without being at risk; the organizers received an opportunity to showcase the sport and get their costs covered, and the sponsors got lots of exclusivity and almost complete protection against ambush marketing ("World Cup USA 94," 1993, p. 11). *Ambush marketing* is when a company advertises in some manner during a major sports event which has official sponsors. The official sponsors have paid for the right to advertise at the event, the ambush marketers have not.

Sport events also allow company executives to mix socially with elite athletes and can provide valuable client entertainment activities. One of the best examples of this is the Sporting Goods Manufacturers Association's annual Super Show. This trade show gives the manufacturers a chance to display their products but also allows for the entertainment of their major buyers. Many companies also have their endorsees (star athletes) there to meet their customers.

More important than the social attributes of sponsoring sport are the business-related objectives of sponsors. You must "look at an event to help meet a marketing objective, then make sure it meets sales promotion, PR and internal employee morale needs" (International Events Group, 1992d, p. 4). One company's director of sponsorships stated this point clearly when he said, "We are no longer satisfied with enhanced image; give us opportunities for on-site sales, well-developed hospitality packages and dealer tie-ins and we'll listen" (International Events Group, 1992d, p. 5)

Sport-related businesses, like most corporations, desire to be seen as community citizens with a responsibility to contribute to the well-being of the communities where they do business. In support of this concept is the message delivered by a special events manager, "Customers want companies that care about them, that give back to the community" (International Events Group, 1992d, p. 5). As an example, a local bicycle shop could sponsor a Triathlon to influence competitive riders and also sponsor a child's bike safety class.

A close examination regarding the reasons your business should become involved in sport sponsorships is essential. Friedman (1990) indicated that understanding how these activities can help accomplish your business goals is one of the key elements in selecting successful sponsorships. These must be specific to each event that the sport marketer intends to approach.

Development of a Winning Strategy

The relationship between your sport organization and event owners involved with sponsorship must include advantages to both parties in which your product's market value and profits are increased. A properly structured sport sponsorship can provide mutual benefits for both the sport organization and the sponsors. A key component in the success is the measurement of return on investment (ROI). Sport managers must be fully cognizant of the data with which to demonstrate the accomplishment of specified corporate objectives. This should be provided by the event owner, but is occasionally collected by the sponsor. Sport organizations that use sponsorship as a marketing tool must be prepared to evaluate sponsorship in the same manner as other marketing efforts. You can also have professional market research firms collect the data for you. One such company is Joyce Julius and Associates, which conducts research in the area of sponsor exposure and publishes the results in a journal titled *The Sponsor's Report.*

Among the sports analyzed in *The Sponsor's Report* are automobile racing, horse racing, college football and basketball, skiing, tennis, and volleyball. According to their calculations, sponsors of the Women's Professional Volleyball Association series averaged $389,270 in television exposure for each event of the season. In college football, the sponsors of postseason bowl games averaged just under $3 million in advertising value from their involvement and television coverage (Joyce Julius, 1991).

Wilkinson (1988) has worked with numerous sports organizations that were interested in using sponsorship to generate operating income. He indicated that sport organizations should match their events and products to corporate objectives by examining the following questions:

1. What type of product or service produced is the best fit for a sponsorship?
2. Does involving a sponsor fit our marketing structure?
3. With what type of program has the sponsor been previously successful?

4. Where does our competition stand with sponsorship opportunity (p. 1)?

One of the aspects of sponsorship that has attracted sport-related companies has been their ability to reach consumers by breaking through the clutter in advertising. Marketing managers have used sponsorship as an avenue to present their message to consumers in a more relaxed atmosphere and to support their other marketing efforts (Wilber, 1988). Sport events are also attractive because they can provide a cross-sectional exposure when compared to other marketing avenues available to the sport marketer.

As marketing and advertising have become more cluttered, sport organizations must concentrate only on those sponsorship opportunities that access specific segments within the market. For example, Reebok signed a sponsorship agreement with the Russian Olympic Committee in 1992 and opened their first retail outlet in Moscow in 1993. Adidas seems to have taken a similar approach by signing up with the Olympic Committee and several NGBs in the People's Republic of China. Nike entered into an agreement with the Kenyan Olympic Committee for $1.26 million in sponsorships, which include $500,000 for sport development and $350,000 in in-kind product (International Events Group, 1994a).

Media attention is another important factor in selecting an event to sponsor. Good events have the potential to generate considerable media coverage. This type of message can be particularly effective because consumers typically see this in a different light than they see traditional advertising. Another related facet of media coverage and sponsorship is that if an event has a media sponsor, you can often obtain discounted or free coverage by tagging their promotional messages. Such a situation exists with the annual Bolder Boulder road race in Boulder, Colorado. The event is sponsored by NBC affiliate KCNC-TV and Nike shoes. Not only does Nike get sponsorship of the race, but it also receives logo presentation on all TV spots promoting the race. Similarly, Nike can benefit from the televised coverage of the race, which will of course have several prominent sponsor banners strategically located for the cameras. There are people who argue that media sponsors give preferential treatment to co-sponsors. Media coverage also provides a reliable and measurable method to calculate return on investment.

Although the number of times the sponsor's name was mentioned by the announcers, the column inches of print devoted to the event, and the number of times the corporation's banner was seen on national television are important, the raw data do not always reflect the whole picture. Take for example an announcer who, in the middle of a race says, "Her Reebok shoes have fallen apart, and she'll have to finish this race barefooted." What is the economic value of that?

Before undertaking a sponsorship, you should develop criteria for evaluating possible opportunities. This process has been discussed extensively (Ensor, 1987;

Irwin & Asimakopoulos, 1992; Mullin,1983; Wilkinson, 1986). Typical factors to be considered include

Budget—affordability, cost effectiveness, tax benefits

Event Management—past history, organizing committee

Image—match to products and services offered

Target Market—demographics, geographical reach

Communications—media exposure, audience size, and demographics

Sponsor Mix—match with other sponsor's products and image

Level of Involvement—title sponsor, in-kind supplier, exclusivity

Other Opportunities—wholesaler tie-ins, on-site displays, signage, product sampling, merchandising.

If an event owner offers a sponsorship that can meet your criteria, is ethically grounded, and gives you service and data with which to justify continuation, sport sponsorships can be a successful marketing tool for sport organizations.

The Olympic Games and Sponsorships

As with other sports organizations "marketing as a basic function and central dimension of the Olympic enterprise, requires specific planning and the performance of distinct activities" (Stauble, 1994, p. 14). Olympic and amateur sport organizations have, over the past several years, become very dependent upon sponsorship income. Stauble (1994) views Olympic organizations as resource-conversion machines. These organizations obtain resources from sponsors and convert them into specific products and services that are provided to the public. To accomplish this, Olympic organizations must create an exchange with the sponsor (Stauble, 1994). Typically, these have been in the form of signage, logo presentation, hospitality opportunities, and identification with high-level teams and athletes. "There are plenty of opportunities for sale in the five ring circus: television, commercials, product licensing, product exclusivity at the Games, team sponsorships, Olympic movement sponsorships, awards presentations, training center support, product endorsements, and almost anything a marketing [person] could devise" (Marsano, 1987, p. 65).

Sport sponsorships between Olympic organizations and corporations have existed for many years. In 1896, Kodak had an ad in the official program of the first modern Olympics, and by 1928 Coca-Cola had begun its long-standing relationship with the Olympic movement (Pratzmark & Frey, 1989). Sponsorship and the Olympics have a longstanding relationship and one that has increased significantly in complexity.

Olympic Television Revenues

One of the most important goals for any Olympic sport organization is revenue generation (Stauble, 1994). The International Olympic Committee (IOC) was in very weak financial condition in 1960. However, a contract to televise the Olympic Games on the Columbia Broadcasting System (CBS) brought them out of financial trouble and into a modern era of profitability (Pratzmark & Frey, 1989). The rights fees paid by American broadcast companies have been a substantial revenue source for the Olympic movement for decades. The costs of Olympic television coverage have risen from $500,000 dollars paid for the Rome Summer Games in 1960 to $456 million generated for the U.S. rights and $275 for the European rights to the 1996 Atlanta Olympic Games (see Table 14.1).

As with any exchange there are questions of leverage. When a corporation puts a product on the market, a viable price must be calculated. Unlike marketing mass consumer products, the Olympic Games are unique and occur only in a 4-year cycle. To establish the fair market value of their product, the IOC puts the Games out for bid. The networks cannot go to another producer; there is only one Olympic Games. For the 1994 Summer Games, NBC had the winning bid of $456 million, with ABC offering $450 million and CBS in third place at $415 million ("NBC Gets Olympic TV Deal," 1993). This clearly shows the leverage of the

TABLE 14.1 - U.S. Television Rights Fees for 1960-1998 Olympic Games

Year	Site	Network	Price
1960	Squaw Valley (Winter)	CBS	$394,000
1960	Rome (Summer)	CBS	$550,000
1964	Innsbruck (Winter)	ABC	$597,000
1964	Tokyo (Summer)	NBC	$1.5 million
1968	Grenoble (Winter)	ABC	$2.5 million
1968	Mexico City (Summer)	ABC	$4.5 million
1972	Sapporo (Winter)	NBC	$6.4 million
1972	Munich (Summer)	ABC	$7.5 million
1976	Innsbruck (Winter)	ABC	$10 million
1976	Montreal (Summer)	ABC	$25 million
1980	Lake Placid (Winter)	ABC	$15.5 million
1980	Moscow (Summer)	NBC	$87 million
1984	Sarajevo (Winter)	ABC	$91.5 million
1984	Los Angeles (Summer)	ABC	$225 million
1988	Calgary (Winter)	ABC	$309 million
1988	Seoul (Summer)	NBC	$300 million
1992	Albertville (Winter)	CBS	$243 million
1992	Barcelona (Summer)	NBC	$401 million
1994	Lillehammer (Winter)	CBS	$300 million
1996	Atlanta (Summer)	NBC	$456 million*
1998	Nagano, Japan (Winter)	CBS	$357 million**

Sources: Stotlar, 1993, p. 195; **Greeley [CO] Tribune*, July 28, 1993, B2; ***Business Week*, Feb. 2, 1994, p. 36

IOC.

Some degree of leverage exists on the television side as well. Television networks must achieve a profit on their involvement and use their leverage with the IOC to make that possible. Typical incidents of this can be seen when the schedule of events has been altered to maximize prime-time TV hours. In addition, the IOC has given a clear message to many of the Olympic sports: "Make your sport more adaptable to television or you will be out of the Olympic Games."

Sponsorship of the Olympic Games

"In 1985, the IOC hired ISL Marketing, whose task it was to create a program to facilitate corporations interested in sponsoring the Olympic Games" (Marsano, 1987, p. 65). The Olympic Programme (TOP) was the creation. According to ISL, TOP "brings together the rights of the IOC as owner of the Olympic Games, the two Games Organizing Committees, and the National Olympic Committees throughout the world as partners in one four year sponsorship programme" (ISL, 1993, p. 3). This process also accomplished another major goal of any sport marketer—make it easier for consumers to buy your product. Another factor in this formula was the IOC's restructuring of the games so that an Olympic Games (Summer or Winter) would occur every 2 years instead of both Games occurring in one year. This would allow for sponsors to gain more long-term benefits and would spread the payments over an extended period.

The system was designed to allow a limited number of sponsors to receive special treatment and benefits on a worldwide basis and achieve exclusivity and protection in their Olympic sponsorship activities (Pratzmark & Frey, 1989). Specifically, TOP Sponsors would receive the following benefits (ISL, 1993; Pratzmark & Frey, 1989):

1. Product Exclusivity. Only one sponsor would be allowed for any product category. This meant that if Coca-Cola and Visa were members of the TOP, then Pepsi and American Express would not be allowed to become involved with Olympic sponsorship on any level, International, National, or with the Organizing Committee.
2. Use of Marks and Designations. Each participant was granted the right to use the solitary Olympic rings and their use in combination with all NOC designations. This gave them worldwide and local impact. Companies could also use the "Official Sponsor" and "Official Product" designations. All Organizing Committee logos were also available to sponsors.
3. Public Relations and Promotional Opportunities. Sponsors were given special tie-ins and media events to increase their exposure.
4. Access to Olympic Archives. The IOC made articles from its archives in Switzerland available to sponsors for special exhibits and displays.
5. Olympic Merchandise and Premiums. Clothing and apparel could be used bearing the Olympic logos for sales incentives and marketing activities. Visa had to reorder company shirts three times in 1988.
6. Tickets and Hospitality. Sponsors received priority access to seating at

both the Winter and Summer Games.

7. Advertising Options. Each participant in TOP was given first chance at souvenir program ads and the option (where possible) to television commercial purchases.
8. On-Site Participation. Point-of-purchase and product displays were included in the package. Companies would also have certain rights to concession areas and space for product sampling.
9. Research. Each sponsor would receive a full research report on the public's perception of their participation and an assessment of the valued-added benefits. Research after the 1988 Games showed significant improvements in product image for TOP participants.
10. First Right of Negotiation for the Next Quadrennial. Those who were satisfied with TOP would have the option to continue in their product category.

For the 1996 Games the corporate sponsorship costs were $10-$40 million for each TOP company (International Events Group, 1994a). For the 1996 Summer Olympic Games in Atlanta, ten TOP sponsors were secured. Since the 1985 development of TOP, sponsorship has become an integral part of the Olympic movement. TOP served two major goals of the IOC: It made the IOC less dependent on television revenues, and it assisted all countries in the world with sport development through a shared-revenue system.

Other Olympic Sponsorship Areas

There are a variety of different types of sponsorships that Olympic organizations can offer to corporations. Each entity provides specific sponsor rights associated with participation (Kelly, 1988). National Olympic Committees exist in all of the 170 countries that participate in the Olympic Games. These organizations can authorize the use of the Olympic rings, but only in conjunction with their logo. For the 1996 Olympic Quadrennium, the USOC secured sponsorships that amount to more than 50% of its $400-million operating revenue (Morganthau, Barrett, Dickey, & Talbott, 1992).

Interestingly, for the 1996 Summer Games, the USOC joined forces with the Atlanta Committee for the Olympic Games and created a program similar to TOP with Atlanta Centennial Olympic Properties (ACOP). Some of their major sponsors included Anheuser-Busch, Champion, Home Depot, IBM, and NationsBank at about $10 million each (International Events Group, 1994a).

In 1992, ACOP attempted to bring the National Governing Bodies into their agreement. National Governing Bodies (NGBs) exist at the base of the Olympic family. They can engage in sponsorship activities separate from those of the IOC and the USOC. Each Olympic sport has an NGB in each country that is a member of the IOC. These organizations can generate sponsorship activities within a single country. The ACOP proposal offered each NGB a package of sponsorships, but also restricted their independent sponsorship activities. The proposal asked the NGBs to

- relinquish 90% of the categories in which they can sell sponsorship
- relinquish all broadcast rights
- refrain from selling cosponsorships, signage or hospitality rights in unprotected areas
- Give ACOP sponsors more rights that NGB sponsors
- Give ACOP sponsors the rights to first refusal of NGB events
- Allow ACOP sponsors to freely grant to "others" - e.g. competitors of the NGB's own sponsors - marketing rights to the federation. (International Events Group, 1992b, p. 2).

Generally, this proposal received little support from the major sport governing bodies. Although few of the high-profile NGBs even gave the offer consideration, many of the lesser known NGBs saw this as a great opportunity.

The NGBs with the greatest exposure and public recognition are engaged in their own sponsorship deals. USA Track and Field has signed agreements with several sponsors. Their $1-million deal with Nike provides apparel, official uniforms, and accessories. Another NGB, U.S.A. Swimming, offers ongoing sponsorship packages ranging from $25,000-$500,000. Their sponsors include Murine, Gatorade, Speedo, and Phillips 66. USA Swimming and USA Track and Field have also signed Fuji as their official film supplier, which undermines the IOC and USOC arrangements with Kodak. USA Gymnastics has chosen several sponsors that are already associated with the USOC. Specifically, they have deals with Visa, Reebok, McDonald's, and Hilton.

USA Basketball, coming off a spectacular sponsorship and licensing arrangement during the 1992 Summer Olympics with the "Dream Team," uses NBA Properties as its agent. This arrangement helps reduce specific conflicts that could occur with the NBA players who constitute the Olympic team (International Events Group, 1994a).

Individual Olympic sports are also involved through their International Federations. International Federations (IFs) are the worldwide organizing bodies for specific Olympic sports. The International Amateur Athletics Federation (IAAF) uses ISL Marketing (as does the IOC) as its exclusive agent in sponsorship negotiation. ISL has signed 12 sponsors and acts as the bargaining agent for the television coverage of the IAAF's World Cup Championships in track and field. The event attracts a multimillion-dollar rights fee for television coverage with a viewing audience of 3.3 billion in 152 countries (ISL, 1993).

Similarly, ISL acts as the agent for FIFA, the IF for soccer. The 1994 World Cup was the most watched event in history with a worldwide audience of 32 billion people in 176 countries (World Cup '94 Organizing Committee, personal communication, December 22, 1994). For 1994, ISL signed 5 Gold sponsors at $20-$25 million each and provided an increase in exposure for sponsors with over 3.5 million people through the turnstyles (McClellan, 1994).

The Olympic Organizing Committees have benefited from both television revenues and from sponsorship agreements. The IOC provides the organizing committee with a share of that income. The organizing committee is free, however, to pursue sponsorships that are not prohibited by the IOC. The Lillehammer Olympic Organizing Committee (LOOC) secured sponsorships totaling over $50 million. Scandinavian Airlines secured the rights as official airline, whereas IBM handled computer software, and Seiko was the official timer for the 1994 Winter Games.

Ambushing official sponsors became a successful strategy when Kodak upstaged Fuji in the 1984 Olympic Games by purchasing sponsorships with the USOC and buying television ads. Although Fuji had purchased the right to be an official sponsor from the Los Angeles Olympic Organizing Committee, the public never really knew that Fuji, not Kodak, was the official sponsor (Marsano, 1987). Visa and American Express have also engaged in similar tactics. American Express even took Visa (a TOP sponsor) to court alleging that they misled the public in their Olympic advertising. Because of tactics like this, each organization must carefully guard its sponsor's rights.

As a sport marketer, one of the most difficult tasks that you will need to perform is pricing the sponsorship. If you own the event that can be sponsored, you must be able to articulate a fair market price. An article in the sponsorship industry newsletter, *IEG Sponsorship Report,* gave considerable detail on the appropriate considerations and calculations for pricing sponsorships. As with all product pricing, a thorough analysis of the market must be completed. The sport marketer must know what other sport organizations are charging for their sponsorship packages and what the buyers are paying for other promotional/media tools (International Events Group, 1992a).

In all sponsorships there are both tangible and intangible components. The tangible components include media advertising, signage, tickets, programs, and sampling. Each of these activities has a market value. Most organizations include advertising in their proposals to sponsors. Often the sponsors get "tagged" to the advertising for the event. In this case, the sponsor simply gets to attach its logo to the promotional ads for the event. The value of these ads for the sponsor certainly does not equate to the full value of the ad. A general guide is about 10% of the value of an identical media buy. If you include more than one sponsor's logo, the value should be reduced accordingly (International Events Group, 1992a). Some sponsorship packages offer complimentary media space for the sole use of the sponsor. These "free ads" are typically obtained as a trade-out from a media sponsor of the event. If the sponsor is allowed full discretionary use of the space, full value can be applied to that piece of the package based on the going advertising rate.

Value calculation for sampling opportunities is more difficult to ascertain. Probably the best approach is to investigate the costs of similar activities at area shopping malls and trade shows. Advertising in programs and event tickets are the most difficult to value for both the organization and for the sponsor. Some organizations simply price all of their sponsor tickets in the VIP section at double the going ticket price. It does not really matter what the organization says they cost because all of the tickets are packaged for sponsors or VIPs. It costs the same to print $50 on a ticket as it does to print $30. The same game is often played with program advertising. To be honest, you should price both tickets and program ads at a competitive rate for both sponsors and nonsponsors.

The intangibles of a sponsorship plan are often the most important to the sponsor, but are the most difficult to value. Sponsors are paying to be associated with your event and will be depending, in part, on your logo. Can this really help sales? Data collected for the 1994 Soccer World Cup indicated that 63% of consumers were more likely to purchase a product with a World Cup USA logo than one without the logo (International Events Group, 1994c). The desire for sponsors to associate with your organization is also dependent on your prestige value. Is your event the "one and only" like the Olympics or the Indianapolis 500, or is it just another softball tournament? Of course, the more prominent and unique the event, the higher the price you can charge.

Supply and demand are always relevant factors in pricing. In the 1990s the supply of sponsorship opportunities has been greater than has been the number of companies with the financial capability to sponsor events. Therefore, sport organizations have to be very competitive on pricing to attract quality sponsors. Finally, a major consideration centers on in-kind donations from sponsors. Some sponsors like to barter their products with you in lieu of cash payments. This situation works out well when the company can offer products that you otherwise would have had to purchase. Take, for example, airline tickets. If you would have had to purchase 10 tickets at $500 each, a $5,000 credit would be acceptable. The airline may also give you upgrades to first class. However, if they value their contribution at $1,000 for first class and you would have only purchased economy, you are not really getting a fair value for your trade. More importantly in the barter business is to accept only in-kind donations that you can use. The 1990 Goodwill games had a deal with San Sebastian Wines that was more trouble than help. The wine company traded several cases of wine as part of its sponsorship deal, but because of liquor laws, the organizing committee could not serve the wine, and consequently neither the organization nor the sponsors received the benefits they desired.

Packages should be priced at about 25% less than the individual pieces. You want to avoid what is called "cherry picking." This is where sponsors will try to cut only the most profitable aspects of your package out and pay for them separately. Some organizations avoid this by refusing to partition packages or by pricing the individual pieces so high that the package is clearly the best buy. As for payment scheme, most organizations require at least 65% at signing with the remainder due prior to the event (International Events Group, 1994c). Do not allow sponsors to negotiate payment plans that postdate the event. If the results the sponsor anticipated were not achieved, getting the sponsor to complete payments may cost dearly in legal fees.

Sponsors should also be reminded that once the sponsorship is purchased, they will need to incorporate it in their existing marketing programs. This also provides a benefit to your organization as it is often carried into additional markets by the sponsor.

Trends

One of the most important trends that sport marketers should examine is that corporations are seeking more grass-roots involvement. Many companies are realizing that speaking to consumers in a local environment may be more persuasive than through nationwide involvement. However, because many local franchises of national firms do not have the resources to sponsor events, the parent corporation may still extend financial support in a joint-venture sponsorship.

The movement to event sponsorship and away from individual endorsement should continue as consumer data show that the credibility of individual endorsers is low. Events can be successful for the sponsor regardless of who wins, and they are less likely to become entangled in controversy. Substantial competition for sponsorships will undoubtedly come from the arts and social causes. In 1994, cause-related and arts sponsorships grew at more than twice the pace of sport sponsorships and totaled $700 million of the $4.25 billion spent (International Events Group, 1994b). Sport marketers can certainly look toward including the arts and social issues in their marketing campaigns. Here are just two noteworthy examples. The Denver Nuggets of the NBA had a very successful program exchanging game tickets for hand guns. For many years, the United States Sports Academy combined a variety of sponsors in support for a sport art museum housed on its campus. In the dynamic worlds of sport and finance, new trends will certainly emerge. The challenge for sport marketers is to keep abreast of the industry and creatively seek opportunities to use sponsorships and endorsements to market their products and services.

Chapter Summary

The purpose of this chapter was to describe how sport organizations could enhance their marketing efforts through athlete endorsements and sport sponsorships. Because of their knowledge and power within certain groups, sport companies can effectively use opinion leaders to increase product sales. Opinion leaders can also be used in product sampling and prototype testing. Endorsement of products by individual athletes has been a marketing practice in sport for decades, yet its popularity has been waning. A credibility problem with individual endorsements exists in that many consumers believe that sports celebrities were endorsing products only for the money. A trend that appears to be successful is cross-promotion whereby several companies band together around an athlete to gain additional exposure. The concern for the future is whether the sport sponsorship and endorsement field are saturated and companies will change to other areas like the arts and regional festivals to accomplish their objectives.

Questions for Study

1. Describe the advantages and disadvantages of having an individual athlete as a product endorser.
2. Compare and contrast the sponsorship rights available through each level of Olympic sports: IOC, NOCs, NGBs, IFs.

Learning Activity

Attend a local sport event where sponsors have signage displayed in the venue. After exiting the event, ask patrons which, if any, of the sponsors they can remember.

Professional Associations and Organizations

IEG Sponsorship Report
International Events Group
213 West Institute Place, Suite 303
Chicago, IL 60610-3175

Suggested Readings

IEG legal guide to sponsorship. Chicago, IL: International Events Group.

Stotlar, D. K. (1993). *Successful sport marketing.* Dubuque, IA: Brown-Benchmark.

Sports Market Place, P.O. Box 10129, Phopenix, AZ.

References

Brubaker, B. (1991, March 11). In shoe companies' competition, the coaches are the key players. *The Washington Post,* p. A1.

Comte, E. (1989, February 27). The 'in' trend: Joint promos. *Sports, Inc., 2,* 5.

Ensor, R. J. (1987, September). The corporate view of sports sponsorships. *Athletic Business, 11,* 40-43.

Friedman, A. (1990, December). Sports marketers must work harder and smarter to score. *Athletic Business, 14,* 22.

Gallup, G. (1988) *An investment in America's future: A sponsorship proposal for Apple Computer.* New York: George Gallup Corporate Consultant.

International Events Group (1992a, September 7). Centerfold. *IEG Sponsorship Report, 11*, 4-5.

International Events Group (1992b, November 2). Assertions. *IEG Sponsorship Report, 11*, 2.

International Events Group (1992c, November 2). Industry news. *IEG Sponsorship Report, 11*, 7.

International Events Group (1992d, December 21). Centerfold: The bottom line on sponsorship. *IEG Sponsorship Report, 11*, 4-6.

International Events Group, (1994a). *Who sponsors Olympic properties.* Chicago, IL: International Events Group.

International Events Group (1994b, December 19). Sponsorship spending to rise 11 percent in 1995. *IEG Sponsorship Report, 13*, 1-3.

International Events Group (1994c, December 6). Assertions. *IEG Sponsorship Report, 13*, 2.

Irwin, R.L., & Asimakopoulos, M. (1992, December). An approach to the evaluation and selection of sport sponsorship proposals. *Sport Marketing Quarterly, 1*(4), 43-51.

ISL Marketing (1993). *The Olympic programme.* New York: ISL Marketing.

Jeansonne, J. (1986, April 13). Amateur sports and the pursuit of the almighty dollar. *Newsday, 18*, 16-19.

Joyce Julius, and Associates (1991). *The Sponsor's Report Almanac.* Ann Arbor, MI: Author.

Kelly, P. (1988, June 6). Olympic sponsorship: Choices and benefits. *Sports Marketing News*, p. 15.

Marsano, W. (1987, September). A five ring circus. *Northwest*, 8, 64-69.

McClellan, S. (1994, June 13). Advertisers hope to net global audience. *Broadcasting & Cable*, 9, 27.

Morganthau, T., Barrett, T., Dickey, C., & Talbot, M. (1992, June 22). Piling up the gold. *Newsweek*, (Special Issue), 56-58.

Mullin, B. (1983). *Sport marketing, promotions and public relations.* Amherst, MA: National Sport Management, Inc.

NBC gets Olympic TV deal. (1993, July 28). *Greeley [CO] Tribune.* p. 2.

Pratzmark, R. R., & Frey, N. (1989, January). The winners play a new global game. *Marketing Communications, 11*, 18-27.

Schlossberg, H. (1990, June 11). Allure of celebrity endorsers starts to fade. *Marketing News, 2*, 7.

Stauble, V. (1994). The significance of sport marketing and the case of the Olympic Games. In P. J. Graham (Ed.), *Sport business* (pp. 14-21). Dubuque, IA:

Brown-Benchmark.

Stotlar, D. K. (1993). *Successful sport marketing.* Dubuque, IA: Brown-Benchmark.

Wilber, D. (1988, July/August). Linking sports and sponsors. *Journal of Business Strategy, 13,* 8-10.

Wilkinson, D. G. (1986). *Sport marketing institute.* Willowdale, Ontario: Sport Marketing Institute.

Wilkinson, D. G. (1988). *Event management and marketing institute.* Willowdale, Ontario: Sport Marketing Institute.

Woodward, S. (1988, May 29). Teams foresee war brewing keeping 'billboard rules' in place. *USA Today,* p. 2C.

World Cup USA 94: Between the lines, (1993, Fall). *Between the Lines: Ernst and Young's Financial Newsletter for the Sports World,* 9, 10-11.

Zbar, J. D. (1992, November). Shaquille appeal. *Advertising Age,* p. 1.

Chapter 15

Using Licensing and Logos in the Sport Industry

Introduction

Licensing is the act of granting to another party the right to use a protected logo, design, or trademark (Irwin & Stotlar, 1993). Although trademark licensing may be traced back hundreds of years, its dramatic growth occurred in the 1970s and 1980s. "Pierre Cardin," "Polo," and "Esprit" became very popular as licensed names on products geared toward teen-agers and adults. Comic book heroes, cartoons, schools, professional teams, clubs, causes, characters, and many other subjects became featured designs on clothing.

Historically, sport organizations found it desirable to initiate efforts to protect the investment in their name and marks through trademark licensing (Irwin, 1990). Through such programs, sport organizations could receive name recognition and substantial revenue. In 1963 the National Football League established its licensing program to bring the protection of team names and insignia under central control. On the collegiate scene, the University of California at Los Angeles (UCLA) began its licensing program in 1973 (Irwin & Stotlar, 1993). Other sport organizations, such as the International Olympic Committee, Gold's Gym, and ABC's Wide World of Sports, have also established strong licensing programs.

On the revenue side, the NFL generated over $50 million in 1990 from licensed products in Europe alone. For 1993, total international sales were estimated at $250 million (Lesly, 1992). If you think this effort is not worthwhile for collegiate institutions and amateur sports, consider that sport organizations such as Notre Dame, Penn State, and the United States Olympic Committee receive revenues that approach $1 million per year based on 7% of gross yearly sales. According to industry data (Irwin & Stotlar, 1993; Lesly, 1992) annual sales of all products bearing sports logos exceed $11.1 billion per year.

In sport licensing, four factors led to the development of organized sport licensing (Irwin, 1990). One of those factors was the increased popularity of sport and the resulting media coverage. Successful athletic teams, especially in football and basketball, have, for many years, been a rallying point for the public. Increased popularity in the last 20 years led to greater attendance at games, leading to increased media coverage. This, in turn, led to increased popularity, higher attendance figures, and even more media coverage. Stadiums and arenas were enlarged, front pages of major newspapers carried the outcomes of major sports contests, and television magnified sports and multiplied their popularity. Today, sporting events get headline coverage virtually year round.

Another development during the 1970s was the technology involved with screen printing or "silk-screening," which greatly expanded the licensing industry. With an investment of a few hundred dollars, an individual could literally set up a printing operation in hours with virtually any logo, slogan, or catchy phrase. Blank garments were easily acquired from a number of mills and could be printed to meet any demands. Printed T-shirts became a communications medium during the 1970s. Adults, as well as children, were part of a market that grew dramatically throughout the 1980s.

In sport, the demand for imprinted goods was advanced through the fan pride, loyalty, and desire to support the team by wearing team colors and designs. Anyone who has attended major events knows the emotions fans generate in support of their teams or favorite player. People found themselves extremely attracted to their favorite school, team, or player and desired a means through which they could express their feelings. As the market for imprinted products expanded, they sought licensed goods as a method of expressing their support.

Throughout the 1960s and well into the 1970s, the sport community seemed to consider most commercialism distasteful; however, the costs of running competitive sport programs was increasing dramatically. As a result, the sale of imprinted sport merchandise was initiated to help build revenues. Parallel with the increases in sales, problems began to occur with logo abuse and counterfeit merchandise. When the abuses became more frequent, sport administrators quickly decided that they needed greater control over the use of their marks to prevent the obnoxious designs, poor-quality merchandise, and product liability risks they were beginning to encounter.

In a sport licensing program, the marketer typically grants a manufacturer the right to use the organization's indicia (marks) in producing and selling merchandise. The licensee is required to sign a contract, pay royalties, and adhere to strict licensing regulations. Royalties for licensed goods typically run about 6% to 8% of the price for which an item was sold.

As a marketing vehicle, licensing enables sport organizations to generate consumer awareness and interest through logoed products, all with minimal capital outlay (Irwin & Stotlar, 1993). The market for such items is no longer limited to the team's home city campus, or local market, but extends around the globe. To ensure standardization and quality, many souvenirs, such as clothing, mugs, or novelties bearing sport logos, are put through rigorous marketing and approval processes. Each item is checked for both quality and design.

Licensing, therefore, is extremely important for sport organizations because it enables them to control the way their name and indicia are portrayed on merchandise. Products of inferior quality can be rejected, and strict labeling requirements can be enforced so the consumers can identify the merchandise as authentic. In addition the product manufacturers can be required to carry product liability insurance, which protects the organization if legal action is filed because of an incident involving a licensed product.

As a result of the growth in the use of sport licensing and trademarks on manufactured items for sale, personnel in various commercial, professional, intercollegiate, and amateur sports organizations must attain a significant knowledge base in this area. There has also been an increasing amount of litigation in this field, and the guidelines governing the use of sports trademarks are still being established in the courts (Wong, 1988). As the national and international markets for merchandise bearing sport logos, names, and indicia develop, sport administrators will be required to seek legal avenues to protect their market, products, and marks. However, most sport management personnel know little about how to protect their marks or how to license legally protectable properties to second parties for commercial use (Irwin, 1990).

The Legal Basis for Trademark Licensing in Sport

The case law governing sport licensing is sparse but has developed rapidly based on traditional trademark law. Sport organizations, therefore, must develop a firm legal basis for requiring that users of their trademarks obtain permission to use the trademarks and for requiring that the users pay royalties for the privilege. In order to more fully understand trademark licensing, you need to be familiar with the following principles, terms, and definitions surrounding trademark law.

Trademark Principles

The Federal Trademark Act of 1946, Lanham Act 45, 15 U. S. C. 1051-1127 (1946), commonly known as the Lanham Act, governs the law of trademarks, the registration of trademarks, and remedies for the infringement of registered trademarks (Wong, 1988). The Trademarks Law Revision Act, which went into effect in 1989, was Congress's first overall revision of the Lanham Act since 1946. The revised Lanham Act created major changes in federal trademark law that are highly relevant to sport trademark registration and licensing. The most fundamental changes were in the definitions of the use of trademarks (Irwin, 1990).

1. Trademark: "Any word, name, symbol, or device, or any combination thereof used to identify and distinguish the goods of one person from those manufactured or sold by others."

2. Service mark "Any word, name, symbol, or device, or any combination thereof used to identify and distinguish the services of one person from the service of others."
3. Collective mark: "A trademark or service mark used by members of a cooperative, association, or other collective group or organization."
4. Mark: "A shorthand reference to any type of mark, including trademarks, service mark, and collective marks."
5. Registered mark: "A mark registered in the United States Patent and Trademark Office, as provided under the Act." (United States Department of Commerce, 1993, p. 1)

Infringement of a Trademark

The Act defines trademark infringement as the reproduction, counterfeiting, copying, or imitation, in commerce, of a registered mark "in connection with the sale, offering for sale, distribution, or advertising of any goods or services on or in connection with which such use is likely to cause confusion, or to cause mistake or to deceive without consent of the registrant" (United States Department of Commerce, 1993, p. 7).

Secondary meaning

Secondary meaning is a mental recognition in the buyer's mind, associating symbols, words, colors, and designs with goods from a single source. It tests the connection in the buyer's mind between the product bearing the mark and its source (Wong, 1988). Certain terms that are selected or invented for the express purpose of functioning as trademarks may be classified as inherently distinctive. Such marks are protectable and registerable immediately on use. One such example would be "Apple" computer. However, some potential marks describe products or services, geographic designations, or personal surnames. To qualify for protection as a mark, the courts require evidence that such a term has acquired secondary meaning; that is, consumers associate the products or services under the term with one particular source (Wong, 1988). The example here is that one shoe company produced a football shoe called Montana. They claimed that it was a generic reference to a geographical region. Former football player Joe Montana, his agent, and eventually the courts disagreed finding that the word Montana had attained secondary meaning in the sport industry.

Laches

Laches may arise when a party fails to assert a right or claim within a reasonable time, and the other party relies on this inaction to claim use to the other party's mark (Battle, III, Bailey, & Siegal, 1991). An example of just this case arose when the University of Pittsburgh tried to stop Champion from producing sweatshirts with the Pitt logo. The court in this case said that because

Pitt had previously allowed Champion to use its logo, it could not now prevent its use by Champion.

Each of the types of marks described earlier is protected equally under the Lanham Act. Sport organization names, team names, and logos may be described as trademarks, service marks, or collective marks (Wong, 1988). Any of these marks used on items such as clothing and novelties as well as services is entitled to protection. Registered marks are not always confined to team names and indicia. In the recent past, sports facilities have registered their names, including the 1988 Olympic Oval in Calgary, Wrigley Field in Chicago, and the Houston Astrodome. Many slogans and sayings are also registered and protected, such as the "Dream Team" of the 1992 Summer Olympics and "Threepeat" referring to the third consecutive NBA championship of the Chicago Bulls in 1993. Ironically, "Threepeat" was registered by New York Knicks coach Pat Riley, whose team was beaten by the Bulls in the 1993 playoffs. Although property rights begin to develop automatically under common law, federal registration of the marks is also available.

Because of the complexity of managing a sport licensing program (integrating financial, promotional, and legal responsibilities), there have been organized efforts to control the use of sport organizations' logos, trademarks, and copyrights. As a result, organizations have been faced with a serious dilemma: internal versus external management (Irwin & Stotlar, 1993). Irwin's (1990) research and subsequent publications shed considerable light on this decision.

Several large companies have entered the business to assist sport organizations in the management of their licensing programs. In these organizations, the licensing agent helps in the protection of an organization's logo or marks. One such company, the Collegiate Licensing Company, developed seven basic goals with short-term and long-term strategies (Battle III et al., 1991). The consortium not only affects its members, but it also directly and indirectly affects nonmember schools. Their goals include the following:

1. "To attract, maintain, and strengthen a prestigious base of universities, bowls, and athletic conferences." (p. 253)
2. "To attract and maintain a base of licensees sufficiently large to cover all potential market segments and wire all marketable products." (p. 253)
3. "To identify retailers that are current or potential carriers of collegiate merchandise and show them the requirements and opportunities of collegiate licensing." (p. 253)
4. "To identify consumers of collegiate products and encourage them to buy licensed products." (p. 254)
5. "To improve the effectiveness of current methods of enforcement and to develop new methods." (p. 254)
6. "To establish marketing programs that can expand the market for

"Officially Licensed Collegiate Products" and take advantage of synergistic marketing, advertising, and promotional programs." (p. 254)

7. "To provide unparalleled services to member institutions and licensees and to develop a database and reports to give management the information needed to analyze, evaluate, and manage progress toward the goals previously listed." (p. 256)

Although private companies handle licensing for some of the nation's large universities, many schools and sport organizations are running their own programs. All of the professional sports leagues (NBA, MLB, NHL) have entities that handle their licensed products pioneered by NFL Properties, Inc.

Research by Irwin (1990) examined the pros and cons of internal versus external management and found that most organizations are better off handling their own programs. Specific factors in program design were established against which sport organizations could judge their programs. A review of these operational factors follows (Irwin, 1990; Irwin & Stotlar, 1993).

Operational Protocol Factors in Sport Licensing

Program Governance and Leadership

Designated internal licensing authority
Principal licensing assignment full-time
Direct report to central administrator
Licensing policy committee assembled
Professional licensing agency assistance

Program Protection and Enforcement

Legal specialist consultation
Majority of logos registered as trademarks
Licensee application and screening process
License issuance and renewal procedures
Basic agreement nonexclusive
Execution of joint-use agreements
Execution of international licenses
Product sample required for quality control
"Licensed Product" identification required
Counterfeit logo detection procedures
Counterfeit logo reduction procedures

Program Promotions and Public Relations

Pro-active recruitment of licensees
Pro-active recruitment of retailers
Licensee/retailer public relations program
Advertising used to promote products/program
Publicity used to promote products/program
Licensing program information published

Revenue Management

Advance payment required
Uniform royalty charged on all products
Written royalty exemption policy
Royalty verifications routinely conducted
Royalty verifications conducted by specialist
Written royalty distribution policy.

The advantages and disadvantages assignable to internally and externally managed licensing programs must be reviewed within the context of the organization's resources. Generally, internally managed programs are more expensive to run, but they yield higher profits. External or agency-managed programs usually offer easier access to wholesale and retail networks and may have better nationwide success.

Sport licensing is a journey and not a single destination. All factors affecting the program must be considered. Irwin's (1990) conclusions prescribed a licensing paradigm. The major components of a licensing system should include

1. An examination of the feasibility of assigning a full-time licensing administrator.
2. An evaluation of the cost effectiveness of internal versus external management of the program based on internal resources and potential markets and profits.
3. Identification of a single administrative authority for licensing agreements.
4. The development of policy for the issuance of exclusive and nonexclusive license agreements.
5. The design of specific royalty and exemption policies.
6. Application procedures for issuance/renewal of licenses.
7. A process whereby licensees must disclose financial stability, distribution intent, and licensing references.
8. A request for advance payments from licensees as earnest money to be applied to future royalties.
9. The establishment of a uniform royalty rate calculated on the net cost of the licensed item sold.
10. The requirement to furnish finished samples of the licensed merchandise.
11. The requirement to furnish certificates of insurance pertaining to licensed merchandise sold.
12. The federal registration of at least one of the organization's marks.
13. The required use of licensee identification on all merchandise distributed

(hang tag, label, etc.).

14. A plan for the allocation of royalties received by the organization.
15. An enforcement policy including the responsibility to monitor merchandisers and issue cease and desist orders.
16. Consultation with trademark law specialists as needed.
17. The performance of compliance review with licensees.
18. The recruitment and recognition of licensees on a sustained basis.
19. The development of licensing brochures or guidelines for distribution to prospective licensees.
20. The reporting structure for the licensing administrator within the organization. (p. 151)

Regardless of the system employed, the major objectives of any sport licensing program are threefold: (a) Protection—to protect the trademarks of the organization, (b) Public Relations—to create a favorable image and positive exposure for the organization, and (c) Profit—to maximize revenues (Irwin, 1990).

Trademark Licensing Agreements

Program-enforcement procedures include all methods of securing and exercising protection of the sport organization's property rights in its name, logo, seals, and symbols. As sport-licensing programs are constructed and policy parameters are established, licensing administrators typically develop contractual relationships with licensees as a part of program enforcement protocol (Irwin, 1990). The primary legal base for this contractual relationship has been the licensing agreement. This agreement should provide for controls, checks, and balances regarding the exclusivity of mark, usage, royalty management, and quality control (Irwin, 1990). Previous empirical data have indicated the authority to grant and execute licensing agreements on behalf of the organization came, primarily, from upper-level administration. Gaston (1984) found that 42% of respondents identified the financial vice president as the source of authority for executing most licensing agreements.

According to the International Events Group (Reed, 1989) the elements that should be examined in a licensing agreement include, first of all, the parties entering into the agreement. The pertinent definitions in the agreement must also be detailed. Service marks and trademarks should be defined with attention to the level of protection through either federal registration or common law use.

The contract should also describe the specific products to be licensed, the duration of the agreement, and terms under which the agreement can be terminated or modified. It is also imperative that the royalty and payment structure be addressed. Specifically, the contract should define the royalty on net sales without deduction for shipping, advertising, or even returns or uncollectable accounts. The agreement should prescribe the reporting procedures and the payment methods and schedule. Other areas traditionally covered would include the types of products to be licensed, the rights for approval, and the territory governed by the agreement. Finally, it is crucial for the organization to restrict the ability of the licensee to assign the license to subcontractors (Reed, 1989).

Chapter Summary

As evidenced by the financial data presented earlier, sport licensing has, since its inception, achieved substantial commercial success. The development of this industry has obviously had a substantial impact on manufacturers, retailers, and consumers. The future of sport licensing seems very bright and appears to be on solid legal ground. A good foundation has been laid and the present billion-dollar market easily could evolve into a multi-billion-dollar industry. However, styles and trends can change as quickly as they evolved. With a clear focus on all three elements of a sound licensing program, protection, profit and public relations, sport organizations can continue to manage successful licensing programs.

Questions For Study

1. What are the laws that affect licensing and trademarks?
2. What factors led to the development of organized sport licensing?

Learning Activities

1. Investigate the origins of NFL Properties, Inc. Who was their first licensing director?
2. Develop a sport logo and determine the procedures and costs for registering that mark in your state.
3. Contact a sport organization with a registered mark(s) and request a copy of their graphics standards manual.

References

Battle, W. R., III, Bailey, B., & Siegal, B. B. (1991). Collegiate trademark licensing. In B. L. Parkhouse (Ed.), *The management of sport: Its foundation and application* (pp. 245-263). St. Louis, MO: Mosby.

Gaston, F. P. (1984). *Administrative decision making: A study of collegiate trademark licensing programs.* Unpublished doctoral dissertation, University of Alabama, Tuscaloosa, AL.

Irwin, R. L. (1990). *Development of a collegiate licensing administrative paradigm.* Unpublished doctoral dissertation, University of Northern Colorado, Greeley, CO.

Irwin, R. L., & Stotlar, D. K. (1993). Operational protocol analysis of sport and collegiate licensing programs. *Sport Marketing Quarterly, 2* (4), 7-16.

Lesly, E. (1992, November 30). What's next, Raiders' deodorant? *Business Week, 21*, 65.

Reed, M. H. (1989). *IEG legal guide to sponsorship.* Chicago, IL: International Events Group.

United States Department of Commerce (1993, September). *Basic facts about registering a trademark.* Washington DC: Patent and Trademark Office.

Wong, G. M. (1988). *Essentials of amateur sports law.* Dover, MA: Auburn House Publishing Company.

Index